DATE			

Digital Typography

An Introduction to
Type and Composition for
Computer System Design

Richard Rubinstein
Digital Equipment Corporation

ADDISON-WESLEY PUBLISHING COMPANY
Reading, Massachusetts • Menlo Park, California
New York • Don Mills, Ontario • Wokingham, England
Amsterdam • Bonn • Sydney • Singapore • Tokyo
Madrid • San Juan

This book was typeset in Goudy Oldstyle by DEKR typesetters, using a Penta frontend system driving a Mergenthaler Linotron 202 digital typesetter. The original manuscript was prepared on-line using an Apple Macintosh computer and an Apple Laser-Writer, the software was Microsoft Word 3.01. Joyce C. Weston designed the book. 🙶

Many of the designations used by manufacturers and sellers to distinguish their products are claimed as trademarks. Where those designations appear in this book, and Addison-Wesley was aware of a trademark claim, the designations have been printed in initial caps or all caps.

Library of Congress Cataloging-in-Publication Data

Rubinstein, Richard.
  Digital typography.

  Bibliography: p.
  Includes index.
  1. Computerized typesetting. 2. Type and type-founding—Data processing. 3. Electronic publishing.
I. Title.
Z253.3.R8 1988   686.2'2544   86-26600
ISBN 0-201-17633-5

ABCDEFGHIJ-HA-898

In memory of my father

Herbert J. Rubinstein

Preface

ALL kinds of people are now typesetting printed documents. Added to the traditional ranks of typographers and printers are writers, publishers, managers, children, engineers, architects, scientists, students, artists, reporters, and secretaries. The rapidly changing methods of preparing and printing documents brought about by digital computers in the last few years can only be described as revolutionary.

Typography is in fact an old and conservative field. Hundreds of years of development have gone into creating our methods of presenting written information, and all literate human beings spend much of their childhoods learning to read printed forms. Books may be the greatest of human inventions. Printing is important to us.

But the world changes, and the means of producing printed material has changed completely several times in this century. The newest method is electronic publishing.

The problem facing the builder of electronic-publishing or -printing systems is to retain high quality while replacing old printing methods. Understanding what is good about traditional printing is surprisingly hard: Typography is both a design specialty in its own right—there is much to know—and an art. The way typographers express knowledge may not be easy for computer experts to absorb. Worse, it may not be possible to express this knowledge in the form of a program. I have written this book to help my fellow engineers and scientists apply computer technology to printing in a sensitive way.

Printing can be beautiful as well as effective. My own interest in typography stems in part from a love of books, which is nourished by their feel and look as well as their content. George Bernard Shaw said, "Well-printed books are just as scarce as well-written ones; and every author should remember that the most costly books derive their value from the craft of the printer and not from the author's genius." When we design and build systems for printing, we can have a profound influence on what written documents look like. Will they be easy to read, or tiring? Will they communicate efficiently, or slow the reader and provoke errors? Will they give pleasure to their owners?

Quality in print is hard to quantify, since it is the result of a hundred subtle factors. Not an absolute, print quality depends on people's expectations and training in reading, and on their abilities to perceive and understand marks on paper or spots on screens. This book provides enough background in typography and in how people see and read to give system builders enough basic guidance that their designs mesh well with human capabilities.

Digital Typography: An Introduction to Type and Composition for Computer System Design is written for anyone who designs, builds, or even selects computer-based systems that produce printed documents or images. The book should also prove useful to specialists in human factors and human interface who need to know how to present type-setting capabilities to users. Equally important, it provides a broad introduction to the technical issues that bear on producing typeset-quality output with computer-driven equipment. Computer scientists, human-factors researchers, and typographers who would like to extend our knowledge of digital typography will find many open questions and projects worthy of their attention. For course use, an appendix provides projects suitable for both undergraduate and graduate students.

The only prerequisites to reading the book are interest, a general knowledge of computer systems, and some experience in preparing documents via word processor, computer, or typesetter. No background in typography or psychology is needed.

I have attempted to express traditional typographic information in a form accessible to system builders, and to describe how computer-based technology affects the quality and effectiveness of printing. I have also tried to translate knowledge from various disciplines, notably typography and human factors, into a form that is useful in engineering. I do this in the hope that this book will contribute to the making of documents that are both beautiful and easy to read.

Wellesley, Mass.   Richard Rubinstein

Acknowledgements

With their encouragement and most of all their patience, my family made it possible for me to write this book. Thank you, Barbara, Adam, and Beth for being who you are. I love you very much.

Charles Bigelow is responsible for much of my typographical education. For all of your encouragement, wisdom, reviewing labors, and enthusiasm for the subject, Chuck, thank you.

Avi Naiman reviewed the manuscript twice in great detail, providing critical comment that was unattainable elsewhere and that improved the result materially. Avi, I owe you one.

I also thank Donald H. Beil, Richard Furuta, and John Gourlay who reviewed the manuscript and provided a multitude of useful corrections and suggestions.

Bob Ulichney and I are working together on a project to understand spatial frequencies in type. He provided all of the power spectra included in the text, and taught me most of what I know about Fourier analysis. Thanks, Bob!

I also acknowledge and thank the many people who assisted in ways too various to detail: Cynthia Carter, Marsha Collins, Sam Fuller, Tom Gannon, Paul Goldenberg, Helen Goldstein, Peter Gordon, Jill Gustafson, Harry Hersh, Kris Holmes, Scott McGregor, Bob Morris, Karen Myer, Larry Samberg, Eliot Tarlin, Joe Vetere, and Bob Williams.

Contents

PART TWO   Lines, Blocks, and Pages

Contents

— 1
Introduction

Printing should be invisible.
—*Beatrice Warde*

JOHANN GUTENBERG, a goldsmith, lived in Mainz in the early 1400s. Gutenberg invented movable type, which made book production far more cost effective than before. He had the essential technical knowledge of casting metal, and also of cutting punches to stamp letters and pictures on metal coins. After 10 years of experimentation, he succeeded in creating economical copies of the handwritten books of his day. His books had to look handwritten because that was the market.

Today, computer technology is being applied to the problems of preparing books. Computer typesetting is just as radical a departure from the tools we had used as movable type was in Gutenberg's time. Today's market is for output that looks printed rather than typed or printed by a computer. While many people have the technical knowledge to make computers do things, few also understand the other technologies needed to make computers print high-quality text, text that readers will perceive as good. Knowledge of typography, visual perception, human factors, computer science, and the detailed behavior of output devices is also necessary.

What is digital typography? Although definitions are rarely complete or entirely satisfying, here is a working one:

> Digital typography is the technology of using computers for the design, preparation, and presentation of documents, in which the graphical elements are organized, positioned, and themselves created under digital control.

Graphical elements include letters, symbols, line drawings, pictures, and other visual elements that are part of the document. Although many documents are predominantly textual, digital typography need not be limited to printed words. More and more, pictures and text are combined on the same page, producing what are called *compound documents*. The freedom to do this is part of digital typography.

An interesting part of this definition is that it includes a range of activities involved in document making for which computers are useful, and in which *digital* typography (as opposed to other kinds) is useful. Traditional design of books and other documents employed paper and pencil. Newer methods use the techniques of computer-aided design (CAD) not only to specify how a book, say, will be structured, but also to enforce that structure by supplying information for use in later stages of production and printing. What makes the design digital is treatment of the form of documents as information to be manipulated and transmitted.

Preparation of text by digital means has become commonplace in recent years. Word processors and personal computers are used to enter text, correct it, store it, retrieve it, and print it out. Treating the content of documents as information is the essence of digital text preparation.

Finally, the presentation of documents digitally on screen or paper is new to typography. The very letters themselves, their shape and position, are grist for the computer mill. Traditional methods of making letters were entirely analog, involving metal cutting, drawing, or photography. Now drawings and pictures are processed and presented under computer control, opening a host of possibilities for controlling both their properties and their quality.

The working definition excludes some conventional uses of computers. For example, it excludes printing with daisy-wheel printers, which form the letter's image on the paper by hitting a ribbon with a letter-shaped type element. Similarly, some early computer-output typesetters allowed controlled positioning of letterforms projected on photographic paper from a master film image. Such methods are also excluded from the definition because they do not involve treating form and content in a general, digital way.

Nonetheless, the working definition is a broad one. The tasks that people performed before digital typography, without thinking about them as information processing, now take on a new perspective. In particular, digital typography includes computer-aided design of the layout of books and other documents, tasks traditionally performed by

graphic artists, typographers, and book designers. It includes the preparation and editing of material that fills out the designed form, the
work of writers and editors. Digital typography includes the design of
the graphical elements themselves, the letters, symbols, and pictures.
It includes typesetting or formatting—the placing of graphical elements into the forms, that is, the realization of the final form of
documents. The technology of doing all of these things well constitutes
the field of digital typography.

Organization of the Book

This book proceeds from the most detailed to the broadest aspects
of digital typography. First, there is a great deal to know about the
shape of letters and symbols, called *letterforms*. The first part of the
book is devoted to the history of letterforms, their role in reading, the
ability of output devices to produce them, and the tools and methods
involved in their design. Letterforms are truly a specialty in their own
right. Here they cannot receive the complete coverage they deserve.
Other graphical objects that may appear in documents also receive
some attention here. Fortunately several good works on both letterforms and image processing are available for further reading. References appear as appropriate.

Next larger in scope is the issue of lines and blocks of text. There is
a technology of choosing the right places to break running text into
lines to make paragraphs. How much space should be placed between
the lines of a paragraph? What parameters affect people's ability to
read blocks of text efficiently?

The final level of concern is the design and formatting of whole
documents. How should the design of a document be represented in
the computer? Given the document design, how automatic can the
placing of text and other graphical elements be? What problems arise
when a document is examined on a screen before it is committed to
paper?

Recurrent Themes

In the consideration of letters, lines, and pages, three themes recur.
The first concerns visual perception, the way in which people see the
world and in particular read and understand documents. People's abil-

ities and predispositions provide a guide for how documents should look. Optimizing human performance is always the primary goal. Examining print in these terms provides a basis for judging quality and making pragmatic choices.

Second, history provides useful input for design. Unless we have data to the contrary, conventional typographic practice can be trusted to provide useful answers to questions and starting points. Thus the second theme is discovering what typographers know about making documents, and using this knowledge to its greatest advantage.

The third theme is engineering and analysis. Issues of perception and document making should be understood in analytic terms that facilitate writing programs and building machines that achieve good results. For this reason, experimental data and mathematical relationships prove useful for expressing knowledge in engineering terms. For example, considering print in terms of its *spatial frequencies,* that is, as periodic patterns spread over a page, provides some insights into the nature of different presentations.

Goals of Digital Typography

Computer and printing trade journals are full of terms like desktop publishing, electronic publishing, demand publishing, computer typesetting, and prepress imaging. These and similar terms reflect different uses of the same digital typography technology that is the subject of this book. For example, desktop publishing is digital typography packaged for personal computer users, while prepress imaging is tailored to the needs of the commercial printer. This book uses the terms digital typography and electronic publishing interchangeably, as generic terms that include all such specialties.

The printing industry is changing. Computers are being used heavily in business for document preparation. Many tasks formerly jobbed out to printers are being done in-house on the user's own equipment. Quality once attained by conventional printing methods and specialists in design and layout must now be attained more or less automatically, with a minimum of user attention. However, it is just plain hard to get good typographic quality out of computers. The issues are complex: Knowledge, art, and skill are required at several points in the process, and hardware is usually not designed with typographic sensibilities in mind.

Printing and publishing are a $100 billion industry in the United States. Indeed they are the third-largest corporate expense today, exceeded only by capital and labor expenditures. The result is a huge corporate market for any technology that reduces cost and lead time, consistent with other requirements of document production. Quality is frequently the strongest such requirement. Therefore manufacturers of electronic publishing systems have a great need for technical means of improving output quality.

This book proposes a number of goals for digital typography. A premise of the technology of human factors is that the purpose of computer systems is to make life easier and better for the people who use them. Text presented by computers should be easy to read, so easy that it does not call attention to itself in any way. This is what Beatrice Warde had in mind when she said that printing should be invisible. To achieve invisible printing, it is essential that the shapes of letters conform to what people read easily. We have a huge investment in decoding letters used in the printed languages we read. People must not be forced to learn new shapes just because a computer creates those shapes. Similarly, the layout of documents should facilitate the absorption of information without being obtrusive.

Thus it is a goal to achieve the highest typographic quality possible using available equipment and development resources, consistent with the other goals and requirements of a particular project. For the most part, good typography is not much more expensive than bad typography, but it does require knowledge and attention.

Another goal is to base choices on traditional typographic knowledge and standards where these apply. The alternative would be to invent printing from scratch, without direct benefit of the prior art. Learning from earlier technologies will save much relearning and many mistakes.

Finally, good engineering means designing the system to match human needs and characteristics. In digital typography, this suggests making good use of human visual capabilities and training. Knowledge of what makes for good printing can be used to drive the detailed design of output devices, for example, to create better output quality.

Digital typography is truly an interdisciplinary field. We can discuss it using the words and concepts of traditional typographers, or those of psychologists who study reading and vision, or those of computer scientists who describe how computers perform typographic tasks.

These three views are all different but equally valid descriptions of reality; all three are useful and will be used here.

What separated Gutenberg from his fellows was a knowledge of several enabling technologies that together gave birth to a new one. The same is true today. Digital typography is in its infancy. We have the pleasure, challenge, and excitement of combining once-disparate fields into a new and seminal discipline.

PART ONE

Individual
Letters ع‍ء

__ 2
Letterforms

Letters are things, not pictures of things.
                                    —*Eric Gill*

Mᴏʀᴇ than 100 trillion letterforms are printed on paper every day. *Letterforms,* for our purposes, are letters, numbers, and other symbols that people can read. Writing and printing have a long and interesting history, but only relatively recently has such a huge quantity of print been produced routinely. Whereas once the number of letterforms that could be produced was limited to the manual efforts of the few scribes, today we make letterforms in such abundance that relatively few of them are ever read by anybody. We produce them so that information will be available and can be read if people so choose. The daily newspaper can be thought of as a vast database that the readers can access selectively according to their needs and interests.

More and more, the technology for producing all these symbols is digital. All the computer equipment involved must be designed, built, and used. How will people produce good-quality printing in a timely and effective manner? How will we know if we are succeeding?

This chapter begins the quest for answers to these questions. After providing a short history of the making of letterforms, it presents three views of the knowledge and issues involved. These views represent the approaches of typographers, psychologists, and engineers to producing and using letterforms.

A History of Letterforms

Only a small part of the history of writing and printing bears on the quality of text printed by computer.[1] The modest history contained in this chapter focuses on how the digital production of print came about.

---

[1] The Bibliography includes several accounts of the history of printing. Bigelow [1981] provides a particularly relevant and concise summary.

Technology	Cost per Glyph	Quality
Clay tablets	high	good?
Stone cutting	very high	excellent
Wood block	high	good
Pen and ink	very high	good
Gutenberg	low	good
Letterpress	low	excellent
Linotype	very low	excellent
Typewriter	moderate	fair to good
Dot-matrix printer	low	fair
Photocompositor	very low	excellent
Digital typesetter	very low	excellent
Laser printer	low	good to excellent
CRT	very low	fair to good

TABLE 2.1 Various writing technologies compared. Cost estimates are very approximate, and are based on glyphs delivered for reading, assuming the normal reproduction means, if any, appropriate to each technology.

Many technologies for the production of letterforms have preceded our modern methods, including stone carving, pen and ink, wood-block printing, movable type, linotype, and phototypesetting. These media for written expression have varying properties, differing in speed, cost, and quality, as indicated in Table 2.1.

In addition to a general improvement in the speed and quality of letterform production, there has been a dramatic reduction in the cost of text presentation. Frequently quality is sacrificed in one way or another when a new technology is introduced. New technologies always strike new compromises with readers in terms of what is typographically good, readable, and commonplace. Pervasive technologies can mold the expectations of readers and, over time, modify the properties of the letterforms themselves.

We owe to stonecutters the lovely shapes of our roman capital letters, for it was the Romans who adapted the Greek and Etruscan writing systems to create shapes that we still use (see Fig. 2.1). Apparently Roman stonecutters lettered with brushes before beginning to chisel. This design by brush before execution in stone gave rise to the following letterform characteristics [Bigelow 1981:3]:

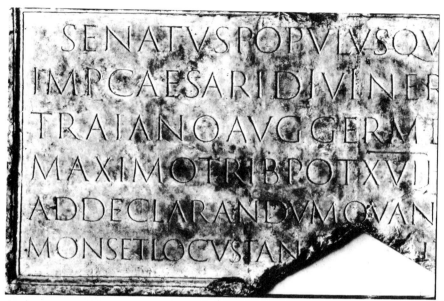

FIGURE 2.1   Our roman capital letters were conceived in stone by the Romans. By the second century A.D., as shown here, the forms were very well developed. They are entirely familiar to today's reader. (By courtesy of the Trustees of The Victoria and Albert Museum.)

- structured contrast between thick and thin strokes;
- tapering serifs at the terminals of many strokes;
- an appearance of geometric symmetry, achieved through asymmetric optical proportions rather than rigid construction;
- varying letter widths and differentiated forms.[2]

Thus the technology of creating letters, as well as the predispositions of the artists creating them, profoundly affected the form of letters.

The recording of less timeless matters was relegated to animal skins and eventually paper, with a pen as the recording instrument. Pen and paper seem at once familiar to us and also far removed from the technology of duplicating and publishing, but as recently as the first half of this century most commercial correspondence was by hand.

---

[2] Reproduced by permission of Seybold Publications, Inc., and Charles Bigelow.

When the proper ink was used, one or two copies could be made by placing the written page in contact with a thin, damp sheet of tissue paper and pressing it in a letter-copying press, a familiar office appliance as late as 1950 in England [Proudfoot 1972:30].

Written letterforms were copied by Gutenberg and later book printers. Gutenberg actually had several versions of many letters so as to replicate the variability of handwriting. His typefaces copied the gothic handwriting of his day (what typographers would now call black letter) to make the result acceptable to a readership accustomed to the handwritten bibles of the time. His font contained more than 300 symbols [McLean 1980:14], compared with the 96 of a modern ASCII character set.

Letterpress technology, also called hand type, is the technological result of hundreds of years of individually modest refinements of Gutenberg's basic ideas. Individual pieces of metal are cast from a master mold for each letter and symbol, as shown in Fig. 2.2. A few multiletter pieces are used, for example, the f-i ligature, which looks like this: fi. This particular pairing is necessary because the dot of the 'i' is not actually present in the combination, and because the correct spacing is tighter than in the pair 'fi'. Letterpress technology also still includes

FIGURE 2.2 Letterpress type. Note the ligature—a single piece of type that prints two or three letters—an f-i combination in this case.

```
Letters are things, not pictures of things.
```
(a)

Letters are things, not pictures of things.
(b)

FIGURE 2.3   Monospaced (a) and proportionally spaced type (b). Compare the relative width of such letters as 't' and 'n' in the two samples.

some variations on letters, allowing the typesetter freedom to choose which form best suits a situation. Advertising and decorative copy today still use variations on individual letters, though they have all but disappeared from commercial and book work.

In terms of overall quality, letterpress may represent the best printing technology to date. It is a reference point to compare with newer methods, and it provides much of the typographic terminology used in digital typography. The characteristics and capabilities of letterpress are one basis for understanding what particular digital technologies can and cannot do. We may also aspire to use computer methods to produce printed works that equal or surpass the quality of letterpress.

Typewriters deserve a brief mention because they provide a recent but noncomputer example of *monospaced* printing. Each typed letter occupies the same amount of horizontal space on the line. Equal spacing represents a compromise between mechanical simplicity in the machine and legibility of the result. This same compromise appeared later in computer terminals as "cell text." Compare the monospaced letters in Fig. 2.3(a) with the *proportionally spaced* ones in Fig. 2.3(b). Note how the proportionally spaced letters adjust in width to provide tight, even spacing.

The apex of current typesetting technology is the high-resolution digital typesetter. It produces photographic masters from which photo-offset reproduction is done. Such typesetters are used today for most book work and ad copy—anything requiring very high quality in a production (cost-sensitive) environment.

The Typographer's View

Traditional typography provides most of the terminology for printing that is used today, even in digital typography. Knowing these terms is essential to discussing typographic issues.

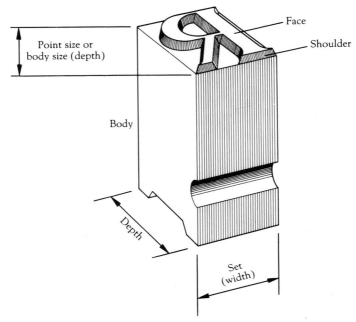

FIGURE 2.4   A piece of type.

An individual piece of metal type, the movable part invented by Gutenberg, is called a *sort* (presumably what apprentices in print shops spent much of their time doing). Sorts are collected into lines, usually spaced by strips of lead metal, giving rise to the term *leading,* which is the space added between lines of print. The size of type is the *depth* of the sorts, as shown in Fig. 2.4. The line-to-line spacing is thus the type size plus any leading.

Printers in the United States and England measure the size of type in *points.* One point measures 0.013837 inches. Thus an inch contains approximately 72.27 points. For many purposes, however, a point is taken to be $1/72$ of an inch. There is also the Didot point, used in Europe, which is slightly larger.

The actual letter that sits on the face of the type body is usually smaller than the size of the type. Some amount of space between lines is thus built in. In fact, the size of the face on the body varies from typeface to typeface, as demonstrated by Fig. 2.5.

Not only does the height of print of the same point size vary, but so

Cloister: abcdefghijklmnopqrstuvwxyz

Goudy Oldstyle: abcdefghijklmnopqrstuvwxyz

Walbaum: abcdefghijklmnopqrstuvwxyz

FIGURE 2.5 Three typefaces in the same point size (body), 14 point in this case, but different-height characters.

does its *set* or width. Different designs are more or less economical of horizontal space, and there may be variations such as *condensed* or *expanded* (also called *extended*) within a set of related designs (see Fig. 2.6).

A *typeface,* really an abstract design idea for how letters are to be presented, is a distinctive design for a set of visually related symbols. The set of symbols normally consists of the alphabet in uppercase and lowercase, as well as various punctuation marks and other ancillary symbols. In the computer context, a character set defines the set of symbols. Times New Roman, Optima, and Baskerville are all typefaces; they are designs for the shapes of symbols for which they are defined. A typeface can be realized in various sizes.

A *font* is a particular example of a typeface, often in a particular size, with symbols for each element of a particular character set. In letterpress type, a font is a collection of pieces of type representing the various symbols in a particular design and size. Many distinct fonts may be associated with a particular typeface. For example, for Times New Roman there may be different sizes, as well as variations such as

Helvetica	abcdefghijklmnopqrstuvwxyz
Helvetica bold	**abcdefghijklmnopqrstuvwxyz**
Helvetica oblique	*abcdefghijklmnopqrstuvwxyz*
Helvetica bold oblique	***abcdefghijklmnopqrstuvwxyz***
Helvetica narrow	abcdefghijklmnopqrstuvwxyz

FIGURE 2.6 Variations in set (average character width) as part of a single design.

bold, italic, expanded and condensed. The individual symbols in a font are called *glyphs* when they have been printed.

Typographers have a nomenclature for describing letters and their relationships on a page. Figure 2.7 shows the names for the various parts of letters.

The basic height of the lowercase letters is called the *x-height*. This is the distance that most of the lowercase letters extend above the *baseline*, upon which they rest. The parts of letters that reach above the x-height are called *ascenders*, and the parts that fall below, *descenders*. Uppercase letters extend a distance above the baseline termed the *cap-height*. There are very substantial differences in design from one typeface to another. Thus no universal relationship exists between the x-height, the cap-height, and the extent of ascenders and descenders.

A few other parts of letters deserve mention. One class of typefaces has *serifs*, small lateral extensions at the ends of strokes. Faces without serifs are called *sans serif* ('without serifs' in French). Serifs have an important role in the readability of type, providing some visual spacing and accentuation to the ends of strokes that may help the reader read faster and avoid fatigue. Serifs also help differentiate the style and mood of type, since there are different kinds of serif. Often the preferences that people express for typefaces depend on whether or not a face has serifs, and if so, on their shape.

Another feature is the *join*. Joins are generally thinner strokes that connect larger ones—for example, between the two vertical strokes in the letter 'h'. Joins often have thin, gentle, oblique curves. A primary vertical stroke is called a *stem*.

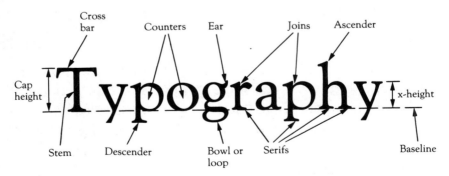

FIGURE 2.7   Parts of letters.

	Noncursive	Cursive
Vertical	**roman**	*script*
Oblique	*oblique*	*italic*

FIGURE 2.8   Composition of oblique and cursive characteristics.

One final round of typographic terminology: There are numerous styles of type, even within a single basic design. These varieties include *roman, italic, oblique,* and *bold.* Roman type is upright and is the normal kind used for running text, as in this sentence. Bold type has a heavier weight, thus being distinguished from roman. Describing italic is a bit more complicated. Italic is slanted or oblique, with curves and joins reminiscent of handwriting, and thus is also termed cursive. Oblique and cursive characteristics are independent, so a typeface may be oblique without being cursive, or cursive without being oblique (see Fig. 2.8). Only if a typeface is both cursive and oblique is it a true italic.

Typefaces are also described in terms of their *weight* and *contrast.* Weight is the heaviness or blackness of the letters. The larger the type, the heavier the lines must be in absolute terms to achieve the same visual weight. Contrast refers to the relationship between vertical and horizontal strokes, and is conveniently assessed by looking at the letter 'o'. In most traditional typefaces, the sides are heavier than the top and bottom. The greater this difference, the greater the contrast.

Using the terminology just presented, it is now possible to describe a useful taxonomy of typefaces. Some of the dimensions used in the taxonomy are discrete, and some continuous. Some properties thus fit into distinct categories, while others are matters of degree (Fig. 2.9).

Figure 2.10 shows some examples of typefaces and analyzes them according to this taxonomy. It would certainly be possible to add other characteristics to the taxonomy, and there are several schemes that describe and categorize typefaces more completely.[3] This is unnecessary for the purposes of this book. However, the ability to make a simple analysis of a type sample, using the scheme in Fig. 2.9, is a useful skill.

---

[3] See *Rookledge's International Typefinder* [Perfect and Rookledge 1983] for one such useful scheme.

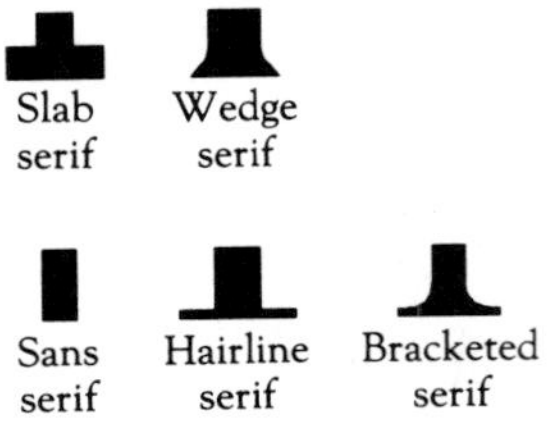

Discrete Categories

		Slab serif	Wedge serif

Serifs: Does the typeface have serifs? What type are they?

Sans serif   Hairline serif   Bracketed serif

Slant: Are the main strokes vertical or slanted?   b p *b p*

Cursive vs.   Are the letters joined or is there the hint of joining,   *abc*   abc
roman: as if written with pen strokes?

Spacing: Are the letters different widths (proportional) or the   **Mill**   `Mill`
               same width (monospaced)?

Thick and   Are the main strokes of equal weight, or do   A   A
thin: they vary?

Continuous Dimensions

Weight: Is the typeface bolder or lighter than others in   W   **w**
               its family?

X-height: What proportion of the ascender height is the x-height?   h   h   h

FIGURE 2.9   Descriptive type taxonomy.

Finally, it is useful to relate this terminology to two terms used in computer science. A *character set* is a numbered set of abstract symbols, independent of their style or appearance. Thus the letter 'A' is part of the ASCII character set. It is number 65, but this information does not specify how it will look, only that people will probably agree that it is an 'A' when they see it.

What computer professionals mean by the term *character* is not always clear. A character may be one of the elements of a character set, that is, an abstract symbol identified (in a computer) by its character code. But the term is also used to identify a glyph printed on a page. The difference did not matter in computer systems until there

Analysis of Type

Bracketed serifs, vertical, roman, proportional spacing, unequal strokes, normal weight, large x-height.

Analysis of Type

Bracketed serifs, vertical, roman, proportional spacing, unequal strokes, heavier weight than first sample, large x-height.

Analysis of Type

Bracketed serifs, slanted, cursive, proportional spacing, unequal strokes, heavier weight, large x-height.

Analysis of Type

Slab serifs, vertical, monospaced, equal strokes, lighter weight, large x-height.

Analysis of Type

Serifs, slanted, cursive, proportionally spaced, unequal strokes, lighter weight, large x-height.

Analysis of Type

Slab serifs, vertical, roman, proportionally spaced, unequal strokes, heavier weight, moderate x-height.

Analysis of Type

Sans serif, slanted, roman, proportionally spaced, equal strokes, lighter weight, very large x-height.

Analysis of Type

Slab serifs, vertical, roman, proportionally spaced, unequal strokes, light weight, smaller x-height.

FIGURE 2.10   Some typefaces analyzed according to the taxonomy. Note that judgments of weight are relative to the first sample. Weights are relative within families, but can be compared between families.

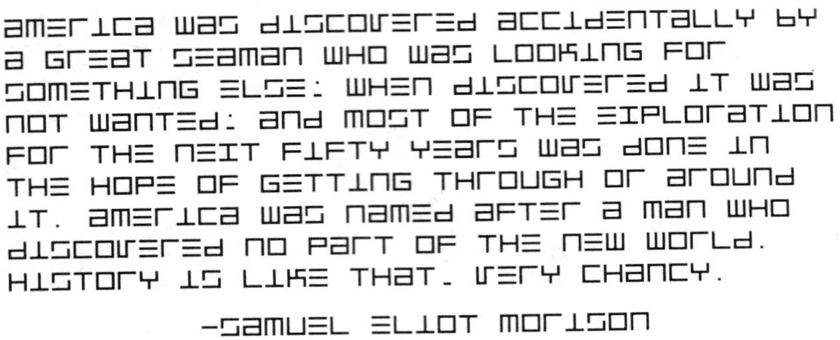

america was discovered accidentally by
a great seaman who was looking for
something else: when discovered it was
not wanted: and most of the exploration
for the next fifty years was done in
the hope of getting through or around
it. america was named after a man who
discovered no part of the new world.
History is like that. very chancy.

                    —samuel eliot morison

FIGURE 2.11   An alphabet with no case distinction, composed entirely of horizontal and vertical strokes.

were choices of typeface in output devices. In this book, the word character will be used in the former sense of an abstract symbol when context does not indicate otherwise.

Legibility

Legibility is the degree to which text is easy to read. The quality of text varies widely, from barely *decodable,* to text that is read quickly and comfortably by all readers.

Figure 2.11 shows a typeface that is decodable at best. It is so bad because it uses horizontal and vertical lines only, without regard to the expectations of readers. Readers have a huge investment in the shapes of letterforms, having spent much of their lives recognizing only certain shapes. Further, the shapes of letters have been tuned over time by printers and type designers to make good use of the abilities of the human visual system.

Interestingly, the quotation printed in Figure 2.11 using this awful typeface is remarkably easy to understand. This is true partly because reading is extremely intelligent behavior in which people make use of a wide range of information from the whole context of the communication, and partly because human beings are extraordinarily good pattern recognizers. To see that this is so, try to identify the individual symbols in Fig. 2.12, which do not form a word.[4]

What is recognizable as a letter, in the limit, includes extreme

---

[4] The answer is ivgearx.

⊥⊔⊡≡⊓⌐⊥

FIGURE 2.12 Some isolated letters in the same illegible typeface.

distortions of the basic letter form. The 'm's of Fig. 2.13 all may be letters in the context of type and print, but they might not be recognized as such in other situations. Ad copy that intentionally distorts letters for effect testifies to this fact (Fig. 2.14). The point is that mere decodability of letterforms does not attest to the quality of the typeface, but is only a rave review of human visual information-processing capabilities.

While the barely decodable text of Fig. 2.11 is an extreme example,

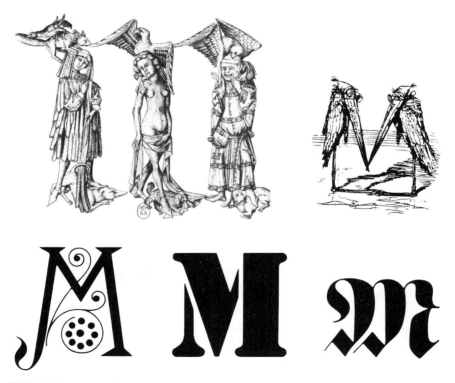

FIGURE 2.13 All of these "symbols" are recognizable as the letter 'm'. (Ornamental initial with figures, ca. 1460. *Phot. Bibl. Nat. Paris.*)

FIGURE 2.14   Advertising relies on people's ability to decode nonstandard forms as letters. These advertising logos make delightful use of our visual flexibility to create visual puns. (The Parkside logo design for Milestone Properties Corp. by S&N Advertising; David Wolfram, art director. Reproduced courtesy of S&N Advertising and Milestone Properties. Belmont Springs logo courtesy of Belmont Springs Water Co., Inc.)

Fig. 2.15 shows a font developed for computer output. It is easy to produce on dot-array output devices, and superficially has well-formed letters. Although more legible than the face shown in Fig. 2.11, it would not be suitable for a book, business letter, or any other running text. Reading very much of this font would be fatiguing, and most people would soon grow weary of a book printed with it. (Try reading the full sample in Fig. 2.15!) Most fonts presented on computer screens today are legible enough for some purposes, but do not pretend to be suitable for running text on paper. Some of the early dot-matrix fonts were of low quality indeed. In contrast, Fig. 2.16 shows a very legible

America was discovered accidentally by a great seaman who was looking for something else; when discovered it was not wanted; and most of the exploration for the next fifty years was done in the hope of getting through or around it. America was named after a man who discovered no part of the New World. History is like that, very chancy.

—Samuel Eliot Morison

FIGURE 2.15   A low-resolution font. (Chicago, a screen font developed for its Macintosh computer by Apple, Inc.)

America was discovered accidentally by a great
seaman who was looking for something else;
when discovered it was not wanted; and most
of the exploration for the next fifty years was
done in the hope of getting through or around
it. America was named after a man who
discovered no part of the New World. History
is like that, very chancy.

— Samuel Eliot Morison

FIGURE 2.16   A more legible font (Monotype Baskerville roman, 12 point).

typeface, one suitable for publication use with running text. It respects
history and the reader's investment in the shapes of letters. It is easy
to read.

Typographic quality arises from a number of qualities of typefaces.
Since their inception in 1816, sans serif typefaces have inspired debates
about their legibility and appropriateness. Today we are so thoroughly
familiar with sans serif faces that some of the controversy of the past
may be hard to understand. While there are sans serif text faces of high
quality, serifed types are generally preferred by typographers and book
designers for running text. Most books, magazines, and newspapers
employ serifed typefaces for the bulk of their content. Similar comments can be made in comparing monospaced and proportionally
spaced typefaces, except that no school of typographers prefers monospaced faces on æsthetic grounds. Monospaced printing is an artifact
of output technologies—typewriters, cell-text terminals, line printers,
and so on—and has very limited typographic utility.

Interletter spacing of letterforms materially affects the legibility of
text. There is a nominal, close spacing built into most typefaces used
for running text (as in books) that is part of our expectations about
how print looks. Irregularities in spacing attract the reader's attention
and reduce the quality of text presentation. Figure 2.17 shows the same
typeface spaced well and spaced poorly. The difference is readily apparent.

A more subtle factor in readability is differentiation of letterform
shapes. Consider the letter pairs 'bd' and 'pq'. In some typefaces, these

America was discovered accidentally by a great
seaman who was looking for something else;
when discovered it was not wanted; and most of
the exploration for the next fifty years was done
in the hope of getting through or around it.
America was named after a man who discovered
no part of the New World. History is like that,
very chancy.

—*Samuel Eliot Morison*

(a)

America was discovered accidentally by
a great seaman who was looking for
something else; when discovered it was
not wanted; and most of the exploration
for the next fifty years was done in the
hope of getting through or around it.
America was named after a man who
discovered no part of the New World.
History is like that, very chancy.

—*Samuel Eliot Morison*

(b)

FIGURE 2.17 Interletter spacing affects legibility. Compare the good spacing in (a) with the poor spacing in (b).

letters are mirror images of each other (Fig. 2.18a). All such similarities
of different letters are called *assimilation.* It is a matter of degree; faces
may exhibit more or less of it. Most serifed designs intentionally break
this symmetry (Fig. 2.18b), creating greater differentiation between
the shapes. It is not only people with dyslexia, a perceptual problem
that can cause confusion of left and right, who are troubled by high
degrees of symmetry in letter shape. Assimilation reduces readability
by eliminating features that are useful in identifying letters and words.

What else are serifs for? One suggestion is that they help to make
the ends of strokes more visible, thus making it easier to identify the
main strokes in a letter. Another observation is that they help differentiate combinations of adjacent letters and minimize ambiguity. For

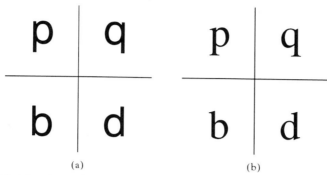

FIGURE 2.18   Assimilation of letterforms results in mirror-image shapes (a). Most serif faces intentionally do not have this symmetry (b).

example, the combination 'rn' in a serif typeface is usually less like an 'm' than in a sans serif face: 'rn'.

Why are there so many typeface designs? One has only to look through a typeface book, flip through a magazine, or select transfer letters in a graphics arts store to discover the diversity of type. There is no single answer to the question. Certainly, commercial exploitation of designs and different technologies have been responsible for the proliferation of type designs, as have differences of opinion and æsthetics. Perhaps many typefaces have been created for too little reason, certainly the case in the digital world. The most important reason for the wealth of typeface designs, however, may be that type is put to a broad range of uses, and the differentiation of purpose drives the creation of so many designs to fulfill the various needs. On this point, Bigelow (private communication) said:

> Literate people like to make letters. It is a reflection of a literate society that typefaces are part of fashion. We even deface our buildings with graffiti made of letters.

How bland the world would be if there were only a few typefaces for books and magazines, a few for advertising, one for phone books, and so on. Thus the diversity serves the useful purpose of providing functional choices for particular uses and typesetting technologies.

What Typographers Know about Reading

Letterforms have evolved over time as production technology has improved and as type designers have gained more and more experience with what works and what does not. One force acting on the development of typefaces is the capabilities of human readers, which provide guidance in the form of preference and effectiveness as change is introduced. It is dangerous to tinker too much with the shapes of letters in defiance of historical practice because many sound reasons for conventional practice do exist.

However, most traditional typographical knowledge is based on experience and æsthetics, not experimental research. Some typographers' beliefs will probably have to be adjusted as a result of psychological experiments, as will be shown later. Nonetheless, typographers do know a great deal that psychologists and now computer system developers are just finding out. Here are a few examples that apply to running text.

Italic text, while generally considered quite legible, is certainly more difficult to read than ordinary roman text [McLean 1980:44]. Although a word or two in italic, used for emphasis, does not slow people down much, whole blocks of italic text are annoying and tedious.

The same can be said of bold type. Boldface stands out more strongly on the page than does italic, and this creates a greater degree of emphasis.

TYPE SET IN ALL UPPERCASE LETTERS IS HARD TO READ BECAUSE THE LETTERS HAVE FEWER DIFFERENTIATING CHARACTERISTICS THAN DO LOWERCASE ONES [NEISSER 1967:109]. THE WORDS ARE ALL RECTANGULAR, UNLIKE LOWERCASE WORDS WHICH HAVE CHARACTERISTIC SHAPES [TAYLOR 1983:185–188]. ALTHOUGH USING UPPERCASE DOES ATTRACT ATTENTION, IT SLOWS DOWN THE READER. A LITTLE UPPER CASE GOES A LONG WAY. CAPS AND SMALL CAPS ARE NO MORE READABLE THAN FULL-SIZE CAPITALS.

According to typographers, sans serif type, like this, is generally harder to read than serifed type, [McLean 1980:44]. Rarely are books set in sans serif typefaces. Nonetheless, readers are quite accustomed to sans serif forms; some magazines are set with them, and signs and advertising abound with these "more modern" letters. Sans serif type has a more functional, up-to-date appearance.

```
Monospaced type is also harder to read, com-
pared to proportionally-spaced typefaces. This
may be because the constraint of equal spacing
interferes with the usual spacing of features in
```

```
sequences of letterforms. Intraword spaces are
unnecessarily large with monospaced type, and
thus it is uneconomical of space on the line.
```

The Psychologist's View

Not only is the knowledge of typographers useful in designing fonts and documents for computer presentation, it reflects intriguingly on the nature of human reading abilities. Psychologists approach letters and reading in terms of human abilities and behavior. They form vision theories and conduct experiments in the hope of developing a better understanding of how seeing works, that is, of *visual perception.*

Much of our knowledge about how people understand words comes from experiments in which people report what they see when words or letters are flashed briefly. Other experimental work has been done on *continuous reading,* also called *reading for comprehension.* Studies of continuous reading are performed by such methods as measuring overall reading speed for various texts, and tracking eye position by computer during reading.

Reading is an amazing feat. In purely computational terms, dozens or even hundreds of symbols can be perceived, analyzed, and decoded every second. Consider this quotation from Flesch [1949:182]:

> Reading is really a miracle: Your eyes pick up groups of words in split-second time and your mind keeps these words in delicate balance until it gets around to a point where they make sense.

Each symbol has features that we use to distinguish it from other, possibly similar symbols. Although reading is not understood in its entirety, the structure and some of the basic information-processing characteristics of the visual system are known.[5] This information bears directly on issues of the typographic quality of printed and displayed images.

The structure of the eye is shown diagrammatically in Fig. 2.19. The *retina,* the structure upon which the *lens* forms images, senses the light and performs the first level of analysis of the image. The retina has a special central region, the *fovea,* where the greatest acuity lies. The neural structures in the retina detect light levels, register color,

---

[5] There is also a large body of research on the reading process. See Taylor and Taylor [1983] for a survey.

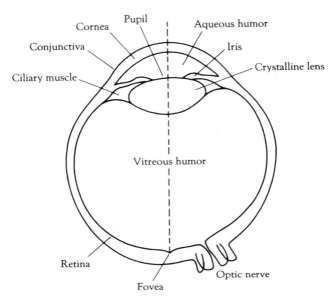

FIGURE 2.19 The human eye.

and enhance the contrast of edges. In fact, the "wiring" of the retina performs a great deal of feature detection and signal processing, creating a partially processed image to send on to the brain for higher-level analysis.

Outside the fovea, the retina is populated mostly by *rods,* cells that can detect light down to very low levels but do not detect color. The fovea, by comparison, contains a high density of color-sensitive *cone* cells. The fovea is small compared with the whole visual field—only about two degrees of visual angle. At a reading distance of 12 inches, for example, this is only a circle about 0.4 inch in diameter, or about 10 mm. This circle is large enough to include only a few letters, maybe a word or two. To see the limits of your own fovea, try this experiment. Close one eye, and focus your attention on a single letter near the middle of this paragraph. Then, without moving your eyes, see how many nearby letters you can actually see clearly. Only a few are clearly visible. Nonetheless, we perceive words, objects, and whole scenes in the world.

The eyeball is rotated by muscles so as to focus different parts of the visual scene onto the fovea. Even when looking at a single spot, as in the experiment just described, the eye actually oscillates continuously. These small motions appear to be necessary to seeing; an image contrived to be stationary on the retina quickly disappears from the perceived view. Larger motions, called *saccades*, each followed by a *fixation*, are combined to scan an image, such as a page of text, so as to take in the parts necessary to see the whole. The brain, of course, does the computational magic necessary to assemble the pieces into a perception.

Spatial Frequencies

For purposes of discussing typography, it is necessary to talk in terms of the information-processing abilities of the visual system. Figure 2.20 shows the sensitivity of the eye to *spatial frequencies*—the number of cycles per degree of visual angle—as determined by the contrast necessary to distinguish any given frequency. The maximum sensitivity is about eight cycles per degree. Above about 50 or 60 cycles per degree, sensitivity is so low that only uniform gray is perceived by most people,

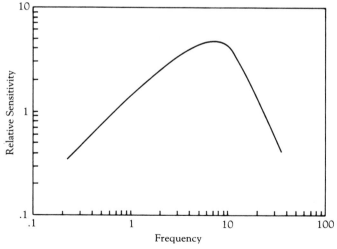

FIGURE 2.20 Spatial sensitivity of the eye. Note the fairly broad peak of sensitivity around six or eight cycles per degree. There is little sensitivity beyond 50 or 60 cycles per degree. (Based on data from *Visual Perception* [Cornsweet 1970:341].)

under normal conditions. There are situations, however, in which greater spatial sensitivity is observed. For example, in the phenomenon of *hyperacuity*, spatial differences as small as 600 cycles per degree can be detected [Westheimer 1979; Geisler 1984].

What are the consequences for typography? First consider the numbers in terms of real reading situations. The visual angle of a feature on paper depends on its physical size and on the reading distance. For example, at a reading distance of 12 inches (relatively close), 60 cycles per degree of visual angle corresponds to roughly 300 cycles per inch (see Fig. 2.21). At 12 inches, lines spaced at 300 per inch would be just discernible as lines rather than gray.

The ability of the eye to perceive detail depends in part on the contrast. Different output media have different contrast. In fact, for many output devices, greater contrast can be attained at greater cost of the device. Thus certain engineering decisions affect the quality of perceived text. More of this in Chapter 3.

One school of vision researchers holds that the overall sensitivity of the eyes to spatial frequencies is in fact the result of a number of spatial filters operating in parallel [Ginsburg 1980; Sekuler, Wilson, and Owsley 1984]. Figure 2.22 shows how this might be so. According to Ginsburg [1980], the presence of these individual channels is verified by biological data. Such an arrangement is not too surprising, considering that an analogous decomposition into temporal frequencies is performed by the ear in analyzing sounds.

That spatial information might be resolved into a number of channels, for processing in the eye and brain, suggests some interesting

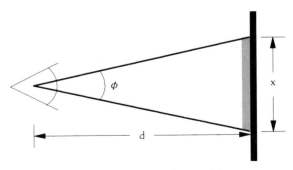

FIGURE 2.21   Visual angle, distances, and spatial frequency. $x = 2d\,(\tan \phi/2)$. If $\phi = 1/60°$, and $d = 12$ inches, then $x = .0035$ inch, or 286 cycles per inch.

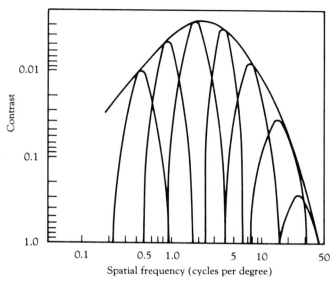

FIGURE 2.22   Spatial sensitivity of the eye as the sum of the sensitivities of many overlapping filters. (Ginsburg, Arthur P.: "Specifying Relevant Spatial Information for Image Evaluation and Display Design: An Explanation of How We See Certain Objects," Proceedings of the SID Vol. 21/3, 1980, Figure 1. Permission for Reprint, Courtesy Society for Information Display.)

conclusions for the perception of letters. First, such parallel processing is consistent with the idea that redundant information makes it easier, not harder, to recognize objects such as letters. Letters may be distinguished from one another solely on the basis of low-frequency information (see Fig. 2.23). This does not mean that the high-frequency information (sharp edges and fine details) is unneeded, but rather that the low-frequency channels contain enough information for basic recognition of letters. The channel theory also suggests that misinformation in one channel or another may make recognition more difficult, even though the information necessary for recognition is present within the signal. This is why understanding a picture containing much high-frequency noise is sometimes easier from a distance.

Visual System Characteristics

A related information-processing characteristic of the vision system is the ability of the eye to define edges and enhance contrast. Indeed,

FIGURE 2.23   Using only low spatial frequencies, letters may still be identified and distinguished from each other. In this example, much of the high-frequency information has been lost, but letters and words can still be identified.

the eye appears to be structured primarily for the purpose of finding edges. An effect called *lateral inhibition* is responsible for edge detection in the retina. Experiments with the visual systems of mammals, including man, reveal neural structures "wired" so that outputs occur only when edges of particular orientations are present in their portion of the visual field. Circular areas of the fovea, like the one shown in Fig. 2.24 respond most strongly when the center is lit more than the surrounding areas. When an edge in the visual field is imaged onto the fovea, those regions around the edge respond, communicating the location of the edge to the brain. This arrangement has the useful

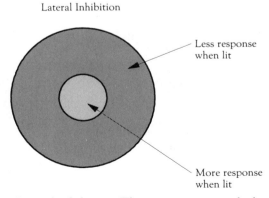

FIGURE 2.24   Lateral inhibition. This structure responds the strongest when partially illuminated, as when an edge passes through its center.

FIGURE 2.25 Simultaneous contrast: The center squares are the same intensity but appear different.

property of being insensitive to the absolute level of light. Thus a black
velvet dress is just as visible in the dim light of a restaurant as in
sunlight, provided that its surroundings reflect a different level of light
does the dress itself.

Our eyes serve us well, but they do not always give an accurate
rendering of a visual scene in terms of the intensities or shapes that an
instrument might measure. Many illusions result from the way that we
see. For example, an effect called *simultaneous contrast* is responsible
for the variations in apparent tone of the center squares in Fig. 2.25.
In fact the centers are the same shade of gray; only the adjacent areas
differ.

Another example is shown in Fig. 2.26(a). This familiar illusion,

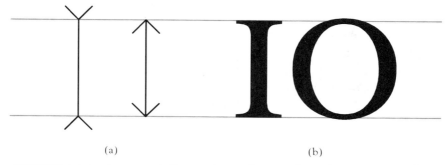

(a)   (b)

FIGURE 2.26 An optical illusion that makes size depend on context and
shape (a) necessitates modifications to letterforms to achieve apparent alignment (b). Here the 'O' has been made slightly larger than the 'I'.

the distortion of length by context, means that letters must be altered in some situations in order to look right, as shown in Fig. 2.26(b).

The temporal abilities of the eye are also of interest for typography. Reading rates are limited by the rate that the visual system can process information. Also, screen displays that flicker or otherwise vary in intensity may interact with time-sensitive characteristics of the visual system. The eye can detect very small variations in intensity when the rate of change is neither too fast nor too slow. In particular, at rates above about 40 cycles per second, even large changes in intensity become imperceptible for most people. This is why motion pictures appear to be steady in intensity. Although only 24 frames are presented each second, each is presented twice by the movie projector [Simon and Schuster 1967:190-191], with a resulting flicker rate of 48 flashes per second. The *critical-fusion frequency* (CFF) is the rate at which a light varying in intensity will appear to be steady for 50% of all people. CFF is a function of the modulation of the signal, the relative intensity of the high and low points in the variation. There are substantial differences in critical-fusion rates from person to person.

Figure 2.27 shows the critical-fusion frequency as a function of intensity modulation. In the case of 100% modulation, CFF is 40 cycles per second. This corresponds to the situation of a motion picture projected in a totally dark room; when the beam of light is interrupted, it is actually turned off and on completely. At 5% modulation, CFF drops sharply, to only 19 Hz. At this same 5% modulation, the low-frequency limit of flicker sensitivity is 3 Hz.[6]

Another area of interest to psychologists is determining how the parts of letters are used in reading words and sentences. As Fig. 2.28 reveals, the information used to decode letterforms is not distributed evenly throughout the symbols. Most people can read the top line (a) in the figure more easily than the bottom line (b), although roughly equal parts of the letters are revealed. The top part of the line contains more useful information than the bottom. That is, there are more features on top that differentiate one letter from another. Interestingly, information density varies from one writing system to another. Hebrew contains more information at the bottom of the line than at the top [Haber and Haber 1981:167].

---

[6] Cycles per second is denoted as Hz, in honor of the 19th-Century German physicist, Heinrich Rudolf Hertz.

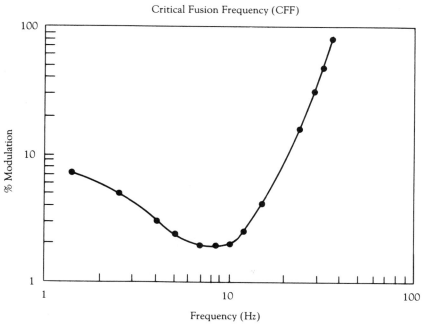

Critical Fusion Frequency (CFF)

FIGURE 2.27   Threshold of sensitivity to intensity variation (based on [Cornsweet 1970:396]). For example, at 5% modulation the range of sensitivity to flicker is between 3 Hz and 19 Hz.

Letterforms are rendered less legible when the high frequencies—the detail-bearing parts—are lost in reproduction, as happens when outputting to a device with low resolution. Substantial loss of quality also results when detailed features are obscured by high-frequency noise in the reproduction. Figure 2.29(a) shows how high-frequency noise can reduce print quality, as any user of a maladjusted photocopier knows. Figure 2.29(b) shows a similar problem, when noise is added by the output grid in the form of dots constituting the symbols. Compare each of these with Fig. 2.29(c).

It is perhaps surprising that perturbations of low-frequency components interfere dramatically with legibility. After all, information theory might suggest that high-frequency parts contain more information than do low-frequency parts. Low-frequency noise takes the form of irregularities in letter size, shape, and spacing. The eye is most sensitive

As quick as thought is an old mode of expression,
used to convey an idea of the greatest rapidity; but
no one, until lately, ever dreamed that a thought
could be sent hundreds of miles in a few seconds;
and that a person standing in London might hold
a conversation with another in Edinburgh, put
questions and receive answers, just as if they were
seated together in one room, instead of being three
hundred miles apart. The Electric Telegraph is
another of the wonderful discoveries of modern times

(a)

As quick as thought is an old mode of expression,
used to convey an idea of the greatest rapidity. But
no one, until lately, ever dreamed that a thought
could be sent hundreds of miles in a few seconds,
and that a person standing in London might hold
a conversation with another in Edinburgh, put
questions and receive answers, just as if they were
seated together in one room, instead of being three
hundred miles apart. The Electric Telegraph is
another of the wonderful discoveries of modern times.

(b)

FIGURE 2.28   Where is the useful information in letters? There is more useful information in the tops of Latin letters than in the bottoms, as this figure
illustrates. Roughly equal parts of the letters are exposed in (a) and (b), but the
sample that exposes the tops of letters, (a), is much easier to read.

to low spatial frequency, and thus detects these "errors" well, but the
basic decodability of the letterforms remains intact. High-frequency
disturbances to shape change details and distinctive features of letters,
characteristics important for letter identification.

Reading Performance

The results of psychological experiments can bear on the best ways
to present textual information. Personal preferences or even informed
professional judgments seem inadequate to measure the quality of a
typeface. An objective standard of measurement of typeface quality
would certainly be useful, but none has yet emerged.

One psychologist, Miles A. Tinker, compared the speed at which
people could read text set in various ways. When typeface was the

Noise interferes with legibility.
(a)

Noise interferes with legibility.
(b)

Noise interferes with legibility.
(c)

FIGURE 2.29 High-frequency noise reduces text legibility. In (a), random dots of white and black interfere with the letterforms. In (b), letters are composed of pixels in a coarse grid, resulting in jaggedness in the letterforms. Compare these with (c), which is set at higher resolution, without added noise.

variable of interest, Tinker observed significant differences in reading performance. Some of his results are shown in Table 2.2 [Tinker 1963b:48].

Interesting questions arise from such studies. Tinker found few significant differences in reading rate with the sans serif types he investigated compared with serifed types. For example, in the experiment summarized in Table 2.2, the 2.6% difference for Kabel Light (sans serif) compared with Garamond (serif) is statistically significant. Nonetheless, readers had a strong preference for serifed type [Tinker 1963b:64]. Such conflicts between the typographer's advice and experimental results demand a refinement of the issues, and a careful comparison of the two sources of information. Either source may be right or wrong. In contrast, experiments have verified the superiority of proportional spacing over monospacing [Payne 1967:125-126; Beldie, Pastoor, and Schwarz 1983].

It is important to understand the operational definition of quality for psychological evaluation of printing. Reading speed is the best measure of type quality that has been found. While other aspects of reading, such as preference for one style of type or another, are certainly relevant, these more subjective responses are hard to measure and relate to quality and effectiveness.

A good typeface design will conform to the range of letter shapes that people expect and read easily. Intentional distortions or deviations from the norm result in lower quality, regardless of how well printed

Typeface	Percent Difference
Scotch Roman (standard)	0.0
Garamond	+0.4
Antique	−0.2
Bodoni	−1.0
Old Style	−1.1
Caslon Old Style	−1.3
Kabel Light	−2.2
Cheltenham	−2.4
American Typewriter	−4.7
Cloister Black	−13.6

TABLE 2.2   Tinker's ranking of the readability of various typefaces. The values are percentage differences in reading speed. A *difference* greater than 2.6% is significant in these data. Thus, for example, Kabel Light and Cheltenham were both found to be significantly less readable than Garamond. Kabel Light is the only sans serif typeface included in this study. (Reprinted by permission from *Legibility of Print* by Miles Tinker © 1963 by Iowa State University Press, 2121 So. State Ave., Ames, Iowa.)

the result may be. Of course, many faces are designed to call the reader's attention to themselves—advertising is full of them. However, these designs score low on the kind of readability tests that Tinker used. His tests were aimed at running text, material to be read in order to receive information encoded in written language (as in a book). Tinker's work, discussed at some length in Chapter 5, provides a useful start towards measuring legibility.

The Engineer's View

An engineer might approach typography by examining the type itself to understand its physical characteristics and structure, with the goal of being able to produce good print economically. Engineers ask questions about what is really necessary in a system to achieve the desired result, and what can be eliminated or restructured to reduce cost. These are useful questions because they challenge us to define typographic requirements for systems and to relate typographic results to a system's effectiveness.

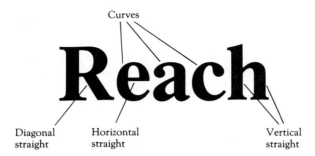

FIGURE 2.30 Primary features of Latin letterforms.

The Physical Characteristics of Letterforms

What is the physical structure of letters? How much information is required to create them? By comparing the answers to these questions with the characteristics of the visual system, it is possible to make engineering decisions aimed at achieving a particular level of quality.

Letterforms have four specific recurring features (see Fig. 2.30):

- straight vertical lines;
- straight horizontal lines;
- straight diagonal lines;
- curves and arcs.

These features have low spatial frequencies, normally in the range of 4 to 8 cycles per degree of visual angle for books read at a comfortable distance. Thus the number of light-dark cycles per degree of visual angle for these features is relatively low. They are the large-dimension parts of letters. Conversely, the high-frequency components of letters are sharp edges and small elements such as serifs.

Technology versus Quality

Among the definitions of 'quality' in Webster's dictionary are (1) degree of excellence and (2) superiority in kind [Merriam-Webster 1983]. The first meaning is a matter of grade or comparison, as with different grades of meat. The second refers specifically to the best grade—an automobile of high quality, for example. Both kinds of statement about letterforms are useful. Relative to some use, one typeface may be superior to another. Again with respect to some purpose, a goal of a project may be to produce the best printing possible,

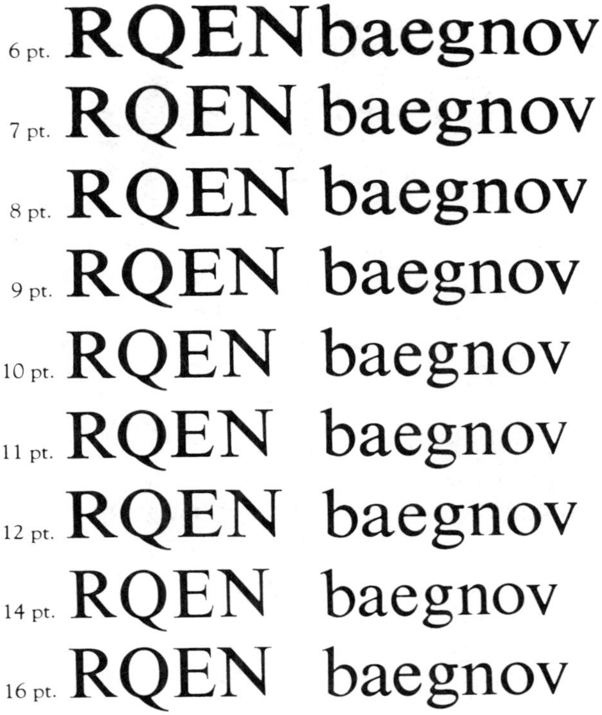

6 pt. **RQENbaegnov**

7 pt. **RQEN baegnov**

8 pt. **RQEN baegnov**

9 pt. **RQEN baegnov**

10 pt. **RQEN baegnov**

11 pt. **RQEN baegnov**

12 pt. **RQEN baegnov**

14 pt. **RQEN baegnov**

16 pt. **RQEN baegnov**

FIGURE 2.31 Typeface features vary with size. The letters shown have been normalized to the same height to make the differences more visible (courtesy of Charles Bigelow).

equal to any done by any means. Unfortunately, a cost is always associated with any given level of quality.

Engineering is compromise, finding good trade-offs among the various aspects and characteristics of a product. Printing technology is no different. Any machine for making letterforms represents a set of choices that favors certain properties to the detriment of others. The process of designing printing and publishing equipment forces engineers to make choices that affect the cost, quality, and effectiveness of the resulting designs. An important focus of this book is those trade-offs that affect the quality of the print.

Phototypesetting machines make good-quality letterforms by imaging them photographically from carefully made film masters. Only one master is usually used to create all of the sizes in a particular style. In traditional type design, however, the shape of letters in the same typeface varies systematically as the size changes (see Fig. 2.31). Smaller letters must be bolder and fatter to retain their legibility and their family resemblance to larger letters of similar design. Larger letters, used for titles and other "display" purposes, have more detail and more visually interesting features. Although manufacturers of phototypesetting equipment included multiple optical masters in their early products to cover the size range better, competitive economics led them to issue many typefaces rather than multiple masters for each face. Quantity seemed to be more salable than quality. The standard master was tuned to normal text sizes. Thus most phototypeset material is less than optimal in small and large sizes, but is fine for ordinary running text. The economics of this new technology were stronger than the apparent necessity to conform to the best typographic practice. As a consequence, readers have been exposed to phototypeset material not quite matching the visual quality of typeset material created using earlier metal-casting technology.

In contrast to phototypesetting, movable metal type is limited in the degree to which letters may overlap each other's space horizontally, and especially in the fineness of the thin, scriptlike strokes that might join two adjacent letters [Flowers 1984]. Figure 2.32(a) shows a type

Letters, these seemingly commonplace little signs, taken for granted by so many, belong to the most momentous products of creative power.

(a)

It is not the attainment of the goal that matters, it is the things that are met with by the way.

(b)

FIGURE 2.32 (a) Isadora, a type design by Kris Holmes. The freely overlapping letters and thin joins would have made this face impractical in metal type (courtesy of Kris Holmes). (b) Old Original Caslon italic, a Monotype metal typeface.

design that would have been extraordinarily difficult to produce and use in metal type. Compare it with Fig. 2.32(b), which displays a typeface designed for metal type.

Each change of typographic technology creates new constraints and new capabilities,[7] which may or may not be exploited. For example, most photocomposition equipment incorporates a coarse-unit spacing system (e.g., 18 different widths) that is a holdover from Monotype typecasting machines, even though no technological limit requires so coarse a unit of width in the new machines.

This same situation arises in digital typography. Digital system designers are now in the position of deciding whether to perpetuate the limitations of photocomposition, or to make use of new capabilities in support of better typographic quality. In phototypesetting, designs that varied with size incurred the cost of making additional photographic masters. In digital systems, greater cost results from creating additional font descriptions that have to be produced, stored in memory, and decoded when needed. Alternatively, software might be developed to automatically adjust typeface features with size, again at some expense. Remarkably, the same set of choices must be made again, and the choices made will probably affect this aspect of typographic quality for some time to come.

These are only a few ways in which type designs have been adapted to prevailing printing technologies. Indeed, the printing method creates many requirements that the type designer must meet in order to get good results, and therefore the style of any period partly reflects its printing technology. Hermann Zapf, an excellent contemporary type designer, describes the situation as it stood a few years ago [Zapf 1970:29-30]:

> When Claude Garamond and Giambattista Bodoni created their famous printing faces (for us still 'archetypes') all printing was done entirely with the hand press upon dampened hand-made paper. Their types had to meet only these requirements. Today, on the contrary, a useful printing type must be suited not only to the content and surface finish of the various printing papers (and what do not the paper mills mix into their paper-brews today!), but suited also to the refined demands of modern high-speed presses. And it must further do justice to the newer processes—

---

[7] Zapf [1968] provides a full historical discussion of this point.

offset and gravure, stereotypes and electrotypes for large runs on rotary presses. The type itself is no longer hand-cast as in earlier centuries, but in fast-running type-foundry casting machines; or in elaborately-devised composing machines, casting either a complete line or single letters. In the electronic photographic way of composition, the letter is designed to an unimaginable speed of reproduction. These problems surely never afflicted Garamond and Bodoni. A modern type will hence avoid narrow counters (producing narrow inner areas in the letters), such as appear in Garamond's e, or the delicate hairlines of Bodoni's or Didot's types. Whoever has heard a printer's explosive language when the tender serifs break in printing (since hardly anyone today takes time or care or patience to replace broken letters), will dream of a type that will not needlessly tax the printer's spiritual equilibrium. All these simple examples will have suggested two fundamental requirements in the design of new type especially for the smaller sizes: open and clear letter forms and a well-defined weight of stroke for the modern technical demands additionally made by the newer technical processes.[8]

It is worthwhile to understand what characteristics of type result from recent printing methods, and especially what requirements current digital methods entail. At the same time, one must remember that digital typography is only the latest in a long series of techniques for achieving largely the same purpose. Many of the problems we have today would be familiar to the practitioners of earlier methods; there is much we can learn from them.

Information Content of Letterforms

The engineering perspective provides an analytic understanding of the physical requirements of creating letterforms. Both understanding and prescriptions for system design emerge from engineering analysis.

The basic engineering tool for attacking the problem of letterform quality is the analysis of spatial frequency. Spatial frequency, as noted earlier, is the rate at which an image changes intensity over space. Just as a musical note from a flute, say, has different frequencies in its harmonic structure, text has a harmonic structure that varies in intensity.

---

[8] Hermann Zapf, *About Alphabets: Some Marginal Notes on Type Design.* Copyright © 1960 and 1970 by The MIT Press. Reprinted with permission.

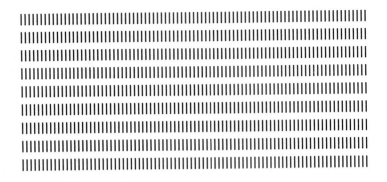

(a)

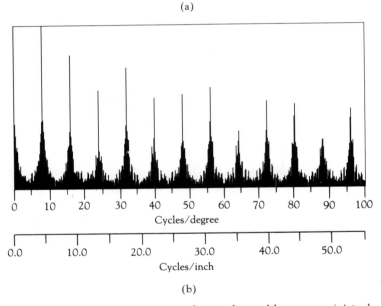

(b)

FIGURE 2.33 The power spectrum of a simple textlike pattern (a) is shown in (b).

Consider the cyclic pattern shown in Fig. 2.33(a). The pattern resembles the main vertical strokes in roman text. Think of it as a signal varying in space from left to right, much as an acoustical waveform might be plotted. Clearly, there is a dominant frequency with a period equal to the spacing of the pattern. If the pattern were sinusoidal, one that varied continuously in intensity, then only this one frequency would be present, not any harmonics or other high frequencies.

However, the pattern has the spatial frequency spectrum shown in Fig. 2.33(b). Text is fundamentally unlike a continuous-tone image, having only sharp transitions from black to white. The successive peaks are harmonics, reflecting the sharp edges of the strokes. While an infinitely sharp boundary has frequency components at all frequencies to infinity, real marks on paper, when analyzed, show declining components at higher frequencies. Also, there is an upper limit to the frequencies that any physical analysis can record.

Spatial frequencies are calculated by a technique called *Fourier analysis*. The representation used here of the frequency components of text is called the *power spectrum*. It is an average measure of the component of each frequency in the original image, and requires a Fourier analysis of a large enough number of samples to be representative. The power spectra in Fig. 2.33 and elsewhere in this book are analyses of the horizontal frequency components of text. They represent the spatial frequencies present in horizontal-line samples through the text, and thus are not sensitive to spatial frequencies in the vertical dimension.

Figure 2.34 shows some text and its horizontal power spectrum. Note the low-frequency part, which corresponds to the main vertical strokes in the letters, and the high-frequency part, which corresponds to fine details. The highest frequencies represent the sharp edges of strokes.

Another view of the information content of letterforms helps explain how shapes copied from traditional typefaces are degraded when converted into digital form. Bigelow [1981:9] describes this situation very clearly:

> Aliasing appears as the diagnostic "stair-case" effects on digital curves and diagonals. At higher resolutions, aliasing roughens these contours. As resolution decreases, roughness becomes jaggedness; flat spots and bumps appear. At still lower frequencies the actual stair-steps become obvious, curved contours become polygonal, and the distinctions between straights, curves, and diagonals become obscured.

Aliasing is a persistent problem in producing letterforms digitally. Other aberrations are added when output devices form images with discrete elements and positions, because shapes cannot be presented

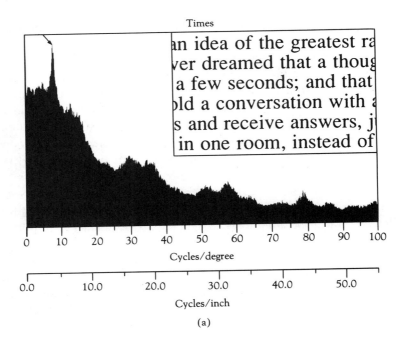

(a)

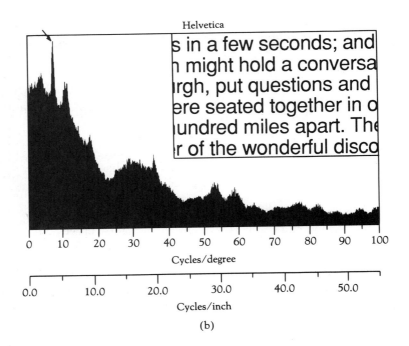

(b)

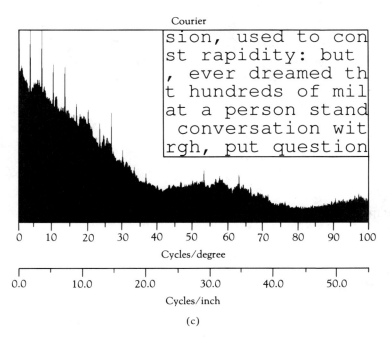

Courier

```
sion,  used  to  con
st  rapidity:  but
,  ever  dreamed  th
t  hundreds  of  mil
at  a  person  stand
 conversation  wit
rgh,  put  question
```

0   10   20   30   40   50   60   70   80   90   100

Cycles/degree

0.0   10.0   20.0   30.0   40.0   50.0

Cycles/inch

(c)

FIGURE 2.34 Samples of text and their horizontal power spectra. The vertical axis is the logarithmic intensity of the frequency component, and the horizontal is the spatial frequency in cycles per degree of visual angle. A reading distance of 40 cm (15.75 inches) is assumed. The peak in the Times typeface (a) at about 8 cycles per degree corresponds to the main stroke spacing. Helvetica (b) exhibits a main-stroke peak, similar to Times, at 7 cycles per degree. These peaks correspond well to the maximum sensitivity of the eye. Courier (c), a monospaced typeface, has no similar peak, but instead a number of sharp harmonic peaks.

to arbitrarily high resolution. Artifacts from the quantized grid, called *jaggies,* are almost always apparent, as Fig. 2.35 shows. On the other hand, the visual system is not perfect either. A good engineering compromise is achieved when the output device produces an image good enough that the eye sees a smooth letterform with the desired shape and position.

Chapter Summary

The creation of letterforms has a long history, encompassing a wide range of technologies, and influenced by human perceptual abilities and expectations. Letterforms consist of strokes of varying shape and

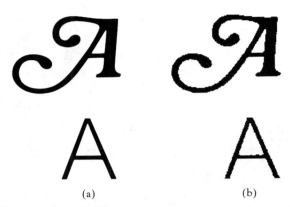

(a)   (b)

FIGURE 2.35   Analog images (a) develop jaggies when digitized and reconstructed at moderate resolution (b).

orientation. The design of a set of related symbols constitutes a typeface. Typefaces come in families of related variations, usually including roman, bold, and italic.

Printers and typographers have been the traditional designers of letterforms, and they have supplied most of the terminology in use today. Psychologists contribute theories and experimental information about the human visual system that are useful for understanding how people see and read. The best measure of type quality is reading speed at a given rate of error.

Finally, engineers excel in making trade-offs that achieve goals. Their analytic tools, including Fourier analysis, provide one basis for understanding the information content of letterforms, and designing technology to produce them. The engineers' choices will determine the properties of the digital machines used for documents preparation; these properties directly affect the quality of print.

— 3
Output Device Characteristics

In order . . . to insure accuracy in the printed Tables, it was necessary that the machine which computed Tables should also . . . supply a mould in which stereotype plates of those Tables could be cast. . . . As each successive number was produced by the arithmetical part, the type-wheels would move down upon a plate of soft composition, upon which the tabular number would be impressed. . . .

The first difficulty arose from the impression of one tabular number on the mould being distorted by the succeeding one . . . I surmounted the difficulty by previously passing a roller, having longitudinal wedge-shaped projections, over the plastic material. This formed a series of small depressions in the matrix between each line. Thus the expansion arising from the impression of one line partially filled up the small depression or ditch which occurred between each successive line.

—Charles Babbage (describing his thinking ca. 1819)

BABBAGE was describing the solution to a problem of output distortion in his mechanical typesetting device, which, though controlled digitally, was not a digital typesetter by our definition. But the output of true digital devices is also subject to distortion. These devices create images in discrete steps, and thus distort output because of aliasing—sampling inaccuracies in the internal representation of shapes. Digital devices are also subject to problems arising from the characteristics of the output mechanism itself. Therefore it is necessary to understand how output devices affect the output, and how to compensate.

Resolution and Related Terminology

The *resolution* of an output device is a measure of the fineness of its spatial divisions. *Pixel*-oriented devices, those that produce images from arrays of marks, are the most interesting and useful for digital typography. The fineness of image that can be produced with a particular machine and its associated computer interface can be described in several ways. First is the *addressing resolution*: the number of dot positions that the computer can specify. Addressing resolution provides the numeric basis for describing positions and sizes in the output. It is usually specified as two integers, one for the x-axis and one for the y-axis. A particular screen display might thus address 512 × 342 pixels in x and y, respectively. A printer could have a resolution of 2000 × 3000.

The *spatial resolution* of a device represents the distance between addressing points when an image is formed. It is described as a particular fraction of an inch (or mm), or alternatively as the number of spots per inch (or mm) in the output medium. A device with a given addressing resolution is considered to have high or low resolution depending on how much physical space is occupied by the addressing resolution. Spatial resolution is usually expressed in *dots per inch* (dpi) or *dots per mm*. Figure 3.1 shows the relationships among these measures.

One complexity in describing resolution is that the mapping between addresses and physical positions is not necessarily in the same ratio on each axis. A given machine could have a horizontal resolution of 150 dpi and a vertical resolution of 75 dpi. In such a case, the device can be described as having a rectangular grid rather than a square one. The ratio of the horizontal to the vertical resolutions is not 1:1, but some other ratio, 2:1 in this case. Further, the pixels themselves need not be square. If in this example the pixels were twice as high as they were wide, the 1:2 ratio of their positioning would be balanced by the 2:1 dimensions of the pixels themselves, resulting in a net 1:1 relationship between addressing and physical dimensions. A square array of bits fed to the device would result in the printing of a square.

The *aspect ratio* of a display describes the overall shape of the output

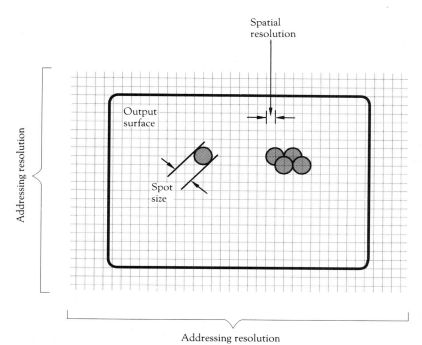

FIGURE 3.1   Addressing resolution, spatial resolution, and spot size.

image. If a particular screen has an image 20 inches wide by 15 inches high, then its screen aspect ratio is 20:15 or 4:3. This ratio is independent of resolution and pixel shape. The standard aspect ratio for television is 4:3.

When told to place a spot or dot at one of the spatial coordinates, an output device produces an image of some size, depending on the device's characteristics. This *spot size* determines the smallest image that can be produced. If the spot size is large compared with the spatial resolution, then the pixels will overlap, avoiding gaps between pixels. Spots or marks produced need not be circular or have sharp edges. The shape of a pixel has a substantial effect on the typographic quality of a device.

The reader is referred to the large body of literature on computer graphics that describes relevant technology and techniques. See [Newman and Sproull 1979] and [Foley and van Dam 1982].

Digitization and Spatial Frequencies

Whether they produce letterforms and graphics with dots, lines, or other shapes, digital output devices all have an inherent limit to their resolution and thus to their image quality. Aberrations always occur. *Aliasing* is the appearance of errors in the shapes and positions of letterforms as a result of sampling them at too low a spatial frequency to resolve the details of interest. At a given resolution, not enough pixels may be available to represent a given shape accurately. Aliasing results in the introduction of low frequencies into the sampled image that misrepresent high frequencies in the original. For example, an almost horizontal line requires very high sampling resolution to resolve properly because very small increments in its vertical position must be detected. If less resolution is used in sampling, the gradual slope is interpreted as a small series of steps, that is, as a step function of long wavelength.

Images may also be distorted by *reconstruction errors* that result from the specific characteristics of the device, in particular the shape of the mark produced when a pixel is specified at a particular value.

A spatial cycle represents the spacing of repeated transitions from light to dark to light, and so on. The *wavelength* of these cycles must be measured between equivalent points in adjacent waves in the cycle, as shown in Fig. 3.2. The spatial resolution of an output device represents the number of distinct positions in which pixels can be placed. To create an image of a given spatial frequency, at least two pixels per

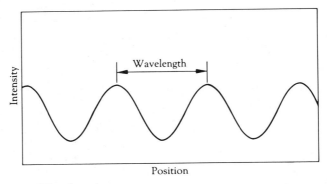

FIGURE 3.2   Wavelength.

cycle are required, one dark and one light. For example, if a laser printer of 300 dot-per-inch resolution can produce distinct lines by alternating pixels on and off (because the spot size is small enough), the wavelength of the resulting pattern would be $1/150$ inch.

On the other hand, the highest spatial frequency present in an output image may be much higher than the spatial resolution. If the device produces sharp-edged pixels, edges in the image will have high-frequency components in the power spectrum of the image. These high-frequency components, while a significant part of the image, may not be under the direct control of the computer. Thus the reconstruction of images by an output device introduces the device's particular characteristics into the output image.

Examining an image, whether with a camera or with the eye, depends on sampling data. The spatial resolution of the instrument used determines the fineness of detail that can be detected. Sampling theory says that the sampling resolution must be at least twice as fine as the size of the smallest feature to be detected. This is called the *Nyquist criterion.* Sampling at too large an interval results in missing transitions between black and white. In the extreme case, alternating black and white parts are sampled only in the black area or only in the white, rendering the image falsely. Thus the term aliasing—a misrepresentation of details, or an alias. A high-frequency component in the original appears incorrectly as a low frequency in the digitized result.

Since the highest spatial frequency most people can see is about 60 cycles per degree of visual angle, it follows that an output device must have a spatial resolution of 120 cycles per degree to prevent aliasing by the eye. This means that at a book-reading distance of about 12 inches, the output device must have a spatial resolution of about 300 lines per inch or 600 dots per inch. (Refer to Fig. 2.21, page 30.) At a distance of 24 inches, this same spatial frequency corresponds to only about 300 dpi. Obviously resolution requirements depend on the use to which the output will be put. In any event, these numbers represent the resolution that engineering analysis predicts will be necessary to match the ability of the eye to see differences.

As noted earlier, the actual output of an output device can contain higher spatial frequencies than specified by the computer when the image was created. The edges of the pixels may be sharper (that is, the transitions may be of smaller dimension) than the spatial resolution. To accurately represent the actual output of a device, for example, when optically scanning (digitizing) an image it has created, still higher resolution is needed. As before, the Nyquist criterion demands a scanning spatial frequency of twice the highest frequency to be captured.

Typographers report that output resolutions higher than 600 dpi result in better quality, and resolutions of at least 1200 dpi are required to achieve the highest-quality printing [Bigelow 1981:13–15]. This higher value may reflect the greater spatial sensitivity of the eye under some circumstances, variation from person to person in visual acuity (with age, for example), the lack of attention to aliasing in the design of typesetters, variations in reading distance, or any number of other factors. Research is needed to determine the need for higher resolutions, which bears on engineering choices in the design of equipment and represents potential trade-offs between quality and cost.

A Taxonomy of Output Devices

To understand the problems of making letterforms and other images appear on digital output devices, it is necessary to understand the physical characteristics of those devices. Many output devices are in use, as shown in Table 3.1. These devices can be described with a

Technology	Type	Color Output?	Approximate Resolution	Typographic Quality
Cathode ray tube	screen	yes	50 to 300	fair to good
liquid crystal display	screen	no	50 to 80	fair
Plasma display	screen	yes	50 to 100	fair
Electrographic plotter	printer	no	about 200	fair
Dot matrix—impact	printer	yes	about 150	fair
Ink jet	printer	yes	240 to 300	fair to good
Laser printer[a]	printer	yes	240 to 600	good to excellent
Digital typesetter[b]	printer	no	725 to 5000	excellent

[a] Paper output.
[b] Photographic paper or film output.

TABLE 3.1 Various output devices and their different typographic characteristics.

taxonomy that analyzes their properties and mechanisms. The broadest categorization is the surface which the output appears; the devices discussed here fall into three such categories: screens, paper, and photographic emulsions such as film or photographic paper. Herein lies the greatest and most obvious difference between output devices— either they are dynamic, presenting a changeable image, or they produce "hard copy."

The ways in which devices form symbols are more complicated to distinguish. Some older printing devices, like phototypesetters and daisy-wheel printers, use a master image that is transferred by some means onto paper. Phototypesetters do this optically, projecting a master image onto the film or photographic paper. Daisy-wheel printers, of course, transfer the image mechanically. Such devices are excluded by definition from digital typography because the letters are not formed under digital control.

Displays form glyphs in one of two ways: Either they draw them with lines or they create them from dots arranged in an array. Line-drawing displays, also called *stroke* or *calligraphic* displays, move a spot of light along paths so as to create each letter, symbol, or graphic image.

The array-of-dots or *bitmapped* display has all but replaced the other types for typographic uses. Images are created by selecting those dots that form the symbol or other image. Both displays and printers operate by this principle.

There is a slight difference between the term bitmapped and the term *raster*. Raster devices scan the entire image area, line by line, selectively marking positions so as to form an image. Television tubes are raster displays. Bitmapping, in contrast, indicates only an array of marks. Some bit mapped displays have electronic control over each position in the array, and are not necessarily scanned point by point, line by line: thus they are not referred to as raster displays. An example is the liquid crystal displays commonly found in calculators and portable computers.

Finally, the image can be formed directly on the output surface, or on some intermediate surface, and then transferred. For example, projection displays form the image internally and then project it to a screen. In printing, the image may be created directly on paper, or may be formed on another surface and transferred to paper. This latter case is of particular interest because it is the basis for all offset printing, the most common form of print reproduction today. Offset is also an important principle in xerography, the technology on which laser printers are based.

Output devices can also be characterized in terms of their resolution in the dimensions of space, time, intensity, and color. As stated previously, spatial resolution must be specified for each axis, as must the relation of spatial resolution to addressing resolution and the aspect ratios. Temporal resolution, which is an issue only for display screens, represents how fast images can be changed. Some devices are *refreshed,* that is, the image they present is renewed by being presented repeatedly. The refresh rate for these devices is the fastest rate that information on the display can be changed.

Intensity resolution is represented by the range of light levels that can be specified for each pixel. Some devices produce only black or white, while others can produce a range of hundreds or thousands of intensity levels. Lastly, *color resolution* represents the number and range of colors that a device will produce.

Most printing technologies cannot produce true *continuous-tone* output. In other words, they do not produce levels of gray at all, but instead rely on placing many tiny spots of ink on the paper to achieve the perception of a gray tone. Photographic output is the exception in the sense that film is exposed directly with the intensity or color desired.

Table 3.2 shows the devices of Table 3.1, analyzed in terms of the taxonomy. A number of these devices are discussed next, in terms of their typographic use in digital typography.

Screen Display Devices

Cathode Ray Tubes Today's most popular screen output device is the cathode ray tube or CRT. CRTs emit light by bombarding a phosphorescent material with a beam of electrons. Although relatively bulky and power hungry, CRTs are inexpensive and show no sign of disappearing, it has been more than 100 years since they were invented.[1]

There are several kinds of cathode ray tube. Early units used electrostatic deflection—a high voltage between two metal plates steered

---

[1] The CRT was invented by Jules Plucker in 1859, although its use as an information-display device is far more recent.

Device	Imaging Surface	Light Source[a]	Dynamic	Character Formation	Image Presentation	True Gray
CRT	phosphor	E	yes	bitmap (raster) or stroke	direct	yes
LCD	liquid crystal	R	yes	bitmap or segment	direct	no
Plasma display	ionized gas	E	yes	bitmap	direct	no
Electrographic printer	paper	R	no	bitmap (raster)	direct	no
Impact or thermal matrix printer	paper	R	no	bitmap (raster)	direct	no
Ink-jet printer	paper	R	no	bitmap (raster)	direct	no
Laser printer	paper	R	no	bitmap (raster) on sensitive drum etc.	offset	no
Digital Typesetter	Photographic paper	R	no	bitmap (raster)	direct	yes[b]

[a] E = emits its own light; R = reflects ambient light.　[b] Rarely used.

TABLE 3.2 A taxonomy of computer output devices.

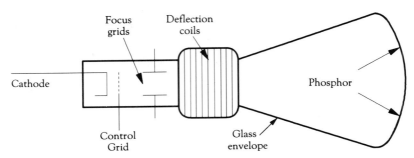

Focus grids   Deflection coils

Cathode

Phosphor

Control Grid

Glass envelope

FIGURE 3.3   A cathode ray tube.

the electron beam to one point or another on the phosphor surface. These *random-access* displays became stroke displays with the addition of electronics to move the beam continuously in a line or curve.

Most computer CRTs today are of the raster, bit-mapped type. They repeatedly scan the entire surface of the phosphor in a fixed, line-by-line pattern. A particular spot, a pixel, is lit depending on whether the electron beam emanating from the tube's cathode is turned on or off at the instant that the beam is positioned to strike that location (Fig. 3.3). Raster tubes typically use magnetic deflection in the form of coils wrapped around their necks, providing the necessary deflection of the beam in each of the two dimensions.

One virtue of the scanning arrangement is that it facilitates a stable image on the screen. Each axis is controlled by an oscillator, with the result that pixels can be made to appear in precisely the same position on the tube surface in each scan. However, *linearity* may vary along the scanning path. Nonlinearity distorts the height and width of images displayed, and may give a pincushion or balloon effect over the entire screen. On a poor CRT, the size of "equal" letters may be noticeably different in one place compared with another.

The temporal resolution of raster CRT displays is determined by the refresh rate. A typical rate is 60 Hz, that is, 60 full images per second.[2] Higher rates, as high as 90 Hz or 100 Hz, are becoming more common because they exhibit less flicker and an apparently steadier image.

---

[2] This rate is used in the United States because it is the power line frequency. In countries with 50 Hz power, 50 Hz refresh is usual.

Also, a higher refresh rate means that the information displayed can be changed more often, allowing for better dynamic images.

One common variation on the refreshing of CRTs is *interlaced scanning*. Instead of scanning every pixel in order, line by line, alternate lines are scanned. First the odd lines are scanned, then the even ones. If each half frame is scanned at 60 Hz, for example, the net rate at which the whole image is replaced is only 30 Hz, or half the rate without interlace.

The effective refresh rate of 30 Hz produced by interlace does not seem adequate because it is lower than the flicker-fusion rate for most individuals. However, interlace is used successfully in television because of two mediating factors. First, if the viewer is far enough from the display that the individual lines are not visible, adjacent lines tend to cover for each other and appear more like a single object flickering at twice the rate. Additionally, adjacent lines in most television images have a very similar image content. This high degree of correlation between lines means that, in terms of intensity at any given location, adjacent lines are good substitutes for each other—they have about the same intensity in each horizontal position.

Interlacing data displays reduces the data rate necessary to keep information on the display—only half the information must be output in each scan. Unfortunately, this works less well for computer displays than for television because the viewer is closer and because there may be little correlation between adjacent scan lines.

Thus interlaced displays can cause serious problems for text display. Small objects like individual letters will flicker noticeably because their individual parts are not being refreshed fast enough for flicker fusion to make them appear constant. For example, a capital letter 'E' might sit with most of its strokes in one interlace frame, and very little in the other. In that case, the whole letter would appear to flicker badly (see Fig. 3.4).

One solution to these problems is the use of a long-persistence phosphor. Light continues to emerge from the phosphor after it has been bombarded by the electron beam. If this emission of light continues at a high-enough level until the next time the spot is refreshed, the perception of flicker will be diminished. The flicker-fusion rate under these conditions has already been described—it is modulation sensitive. (Refer to Fig. 2.27, page 36.) Residual glow in the phosphor

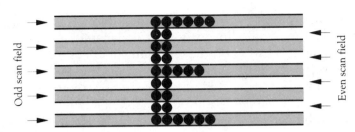

FIGURE 3.4 Flicker problem with interlaced displays. Most of a given letter may be in one field, as is the case with this letter E. It is only refreshed at half the rate and may appear to flicker.

at the time that a spot is refreshed results in a reduction of the modulation of the flickering image. That is, the ratio between the high and low output levels of the spot is lower, diminishing the perception of flicker.

Thus long-persistence phosphors can avoid flicker problems. Such phosphors are not very popular for general-purpose computer displays because they cause moving images to blur. When text is primarily displayed, however, this may not be a problem—slower refresh and, as a result, higher resolution are the rule. When dynamic images must be presented, only moderate-persistence phosphors may be used, and they are less useful in suppressing flicker.

The cathode ray tube display is characterized by pixels without sharp edges. Rather, there is an intensity "tail" around an isolated lit spot, giving a soft, rounded edge (Fig. 3.5). As noted in Chapter 2, because of edge enhancement the eye tends to see these soft edges as sharper than they actually are. As usual, the human visual system is a significant component of the total man-machine system.

When the edges of the scanning spot are soft, adjacent pixels may merge on the display. The width of the illuminated spot is measured between the 50%-intensity-level points on opposite sides of the spot, but this dimension can be misleading because there is illumination far outside the circle defined by the spot-size dimension.

The *image contrast* of text and graphics images is one significant determinant of their quality. Image contrast is the ratio of the highest and lowest intensities in the image—the amounts of light reflected or emitted:

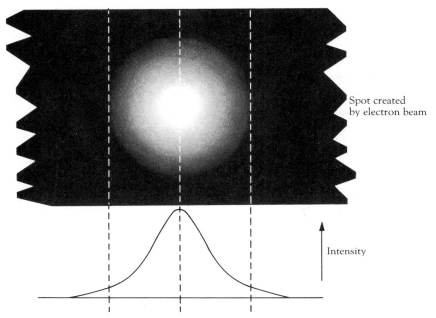

FIGURE 3.5   Generic intensity profile of a CRT electron beam.

$$K = \frac{I_{max}}{I_{min}} \, .$$

The highest text quality results from ratios of about 50:1 or higher. Improvement beyond 50:1 is not useful, however, because people do not express any preference for samples with higher contrast. A ratio of 20:1 is more typical of a TV picture tube in a lit room. Achieving higher contrast ratios might require considerable design effort to be applied to the tube itself.

As Fig. 3.6 shows, three sources of light contribute to I_{max} and I_{min}:

1. Light emitted by the phosphor;
2. Ambient light reflected off the tube surface;
3. Light from (1) or (2) that emerges from within the glass after internal reflection.

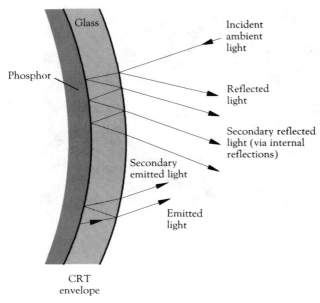

FIGURE 3.6   Internal reflections reduce contrast.

If light reached the eye from only the phosphor, then the eye would receive no light from black parts of the image, resulting in infinite contrast. But stray light from sources (2) and (3) lowers contrast. Ambient light can be controlled at its source: The display can be used in reduced light, or can be shielded from the room lighting. Also, coatings on the surface of the CRT are used to reduce surface reflection of ambient light. Source (3), internal reflection, which is responsible for much loss of contrast, is harder to control. Both ambient light and light from the phosphor get "trapped" within the glass envelope, reflecting one or more times and finally emerging in areas that are supposed to be dark. This is a particular problem with large light-colored fields in the displayed image. Light from the phosphor, originating some distance away from a black displayed feature, can reduce contrast when it emerges from the tube within the black area.

Internal reflection can lead to a situation in which the contrast of a black-on-white image is different from that of the same image reversed, that is, shown white on black. This asymmetry of contrast is of interest because publishing systems are called upon increasingly to represent paper with black-on-white images. This effect tends to reduce the contrast of such images, and thus their quality.

Two other effects result in an asymmetric relationship between images presented as black on white versus those presented as white on black. Consider an isolated white pixel on a black background, as shown in Fig. 3.7(a) The full-intensity tail of the spot is visible, and thus the spot may fill more than its intended space—assuming the usual case where the spot size is a bit larger than the spatial-resolution unit, that is, than the distance between pixel centers. In any event, a relatively broad spot appears. Now consider the inverse situation, a single black pixel in a field of white (Fig. 3.7(b)). The tails of the two adjacent lit pixels are in the space occupied by the unlit one. Therefore the black spot is smaller than the corresponding white spot of the reversed image.

Similarly, as Fig. 3.8 shows, an isolated black spot tends to be narrower than an isolated white spot because the length of time re-

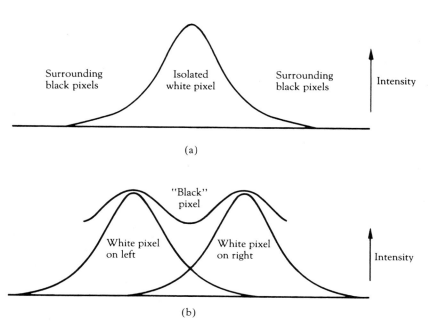

FIGURE 3.7   Isolated white and black spots have different intensity distributions. A lone white pixel (a) may be of higher contrast than a black one (b).

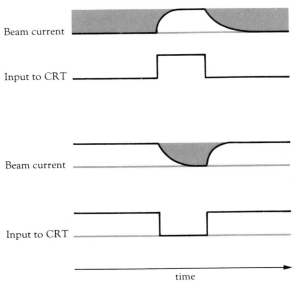

FIGURE 3.8 Asymmetry of beam on and beam off. (a) Isolated white pixel; on-time ≈ 1.5t. (b) Isolated black pixel; off-time ≈ 1.0t.

quired to turn the CRT beam on may not be the same as the length of time required to turn it off: In many CRTs, the beam will turn on faster than it will turn off. This accentuates the width of white regions and narrows black ones.

The combined effect is called *polarity asymmetry*: The same bits that give a good image for white-on-black images will not be optimal for black-on-white, and vice versa. Different font designs may well be required for the two situations. In particular, designs that use a single pixel for the width of vertical strokes (stem width) may look good when presented as white on black, but very anemic as black on white. This assumes that scanning is horizontal across the CRT tube, as is usual. However, the comments also apply to tubes that make vertical scans, which affect horizontal lines in the image. Also, rotating text on a given display will result in differences of appearance because of the difference of scan direction with respect to the symbol.

The term *anisotropy* is used to describe the difference in the characteristics of an output device on different axes. Devices other than CRTs also exhibit anisotropy in their output.

Good font designers not only take these characteristics into consideration when designing screen fonts, they use them to advantage.
Variation in line width can be a resource that allows more subtle
characteristics to be included in a design. Figure 3.9(a) shows a design
for the letter 'r'. On a CRT, the join between the vertical and horizontal strokes appears smoother and more slender (Fig. 3.9b) than would

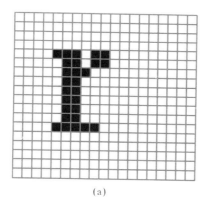

(a)

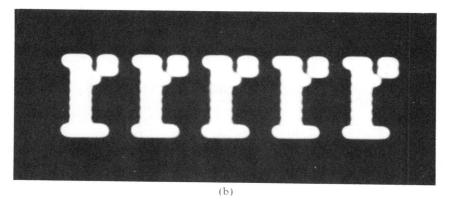

(b)

FIGURE 3.9   Subtle use of CRT characteristics to good effect. (Letterform
design) Bigelow & Holmes, 1981; courtesy of Bigelow & Holmes.) Bits (a)
produce appearance (b).

be expected from looking at the bits. Thus font design done in the context of the output device characteristics can give excellent results. Note, however, that CRT characteristics vary from model to model (and as a result of user adjustment). Therefore, font-design ideas must be tested on the actual display on which they will be used.

Color CRTs are becoming more and more popular, especially in business and engineering applications for which real images or color encoding of information are useful. CRTs currently provide the most economical color display. A common type of color tube uses a shadow mask and three separate guns, one for each primary color. Mixtures of the primary colors create the perception of other colors. The geometric arrangement of the guns and the color phosphors is such that electrons from the red gun, say, can reach only red phosphor dots, and so on. Figure 3.10 shows how this works.

Some tubes have a triangular arrangement of the phosphor dots, while others (such as the Sony Trinitron) use thin parallel strips of the three phosphors (Fig. 3.11). The structure of the CRT, especially the arrangement of the phosphors, affects the typographic characteristics of the particular tube.

Color CRTs create many challenges for font design. Like the pixels created on monochrome displays, those created on color tubes do not have sharp edges; the electron beam is stronger at its center than at its periphery. But phosphor is not present everywhere the beam hits the front of the tube. In the triad dot arrangement, there is phosphorless

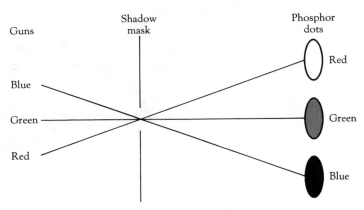

FIGURE 3.10   Shadow-mask CRT arrangement.

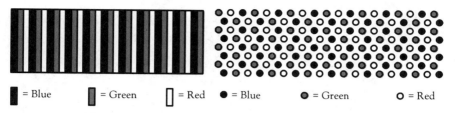

= Blue　　　= Green　　　= Red　　● = Blue　　● = Green　　○ = Red

FIGURE 3.11　Two phosphor arrangements.

space between the dots. Of necessity, the beam size is a good deal larger than one phosphor dot, or even a group of three dots. The result is that a pixel is actually a collection of smaller phosphor dots illuminated with varying intensity. A similar situation exists with phosphor strips.

One typographic consequence of this situation for a color tube, as for black and white, is that black letters on a light background will lack contrast if the strokes are thin (for example, one pixel wide). This is because phosphor dots within the dark parts of the letter may actually be illuminated by the beam (see Fig. 3.12). Presenting the same image reversed—light letters on a dark background—avoids the problem. When the normal black-image-on-light-background arrangement is needed, the solution is to use broader main strokes.

The shadow mask itself gives rise to another kind of problem in color tubes. When much of the screen is illuminated, the shadow mask is hit by the electron beam over a large area. The mask, actually a flimsy metal screen, is heated by the bombardment. It may become substantially warped under the thermal stress. The result is an uneven background. The higher the resolution of the tube, the more it is subject to the problem of unevenness after it has warmed up. Thus a trade-off must be made between resolution of the tube and quality of the typography. At lower resolutions, quality suffers because the image lacks information. At higher resolutions, the letterforms are better constructed, but the background may have distracting variations in intensity.

The lens in the eye focuses light of different colors at different distances. If a person is focusing on a red patch on a screen, an adjacent blue patch will be out of focus by one diopter [Cowan and Ware 1985:106]—a substantial amount. This defect in the eye is called

FIGURE 3.12 Dark on light on a color tube. Phosphor dots within "black" stems are actually illuminated.

chromatic aberration. Also, the eye is less sensitive to blue than to other colors. As a result, the shape of blue objects is not perceived as well as shapes of other colors.

In choosing foreground and background colors, it is important to remember that high intensity contrast is required for good-quality text. Contrast of color alone does not work well. Research shows that the visual system detects edges based primarily on intensity rather than color. In fact, one model of the perceptual system, *opponent color theory,* describes three information-processing channels that work with the same input signal (light acting on the retina) but use the information differently. The light-sensitive cones in the fovea are of three types—those that respond to red, green, and blue. Two color channels deal with color, transmitting a red-versus-green signal and a yellow-versus-blue signal. Yellow, of course, is the sum of red and green. The remaining channel, the achromatic or luminance channel, ignores color and communicates only intensity. In opponent color theory, the achromatic channel is responsible for edge detection and ultimately the decoding of shape [Cowan and Ware 1985:62; Cornsweet 1970:422].

The problems of presenting line graphics are similar to those of presenting letters. Very thin black-on-white lines will have little contrast and will not be very visible. The crucial determinant of quality is good intensity contrast between lines and their background. Color contrast alone is insufficient.

Color tubes are limited in the colors they can produce. Figure 3.13(a), the CIE chromaticity diagram, shows the range of colors that the human eye can see. (CIE—Commission Internationale de l'Éclairage—is a committee that establishes standards for describing and comparing colors.) Colors as human beings see them can be described in terms of *hue, brightness,* and *saturation.* Hue, the perception corresponding to the wavelength of spectral light, is what people are describing when they say an object is yellow, blue, green, red, and so on. Brightness is familiar, being the perception of how much light is present. Finally, saturation is the perceived purity of the color. The more white that appears to be mixed with the color, the less it is saturated, and vice versa.

In the CIE diagram, brightness is not represented directly. All colors within the closed figure have the same brightness. Colors at the periphery are more saturated; those closer to the center are less saturated (pastel). Different hues correspond to different positions around the periphery, as indicated by the wavelength numbers, which correspond to spectral light. The colors that can be produced by mixing two colors correspond to the points on a line that connects them within the closed figure. Similarly, the colors that can be produced by mixing three colors are contained within a triangle, with the three original colors as vertices.

An important issue in computer graphics for the technology of human factors is how to present the color space to the human being in a conceptually simple and useful way. One criterion for choosing among the many proposed systems is perceptual uniformity: An equal perceptual difference should separate adjacent colors in the color space [Meyer and Greenberg 1980].

A color CRT has phosphors that produce three primary colors— red, green, and blue—and creates the perception of other colors by mixing these three. Figure 3.13(b) shows the portion of the full color space that is accessible in principle using a representative set of phosphors. Note that this set of primaries cannot produce all the colors that people can see.

In fact, CRTs are even more limited in range than Fig. 3.13(b)

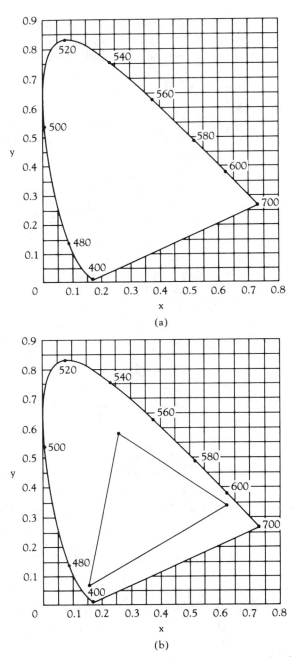

(a)

(b)

FIGURE 3.13   Compare the colors that the eye can see in the first CIE diagram (a) with the range of colors that can be produced by a typical CRT (b).

suggests. There is a limit to the intensity that can be produced by each phosphor, as determined by the electron gun, the tube geometry, and the nature of the phosphor itself. The most intense light output from a color CRT, a white, is produced when each of the three primaries is at its maximum. A red, orange, green, or blue light, or one of another color, cannot be produced at the same intensity, because this would require more light from one or two of the phosphors than the tube can produce.

In the United States, about 8% of males and 0.4% of females have some color-perception deficiency [Grolier 1986:V,113–114]. It is therefore a general requirement of color displays that the information they present be available in the intensity domain as well as the color domain. Information that is encoded with color is thus presented redundantly, making it at least somewhat accessible to color-blind people.

Because of these difficulties, color presentation of text must be approached circumspectly. Very saturated colors are undesirable for either foreground or background. Pastels have better intensity, and thus better image contrast. Saturated blue should not be used as a foreground or background color because it makes boundaries hard to see.

Color also interacts with the perception of flicker, in the sense that different phosphors have differing persistence. If the tube has a longer-persistence green phosphor, a pastel-green background is useful for suppressing the appearance of flicker. Long persistence is not required in every phosphor to improve the stability of the image. The eye will see the entire image as flicker free if the green component alone has long persistence.

The perception of color is complex. For further details, the reader is referred to the psychological literature.[3]

Liquid Crystal Displays   Devices such as portable computers that must have a more compact display can use *liquid crystal displays* (LCDs). These displays contain optically active organic compounds that selectively control the reflection of ambient light. LCDs are lightweight and consume very little power. Typographically they are characterized

---

[3] Among other sources listed in the Bibliography, see [Cornsweet 1970] and [Cowan and Ware 1985].

by their very sharp-edged, round, or square pixels. (Other shapes are possible, but these are the usual ones for bitmapped displays.) Figure 3.14 shows a typical device in cross section. LCD resolutions today are more limited than are resolutions on CRTs, and as a result each pixel is usually visible individually. The structure of the display requires that the pixels not overlap, although they can be made to almost abut. This creates a typographic handicap in font design because the ability of the eye to sharpen fuzzy edges cannot be used to advantage, as it can with CRT displays. When displayed on liquid crystal displays, text tends to look like that in Fig. 3.15.

Smooth, sharp edges cause trouble in both graphics and text by adding the artifact of the pixel shape to the contour of the displayed image. The interference comes from the presence of high-spatial-frequency components in the image that are visible, but not part of the structure of the letterforms. In other words, these sharp-edged square or round pixels add noise to the image.

LCD displays with abutting pixels are materially better at displaying text, but the best shape for a pixel is open to question. Square, abutting pixels result in all-too-familiar edge artifact for diagonal and curved lines (Fig. 3.15). Isolated circular pixels create a different sort of artifact. Perhaps a better approach would be the hexagonal honeycomb arrangement shown in Fig. 3.16. In any event, higher resolution is needed to achieve high typographic quality.

Liquid crystal displays do not usually have flicker problems. Although electronically the displays must be scanned to refresh the information being displayed, the scanning can be fast compared with the time it takes pixels to change their state. Further, a whole row or column of pixels can often be refreshed simultaneously; there is no need to scan one pixel at a time. Also, LCDs do not exhibit polarity asymmetry, since the size of the pixels is fixed geometrically.

Color is not currently an option for LCD computer displays, although it is feasible. The emphasis in developing new LCD displays has been on larger size, lower power consumption, better contrast, and reduced costs, rather than on increased resolution or better pixel arrangements for typographic use.

Plasma Displays   A plasma display consists of an array of individually-addressable, gas-discharge cells. A cell that is turned on produces a small, glowing dot—a pixel. Plasma displays are similar in their

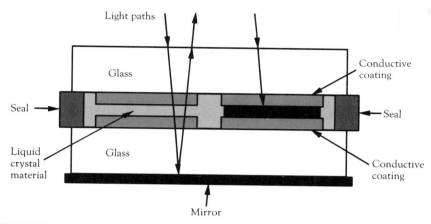

FIGURE 3.14 Liquid crystal display cross section.

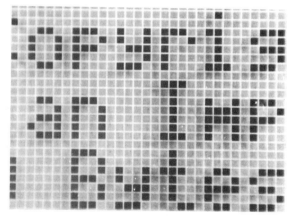

FIGURE 3.15 Text on a liquid crystal display.

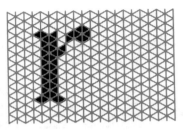

FIGURE 3.16   Proposed hexagonal arrangement of triangular LCD pixels.

typographic properties to LCDs: Their pixels have sharp edges and do not overlap. They do not exhibit polarity asymmetry or anisotropy, and they provide good contrast.

Printing Devices

Nonphotographic printing technologies rely on transferring ink or toner to paper in a controlled way. A great many schemes for placing the ink on the paper have been devised. Letterpress and wood-block printing are traditional examples of *relief printing* in which ink is applied to a raised surface and then transferred to the paper by direct contact. Striking a ribbon with a relief letterform, as in a conventional type-writer, is a similar method. Another traditional means, still the work-horse for production printing, is *offset printing*. In this method, the image is formed on an intermediate surface and transferred (offset) onto the paper by contact. Offset printing has many advantages, among them that the formation of the image is independent of the printing on paper—in both time (there can be a delay) and space (it can be near or far, and image formation need not occur directly on paper). Modern methods of printing directly with a computer output device are much like their traditional cousins in the way that ink is transferred to paper.

Three types of raster printing devices are in common use. First, dot-matrix printers have long met the requirement for low-resolution, low-cost paper output. Second, laser printers, recently improved and re-duced in cost, have put better-quality printed output within the reach of small-computer users. And third, at the high end of performance and price, digital typesetting equipment provides high-resolution output on photographic paper, creating a master image for printing by offset or other photographic means.

Printers also have characteristics that require the attention of font designers. There are many kinds of printers. As with CRTs, the critical issue is how the visual output differs from the literal input. When systematic differences exist, the same situation results: Letterform designs must be tailored to accommodate the differences. However, when additional quality is worth the cost of an extra design effort, peculiarities of printing devices can be used creatively to create excellent designs.

Dot-Matrix Printers   Four kinds of dot-matrix printer in common use provide paper output in bitmap form. Electrographic dot-matrix printers and plotters have one or more rows of electrodes that deposit charges directly on the paper, which is then "developed" by contact with toner and fixed with heat. A common resolution for these machines is 200 dots per inch.

Dot-matrix printers have been available for some years for plotting graphs, often in large paper sizes. Because of their modest resolution and high cost, these printers have been used for typographic work only occasionally. They are characterized by well-defined dots, often not touching each other, and a fair amount of background "noise" resulting from stray toner's attaching itself to the paper.

A similar device uses thermal paper that is passed by an array of tiny heating elements, changing color wherever it is heated. More familiar in printing calculators, this thermal technology is also characterized by discrete, isolated pixels. Thermal paper has the additional drawback of low contrast because the darkened dots are actually not very dark, typically a medium-dark blue. Other devices use the same thermal principle but produce higher-quality images. Finer dot arrays, thermal transfer of ink from a ribbon, or more sophisticated heat-sensitive paper, for example, improve the resulting print.

The third type of dot-matrix printer uses a ribbon, and an array of pins as the print head. Solenoids drive the pins against the ribbon and into the paper (see Fig. 3.17). This technology is thus a relative of the traditional typewriter. These printers have resolutions in the 150–200-dots-per-inch range. Very inexpensive, they provide modest-quality output for personal computers and computer terminals. With a resolution approximately twice that of many CRT screens, they offer a

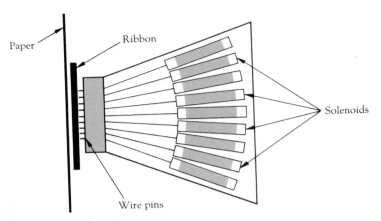

FIGURE 3.17   Impact matrix printer.

reasonably good match of the image quality on the screen, and are used for drafts, screen copying, and "near-letter-quality" printing of both graphics and text. They are used frequently to proof output before it is committed to another device such as a laser printer, film plotter, or typesetter.

The typographic output quality of impact printers is quite variable, depending on the particular design, the resolution, and, in particular, the fonts used. At low resolutions, individual pixels are quite visible, sparse, and disconnected from each other. The better units, operating at or above 150 dots per inch, produce images in which the pixel dots coalesce. Some devices have greater horizontal than vertical resolution—144 × 72 dpi is one combination in use. The images are nonetheless somewhat fuzzy when a cloth ribbon is used. Printers that use carbon or thermal ribbons give sharper images, at the expense of making pixel edges sharper.

Substantial differences in quality can result from variations in font design, even with the same printer. Ribbon "squish"—spreading of the dots at their edges—can be used in a font design in much the same way as can erosion of black-on-white areas on CRTs.

Ribbon spreading creates polarity asymmetry like that of CRTs. It has the effect of broadening black lines and softening the edges at black-white boundaries. Conversely, this effect narrows white-on-black images. The effect is in just the opposite direction from the

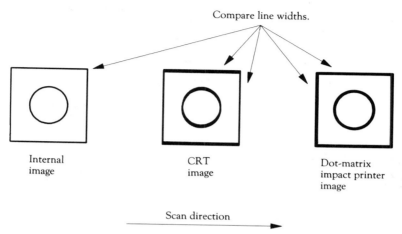

FIGURE 3.18 · Divergence of line width: CRT versus dot-matrix printer.

various CRT effects that make black images narrower and less contrastive. On the other hand, this kind of printer exhibits no anisotropy. Horizontal and vertical images yield the same results, differences in resolution notwithstanding. The result is that pixel-for-pixel copies will not match very well between CRT and paper copies (see Fig. 3.18). As usual, remaking the image with some sensitivity to the device characteristics will improve both the image and improve the perceived match between the screen and paper copies.

Ink-Jet Printers Ink-jet printers have also gained some popularity. They are quite unlike traditional printing machines. Under digital control, ink is squirted in a fine jet at the paper. Using several jets allows color printing. Because the only mechanical motion required is that of the print head and paper, these devices can print relatively fast. Images may have soft edges due to the spreading of the ink. Thus the typographic characteristics of ink-jet printers are similar to those of dot-matrix, impact printers.

Laser Printers Laser printers are essentially photocopiers in which an image is created by scanning a laser beam under computer control, rather than optically from an original document (Fig. 3.19). A number of interesting effects occur because of the electrostatic

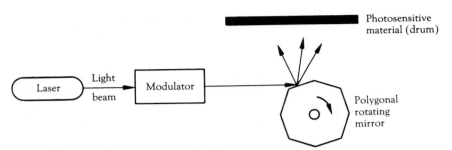

FIGURE 3.19 How a laser printer works. An electrostatic image is formed on the photosensitive surface by scanning a modulated laser beam across it. Then the image is developed with toner, the toner transferred to paper, and the toner is fixed with a heat fuser.

nature of the imaging process in these printers, as well as the physics and chemistry of the toner itself when distributed onto the paper.

Like CRTs and dot-matrix printers, laser printers exhibit polarity asymmetry—the shape of the resulting forms depends on which polarity is used to create them. If a given printer is used to print a white image on a black background, the result will not be simply a "negative" of the same data printed with the polarity reversed.

One striking difference among laser printer engines is that some write a black image on the drum during formation of the image, while others write the white part of the image. Note that this characteristic is independent of the polarity of the output image, say black on white (the usual polarity). Because of the way the toner is attracted to the resulting charged image, one image will be bolder than the other, even though *exactly the same array of dots* is specified. A font designed for one printer may give dramatically different results on another, as the comparison in Fig. 3.20 shows.

In fact, various electrostatic effects result in toner's not being placed on the paper exactly as the bit image specifies, whatever the overall polarity. Consider a sharp convex part of a black image (Fig. 3.21a). Instead of producing a sharp corner, a rounded corner results Fig. 3.21(b). The solution is to make the corner sharper than the desired result, resulting in a more accurate image (see Fig. 3.22). Exactly the reverse happens with concave sections; compensation will also restore these images to the correct shape.

A final characteristic of laser printers actually allows a dramatic

THE GRAPHIC SIGNS CALLED LET
BLENDED WITH THE STREAM OF
PRESENCE THEREIN IS AS UNPER(
A CLOCK IN THE MEASUREMENT
OF ATTENTION DOES THE LAYM/
AT ALL. IT COMES TO HIM AS A S
SIGNS SHOULD BE A MATTER OF
CRAFTS OF MEN. BUT TO BE CON
LETTERS IS TO WORK IN AN ANC
MATERIAL. THE QUALITIES OF LE
ARE THE QUALITIES OF A CLASSI
SIMPLICITY, GRACE. TO TRY TO L
EXCELLENCE IS TO PUT ONESELF
SIMPLE AND SEVERE SCHOOL OF

The full practice of typography i:
process of learning and a challen
skill, imagination and common se
not imply exhibitionism; authent
need to proclaim itself. OLIVER S

(a)

THE GRAPHIC SIGNS CALLED LET
BLENDED WITH THE STREAM OF
PRESENCE THEREIN IS AS UNPER(
A CLOCK IN THE MEASUREMENT
OF ATTENTION DOES THE LAYM/
AT ALL. IT COMES TO HIM AS A S
SIGNS SHOULD BE A MATTER OF
CRAFTS OF MEN. BUT TO BE CON
LETTERS IS TO WORK IN AN ANC
MATERIAL. THE QUALITIES OF LE
ARE THE QUALITIES OF A CLASSI
SIMPLICITY, GRACE. TO TRY TO L
EXCELLENCE IS TO PUT ONESELF
SIMPLE AND SEVERE SCHOOL OF

The full practice of typography i:
process of learning and a challen
skill, imagination and common se
not imply exhibitionism; authent
need to proclaim itself. OLIVER S

(b)

FIGURE 3.20   The same bits imaged by a laser printer that writes the white part (a) and one that writes the black part (b). Note the difference in blackness of the letters. (Courtesy of Bigelow & Holmes.)

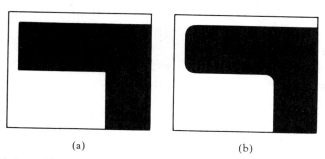

(a)   (b)

FIGURE 3.21   Charge leaks at a point in the image (a) to give the printed result (b).

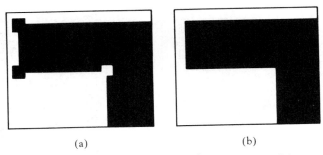

(a)   (b)

FIGURE 3.22 Compensation for charge leaks: The image (a) gives the printed result (b).

increase in the quality of letterforms at a given resolution. Because of the way in which toner goes onto the paper, usually an isolated pixel will not produce a spot on the paper. That location will take on the color of the pixels that surround it. By intentionally creating certain kinds of ragged edges and included voids in letterforms, the toner can be coerced into occupying positions intermediate to the resolution increments. This technique is called *half-bitting* or *dentation*. Figure 3.23(a) shows the design of a letter 'h' incorporating this treatment. Note the apparently rough edge and the isolated white pixels. The result, however, is a more attractive letterform with more subtle curves. Compare this result with Fig. 3.23(b), which shows a letter 'h' without this treatment.

Half-bitting is an example of usefully outputting more spatial information in an output image than the addressing resolution seems to allow. Thus a 300 dpi printer may produce letterforms with greater positioning accuracy than $1/300$-inch. The size of the effect depends on the characteristics of the particular printer. The result for a particular printer could be the equivalent of $1/450$-inch feature dimensions for the affected parts of the letterforms.

For the same reasons that some photocopiers do not reproduce black regions well, printing large black areas is difficult for some laser printers. To print a black region, a great deal of toner must be distributed. When it is not distributed evenly, the result is a mottled or banded region. For a printer in which a black region corresponds to a charge on the photosensitive surface, the effect of the charge on the toner

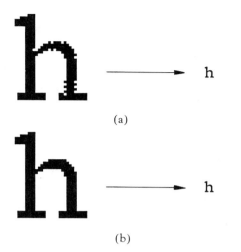

(a)

(b)

FIGURE 3.23 Dentated 'h' as designed and as it actually prints (a). Compare results without dentation (b). Note the subtlety of the resulting curve. (Letterform design courtesy of Bigelow & Holmes.)

will be greater at the edges of the region than at the center, leaving the central area lighter than the periphery.

Digital Typesetters Typesetters are high-quality, relatively expensive machines designed expressly to produce images of good typographic quality. However, they are generally slower and more expensive than laser printers. They usually have resolutions above 1200 dots per inch, although machines used for newspaper work may be as low as 725 dpi. The usual output medium is photographic paper. Typesetter output is expensive on a per-page basis because of the cost of the machine, and especially the cost of the photosensitive paper. The paper alone may cost 25 cents a sheet. Thus other devices such as laser printers are used to proof material to be typeset before a commitment to the typesetter and the associated expense and time.

One problem in using a typesetter is to make the proofing device accurately represent the typeset output, without compromising the quality of the typeset image as a result. This problem, similar to the What You See Is What You Get problem in making screens and paper output match, discussed in detail in Chapter 6, will also be taken up in detail there.

The resolution of typesetters is generally high enough that tricks such as dentation are neither necessary nor particularly useful for improving typographic quality. The primary determinant of quality is the shape of the letters themselves; traditional typographic and æsthetic design considerations apply. As with any printing method, adjustments of letterform design that reflect the final offset-printing process are still necessary. Because typesetters have been used for years for commercial typesetting, a great many fonts are available for most units.

The typographic issues that arise when documents are prepared with a digital typesetter are those of justification, line spacing, layout, paging, and other topics more macroscopic than the design of the fonts themselves. Chapter 5 considers these concerns in detail.

Digital Images

Not only text but images can be displayed and printed with digital systems. Digital image processing is a relatively mature field; there is a technology of capturing images, compressing the data that result, and using the data to print images. Digital images can be stored readily and then printed simultaneously with text, resulting in a compound document. The images can even be modified in various ways in the course of preparing a document for printing.

The resolution needed to portray digital images deserves some discussion. Images may be continuous tone, having a large but finite number of tones, or they may only have a few tones. For example, line drawings are two tone; they are also referred to as binary valued or bitonal. Independently, images may be in color or in black and white, as shown in Fig. 3.24.

Resolution requirements for images depend on the amount of detail in the image, the kind of image, and the capabilities of the output device. Continuous-tone images are easier to render well on output devices that can produce graduations in tone directly. Thus CRTs are readily amenable to continuous-tone output, but most printing technologies are not.

To accommodate continuous-tone images in output devices with few tones, graduations in tone must be simulated with discrete images.

Tonal Range

		Discrete	Continuous
Number of Colors	Few	Line drawings, halftones	Black-and-white photos
	Many	Charts, maps, graphs	Color photos

FIGURE 3.24   Kinds of digital image.

In traditional printing a *halftone* is generated optically, using a screen. Early optical methods used the screen to create a diffraction pattern on the photographic paper. Each spot on the paper represented the average intensity of a small region in the original image. Because of the thresholding inherent in the paper, a spot of area proportional to that intensity resulted (see Fig. 3.25). Modern optical methods achieve the same effect by simpler means.

The digital equivalent of the optical halftone uses discrete pixels to achieve a similar effect. There are various techniques for generating

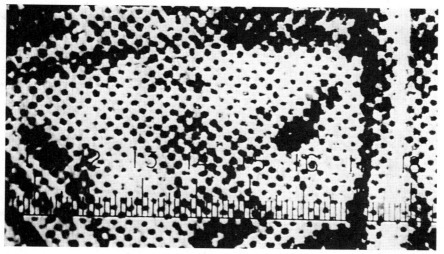

FIGURE 3.25   A traditional optical halftone image from a newspaper. The reticle marks in this microphotograph represent millimeters. (Courtesy of The MIT Press and Robert Ulichney.)

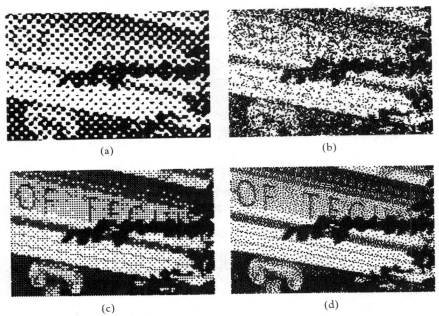

FIGURE 3.26 A comparison of four spatial dithering methods. Clustered-dot ordered dithering is a simulation of optical methods (a). Using white noise (b) eliminates some of the structure artifact of the grid, but also introduces some low frequencies; which are seen in the grainy appearance. Dispersing error improves both methods. Image (c) shows ordered dithering with error diffusion, and image (d) shows aperiodic dithering using blue noise and error diffusion. The effect of blue noise is to suppress the low-frequency problems that resulted in the graininess of image (b). (Courtesy of The MIT Press and Robert Ulichney.)

digital halftones [Roetling 1977; Ulichney 1987]. Using patterns of pixels to create digital halftones is called *spatial dithering*. If repeating patterns are used, the technique is *ordered dithering*; the alternative is *aperiodic dithering*. Dithering tends to introduce artifact—visible structure—into images, the worst case being areas of constant tone, areas that are uniform in the original image.

The simplest periodic dithering method, called the *clustered dot* method, is the simulation of optical halftones. This method is illustrated in Fig. 3.26(a). Note the prominance of the screen pattern. Relief and offset-printing methods are not necessarily able to reliably deposit minuscule spots of ink, which resulted in the need for dots of varying size in conventional halftones. Many digital devices, however, can produce arbitrary patterns (within the limits of their resolution). Some laser printers, for example, can produce a dot specified by a single, isolated pixel. Under these liberalized conditions other arrangements of ink are possible.

Fig. 3.26(b) shows an aperiodic dithering method, one that uses white noise to eliminate the periodic structure effects. At each pixel position, the image value is compared with a random threshold, and a spot printed when the value exceeds the threshold. Another means of structure suppression, called *dispersed-dot ordered dither,* is shown in Fig. 3.26(c). Here the error associated with any particular spot, relative to the correct value in the image, is corrected by adjustments in the vicinity of that location. An even more sophisticated method uses blue noise, that is, white noise with the low frequencies removed– [Ulichney 1987:233–331]. This aperiodic dithering method can be combined with error diffusion to good effect, as shown in Fig. 3.26(d).

The spatial resolution of digital typesetting equipment often exceeds 2000 dpi. Such high resolutions are not needed for printing text, but have been used for halftones to simulate fine-mesh optical screens. The dithering methods just described, combined with methods of image enhancement, can nonetheless produce useful results at lower resolutions. Figure 3.27 compares the clustered-dot method with aperiodic error-diffusion dithering in a larger picture, printed (originally) at 300-dpi with a laser printer.

Line art and images can enter a digital document-preparation system by optical scanning. A scanner measures the reflectivity at points in a rectangular grid on an original paper image. Because of the limitations of sampling (as described by the Nyquist criterion), at least twice the spatial resolution of the useful detail of the image is required in the scanning. Note that scanning a photographically enlarged original is equivalent to scanning a smaller original at higher resolution. What matters is the amount of information available for each point in the output image, not the absolute resolution of the scanning device.

Scanned image quality can be improved by enhancement algorithms [Pratt 1978:307–468]. These algorithms do not add information to the image. Rather, they use knowledge about the image to reduce noise and error in the stored image. For example, if an image is known to be a line drawing, and thus bivalued, an enhancement algorithm can

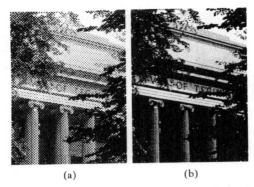

(a)   (b)

FIGURE 3.27   Simulating a classic halftone screen (a) does not make the best use of the available information content. Using more sophisticated techniques, in this case error diffusion and blue noise, a far superior result is possible with the same resolution, 300 dpi in this case. (Courtesy of The MIT Press and Robert Ulichney.)

use this fact to increase contrast and smooth edges. Thus an image more like the original is inferred from both the data and some meta-knowledge about the image.

Some Thoughts on Output-Device Design

Output devices can be designed with the characteristics of type and the problems of typography in mind. There are many creative opportunities of this sort. For example, laser printers can be designed with carefully controlled characteristics aimed at half-bitting. In CRTs, greater spatial resolution in screens can be traded off against dynamic performance (lower refresh rate) and overall screen size. If these characteristics of the device were designed in, typographic performance could be improved.

The following design principles provide basic guidance in the design of output devices for typographic use. They are, of necessity, very broad; finer principles will be discussed in later chapters.

- *Base specifications on system-level requirements.* The output components of an electronic publishing system cannot be designed in isolation. They depend on the use to which the system will be put, as well as the way the system will be used. Specific decisions in these areas will mold the specifications for the output devices to be used.

- *Specify capabilities in terms of perceptual dimensions, plus cost and performance.* As discussed previously, the dimensions of interest are spatial resolution, temporal resolution, intensity resolution, color resolution, and contrast.
- *Do not refine the product beyond the human ability to sense the difference.* There is no value in providing more resolution than the eye can see, faster refresh than the flicker fusion frequency, or contrast greater than the user can appreciate.
- *Design in adaptations to specific output devices.* Because of variations in the characteristics of various devices, consistent results from machine to machine call for modifications of input. For example, different fonts may be required to obtain the same result from two different printers.

Keeping these principles in mind, it is now possible to discuss the design of letters for digital use, which is the subject of the next chapter.

Chapter Summary

Most devices used for output in digital typography are bitmapped. They can be characterized in part by their addressing resolution, spatial resolution, and spot size. Horizontal and vertical spatial scales need not have the same unit, and the pixels themselves need not be of equal height and width. A page or screen aspect ratio indicates the shape of the entire display surface.

The spatial resolution of the eye suggests that, at a normal reading distance for paper, about 600 dpi is sufficient to provide all the detail the eye can see. However, this conclusion is still open to some question experimentally. The output quality of any device depends intimately on its specific characteristics, making generalizations about resolution unreliable.

A taxonomy of output devices takes into account the surface upon which output appears, how symbols and other images are formed, and whether the image is created directly on the output medium, or formed on an intermediate surface and transferred.

The resolution of any output device can be described in terms of space, time, intensity, and color. Some displays are refreshed; the refresh rate determines their temporal resolution. Intensity and color resolution determine whether the device can produce true continuous-tone output, or must instead rely on dithers to simulate intermediate tones.

Cathode ray tubes are common to display information dynamically. They can be refreshed with or without interlacing. Interlaced displays are more subject to flicker when showing text and line graphics. A long-persistence phosphor can eliminate flicker, but at the expense of temporal resolution. CRTs also suffer from low contrast due to stray light that travels to the eye from parts of the tube surface that would otherwise be dark. Color CRTs, while useful for pictures and graphics, causes difficulties for text and line drawings.

Two other display technologies are liquid crystal displays and plasma displays. Both present well-defined pixels with sharp edges, and thus produce text (in particular) of low quality compared with CRTs at the same resolution.

Digital printing devices transfer ink or toner to paper by direct contact, like dot-matrix impact printing, or indirectly, like laser printers. Laser printers are photocopiers in which the image is created by scanning laser light under digital control, rather than by light reflected from an original document. Digital typesetters operate by exposing photographic film or photographic paper, thereby creating a master for reproduction by conventional printing methods.

Most digital output devices exhibit polarity asymmetry. Inverting each pixel, creating the equivalent of a photographic negative, does not produce an exact inverse image. Similarly, many devices have anisotropy—differences between the horizontal and vertical axes in the rendition of images. For good results, accommodations must be made in the data sent to the devices.

— 4
Making Digital Letterforms

I think no virtue goes with size.
— *Ralph Waldo Emerson*

Designing digital typefaces, like designing traditional analog ones, is specialized and difficult work. Very few people can design
digital faces well; they must have an interdisciplinary background and
mind-set as well as substantial skill and experience, and a good æsthetic
sense. The best digital type designs for general reading are still produced by relatively few individuals. Indeed, type design is not a task
to be undertaken lightly. Years before computer-aided design of letterforms was possibile, the traditional typographer Frederic Goudy
[1940:155] warned, "Letters should be designed by an artist and not by
an engineer."

On the other hand, a basic understanding of typeface design is
essential for selecting digital fonts and for using such fonts in the
context of a system. Further, special symbols and specialized fonts are
required frequently in a system; such design tasks are more approachable than the design of whole character sets aimed at readable text for
general use. Also, the tools used to create digital fonts may make the
task somewhat easier than if paper and pencil were the primary design
tools.

Another reason to study design, even if one does not intend to do
it oneself, is that it is helpful in programming automatic font-synthesis
programs. Font creation can be mechanized in large part, but programs
that make fonts are subject to some of the same constraints and difficulties facing people who undertake font design. In particular, many
systems now create fonts 'on the fly' for use as needed for a particular
variation on a stored font. Systems make variations in size, oblique or

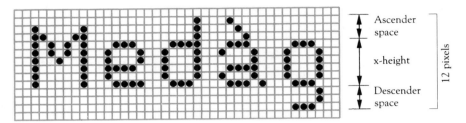

FIGURE 4.1   A few pixels must express the shape of lowercase letters at 72 pixels per inch.

bold, higher or lower resolution, and so on. The topics of this chapter apply equally well to these font-making programs.

Issues in Font Design

All font designs must deal with issues that affect the visible result of the work. One goal in design is to control the characteristics of letters, such as their weight and x-height, as size and resolution vary. Fonts for low-resolution devices are particularly hard to control because very few pixels are available for creating the shapes of letters. This limits the range of choices for letterform features.

For example, many screens operate at 70 to 80 pixels per inch, or roughly one pixel per printer's point. The perception of the size of a font depends principally on its x-height because most of the letters in running text are lowercase. Generally, x-heights range from 40% to 60% of the font body size. At 72 pixels per inch, a 12-point font with a 50% x-height has six pixels available vertically to form the lowercase letter shapes (Fig. 4.1). The only other choices within this percentage range are five pixels and seven pixels, which would be x-heights of 42% and 58%, respectively.

Designs with relatively large x-heights are attractive at lower resolutions because they make better use of the available space, and simultaneously appear larger on the screen with the same line height, than designs of smaller x-height. This fact accounts in part for the popularity in desktop publishing of versions of Times New Roman and Helvetica, two traditional faces with larger x-heights.

One measure of overall blackness of a typeface as it appears on the page, called "color" by typographers, can be assessed via this relationship:

$$\text{color} = \frac{S_{a-z}}{T_v},$$

where S_{a-z} is the set of the lowercase alphabet and T_v is the vertical stem thickness.

The alphabet set, S_{a-z}, is simply the horizontal space occupied by a lowercase alphabet printed out without letterspacing. Table 4.1 shows the color values for a number of traditional typefaces, versions of which are still very much in use. Low numbers indicate dark faces; high numbers, light ones. The color formula is useful for assessing the overall blackness of a typeface, but is less useful in practice for design because the entire lowercase alphabet would have to be designed, at least roughly, to calculate the color.

A measure of the heaviness or boldness of type more useful in font design is *its weight*, which can be expressed as

$$W = \frac{T_v}{x},$$

where T_v is the vertical stem thickness for lowercase letters and x is the x-height.

The larger the value of W, the darker each letter will appear. However, the formula only approximates what people describe visually as weight. It assumes an average width (set). Very narrow faces appear darker (higher color value), and wide faces appear lighter, other things being equal. Furthermore, the stem width of some designs varies from letter to letter. The waist measurement of a letter 'l' can be used as an approximation, or an average value can be used. Note also that some typefaces have heavier stems for uppercase, but this does not much affect the overall weight of a page of mixed-case text.

Table 4.1 also shows values for weight. Weights higher than about 1:5 ($W \geq 0.2$) result in darker typefaces that are not generally easy to read. If W drops below about 1:7 (0.15), the face will appear too light and spindly.

Typeface[a]	Color[b] $\dfrac{S_{a\text{-}z}}{T_v}$	Weight[c] $\dfrac{T_v}{x}$	Contrast[d] $\dfrac{T_v}{T_h}$	Sample	
Bembo	184	0.16	2[e]	if the letters, however pretty combine automatically into	
Bulmer	140	0.22	4	**if the letters, however pretty in t automatically into words; if the**	
Centaur	212	0.14	2	if the letters, however pretty in th automatically into words; if the fo	
Garamond	208	0.15	3[f]	if the letters, however pretty combine automatically into	
Helvetica[g]	163	0.16	1	if the letters, however pretty i combine automatically into	
Perpetua	170	0.18	5½	if the letters, however pretty in the automatically into words; if the	
Plantin	144	0.19	2[h]	if the letters, however pretty combine automatically into	
Times	156	0.17	2	if the letters, however pretty combine automatically into	
Van Dijck	191	0.15	2¾	if the letters, however pretty in th automatically into words; if the four	

Legend:
■ Color
▨ Weight
□ Contrast

[a] Typeface names in *italics* have designs in which T_v varies from letter to letter.
[b] From [Williamson 1956: 398].
[c] Calculated from data in [Williamson 1956:396].
[d] Based on measurements performed by the author.
[e] Measured on an 11-point sample.
[f] Intertype version.
[g] Linotype version.
[h] Measured on a 10-point sample.

TABLE 4.1 The color, weight, and typographic contrast of nine typefaces as measured in a 12-point font, shown with a sample of each face. All values are approximate in terms of the appearance of type on paper, which depends on the printing technology and the conditions of printing for any particular sample.

A final typeface quality worth attention is called *typographic contrast* (as distinct from intensity contrast). Typographic contrast refers to the ratio of the weights of vertical to horizontal letter elements:

$$C_T = \frac{T_v}{T_h} \, ,$$

where T_v is the vertical stem thickness of lowercase letters and T_h is the thickness of horizontal strokes of lowercase letters.

The same caveats that apply to the precision of the weight measure apply here. Many traditional typefaces have high contrast, in excess of 3.0, giving them a look that typographers term brilliant or glittery. Extremely high contrast results in striking, but less legible typefaces. Low contrast ratios, those close to unity, describe faces that appear monotonous and flat overall. Compare the typefaces in Fig. 4.2, which are quite similar, differing only in contrast. The good legibility associated with traditional faces is related in part to their contrast, although some faces succeed in spite of somewhat lower contrast. A contrast of less than unity would result on a CRT when using one pixel for both horizontal and vertical elements (black on white) because of the erosion of the verticals. The look of such letters is distinctly unnatural compared with most printed letterforms encountered in reading (Fig. 4.3).

Not all traditional typefaces have high contrast. Most sans serif designs have contrast near unity. If the intent is to reproduce such a typeface, or to produce a new design in which low contrast is a desired feature, then of course the designer must produce contrast that matches the typeface design.

The measures just discussed serve as specifications in fonts design. A particular typeface will have a certain x-height, weight, and contrast that contribute substantially to its overall look and quality. One goal of font design is to match these parameters in fonts that are supposed to be the same on different output devices or at different resolutions. Related typefaces will have similar values.

When only a few integral values are available for T_v, T_h, and x-height, the range of choices is limited to the available combinations. Continuing the example of a 12-point typeface on a 72-pixel-per-inch screen, the designer can make a table of plausible possibilities (Table 4.2). The table can be worked out with a spread-sheet program, as was this example, calculating the weight and contrast for each proposed

AFTER THE PRIME necessities of life nothing is more pre–
cious to us than books. The art of Typography, their creator,
renders a signal service to society and lends it invaluable
support, serving as it does to educate the citizen, to widen
the field for the progress of sciences and arts, to nourish
and cultivate the mínd to elevate the soul and generally,
taking upon itself to be the messenger and interpreter of
wisdom and truth it is the portrayer of mind. Therefore we
may call it essentially the art of all arts and science of all
sciences. Before the discovery of printing mankind made
slow progress in the paths of knowledge. The pursuit of it
demanded arduous labour and constant vigils, as men dug
deep for it in Natures bosom. And if the more widespread

(a)

AFTER THE PRIME necessities of life nothing is more precious to us than books. The art of Typography, their creator,
renders a signal service to society and lends it invaluable
support, serving as it does to educate the citizen, to widen
the field for the progress of sciences and arts, to nourish and
cultivate the mind to elevate the soul and generally, taking
upon itself to be the messenger and interpreter of wisdom
and truth it is the portrayer of mind. Therefore we may call
it essentially the art of all arts and science of all sciences. Before the discovery of printing mankind made slow progress
in the paths of knowledge. The pursuit of it demanded arduous labour and constant vigils, as men dug deep for it in
Natures bosom. And if the more widespread was the search,

(b)

FIGURE 4.2 Similar typefaces of different contrast in the Lucida family.
Sample (a) is the standard roman, and (b) is a brighter variation (higher contrast). The Lucida Bright variant is the typeface now used in *Scientific American,* and is produced on high-resolution digital typesetting equipment. (Courtesy of Bigelow & Holmes.)

ABCDEFGHIJKLMNOPQRSTUVWXYZ&
abcdefghijklmnopqrstuvwxyz
1234567890$

FIGURE 4.3 Trylon, a typeface with a typographic contrast of less than one. A few such faces are used in advertising, but they are unacceptable for running text.

T_v	T_h	x-height	W	C_T
1	1	4	0.250	1.000
1	1	5	0.200	1.000
1	1	6	0.167	1.000
1	1	7	0.143	1.000
2	1	4	0.500	2.000
2	1	5	0.400	2.000
2	1	6	0.333	2.000
2	1	7	0.286	2.000
1	2	4	0.250	0.500
1	2	5	0.200	0.500
1	2	6	0.167	0.500
1	2	7	0.143	0.500
2	2	4	0.500	1.000
2	2	5	0.400	1.000
2	2	6	0.333	1.000
2	2	7	0.286	1.000
3	1	4	0.750	3.000
3	1	5	0.600	3.000
3	1	6	0.500	3.000
3	1	7	0.429	3.000
3	2	4	0.750	1.500
3	2	5	0.600	1.500
3	2	6	0.500	1.500
3	2	7	0.429	1.500

TABLE 4.2 Spread sheet showing various combinations of vertical stroke, horizontal stroke width, and x-height, and the consequent weight and contrast.

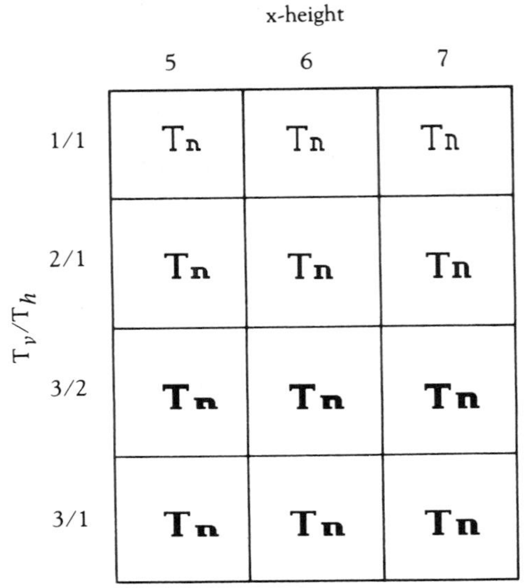

FIGURE 4.4 Appearance of letters with various x-heights, vertical stroke widths, and horizontal stroke widths.

combination of values. These numbers correspond to letters like those shown in Fig. 4.4.

Plotting the contrast against the weight for the values that result gives a chart like the one in Fig. 4.5(a). Unfortunately, most of the possibilities give either very low contrast or very great weight, compared with the values for traditional faces (the shaded area in Fig. 4.5(a)).

As the last chapter showed, the widths of strokes on some output devices, notably CRTs, vary from integral multiples of pixel widths. Therefore another consideration at this point is whether the integral values for numbers of pixels actually represent the dimensions that will appear on the output device. As an example, consider a CRT displaying black text on a white background. The erosion of the vertical stems might be about 0.4 pixels for a particular display unit, giving rise to a revised chart (Fig. 4.5(b)). Different combinations of height and stem width may come closer to the typographically acceptable ranges when these device characteristics are considered.

Figure 4.6 shows the choices when more pixels are available in the

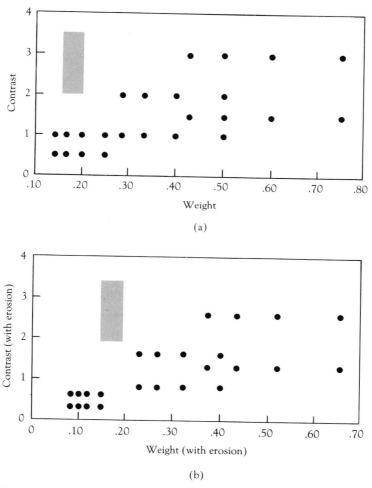

FIGURE 4.5 Possible weights and contrasts in a 12-pixel-high cell. The shaded area represents the ideal range for text typefaces. In (a), pixels are assumed to have their nominal dimensions. In (b), it is assumed that vertical strokes will be eroded by 0.4 pixels, as might be the case for a CRT of a particular design.

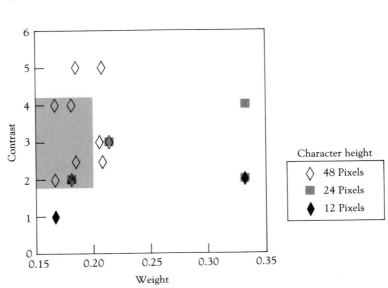

FIGURE 4.6   Possible weights and contrast with three cell heights. The shaded region indicates the approximate desired ranges of weight and contrast for text typefaces.

same height. The possibilities have been restricted here to those closest to the acceptable range in weight and contrast. Resolutions of twice and four times the previous example are considered, which means that 24 and 48 pixels are available vertically.

Observe that at higher resolutions many more potential choices are available because each dimension takes on finer increments. If the goal is to match the appearance of fonts presented at different resolutions, one consideration is to find similar values for weight, contrast, and x-height at the resolutions in question. Figure 4.6 suggests that this may not be possible for the lowest resolutions; only at higher values are there points in reasonable proximity. Similar comments apply to matching typographic color at different resolutions.

One possibility for improving the range of choices of x-height and stem width at low resolution might be to use pixels with an aspect ratio other than 1:1. For example, a display could have fat pixels—say, two times as wide as they are high. There is some precedent for doing this. Some commercial typesetters use ratios other than 1:1.[1] Although

---

[1] An example is the Hell typesetter, manufactured in Germany, which uses a ratio of 6:5.

designing fonts for nonsquare-pixels is considerably harder, the results may well warrant the effort in some cases. Also, when fonts are created automatically in systems, the difficulty of manual font design is not a consideration, so nonsquare pixels may be all the more desirable.

A final issue in font design is the relationship of x-height, cap-height, and ascender and descender lengths. The vertical height of the text is a scarce resource indeed, as the preceding discussion of x-height indicates. Allocating space is a difficult compromise: Vertical space is also needed between lines, and for accent (diacritical) marks. In designing fonts with accents, space above or below certain letters is used for these marks, resulting in tighter constraints on the entire design.

Cap-height is a particular problem, but some happy solutions exist in certain cases. Capital letters must be higher than the x-height, but many typefaces have capitals a bit shorter than the ascenders. If capitals must have diacritical marks, however, much space may be wasted above most of the symbols in order to leave room for these highest ones. There are three choices. The designer can accept the blank space and consider it part of the interline spacing inherent in the design. Or the designer can choose to reduce the cap-height. Of course, if the face must match another with a large cap-height, this approach will not work. One virtue of smaller capitals is that all-uppercase words such as acronyms will look better and may not require small caps, which are often used to accommodate all-cap words to running text.

A third possibility also has precedent in print typefaces. Since the problematic letters are capitals with diacritical marks, those and only those capitals could be shrunk relative to unadorned capitals in the font. This makes these letters look unusual, but the result may be acceptable if they are either used rarely or seldom used next to ordinary capitals that would invite visual comparison. The three strategies are diagrammed in Fig. 4.7.

Descenders are slightly less important than ascenders in terms of readability because readers depend more strongly on the tops of letters to decode them. Very shallow descenders do cause problems, though, such as possible confusion of lowercase g with the number 9. If interline space inherent in the design (exclusive of additional leading) is included between lines, descenders can extend into this space even though they do not have its exclusive use. Some designs even share interline spaces between ascenders (and diacriticals) and descenders

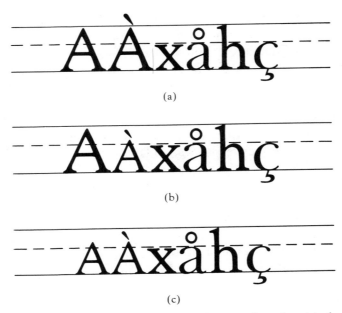

(a)

(b)

(c)

FIGURE 4.7   Three compromises of vertical space when diacritical marks are required.

from the line above. Depending on their use, overlaps may be rare enough that the price is acceptable to gain greater x-height.

Methods of Font Design

There are three general approaches to typeface design: top down, bottom up, and collateral. If an idealized design of high resolution is used as the basis for a type family, with lower-resolution fonts derived from it, it is called a top-down design. Conversely, if an individual font or two of low resolution is used as the basis of the family, it is called bottom-up design. Finally, collateral design seeks to optimize among the various fonts required, compromising some local improvements for the best overall result.

Top-down Font Design

The top-down approach proceeds from the belief that the best designs are those expressed accurately at high resolution. The source of high-

FIGURE 4.8   A letterform design expressed as an outline.

quality letterform designs for this purpose may be traditional typefaces, transferred from other media such as phototypesetting masters, or possibly new designs created with the digital medium in mind. The source design will usually be expressed as an outline, as shown in Fig. 4.8.

Consider a musical analogy to the top-down philosophy. A score represents a musical idea that can be realized more or less well when performed by musicians using instruments. The musical idea may come through to the listener even when musicians make mistakes or instruments do not produce ideal sounds. Similarly, in top-down typeface design, it is hoped that imperfections in rendering the design at various resolutions and for various devices will not prevent the reader from perceiving the overall design.

There are difficulties, however, in representing an ideal design digitally. As a practical matter, all digitized outlines must be edited and adjusted, even if the source is a well-made photographic image scanned at high resolution. This is because many variations in letters arise in printing and digitizing, and these imperfections must be corrected.

Imagine starting with a sample of a traditional design, carefully printed so that it can be digitized. Why does this sample not provide the correct shape for the letters? Fig. 4.9 shows a sample of some traditional letterforms by John Baskerville, one of the most meticulous font designers and printers of the eighteenth century. Despite care, the sample letters will always deviate from their nominal forms. Baskerville was extraordinarily skillful at inking his type, achieving an evenness on each page and from page to page unrealized by his predecessors. But the amount of ink in the particular sample at hand determines the extent to which the letters are broadened by ink "squish" (spreading under pressure) when the impression is made. Is the correct

THE

CONTAINING THE

OLD TESTAMENT

AND

THE NEW:

Tranflated out of the

AND

With the former TRANSLATIONS

Diligently Compared and Revifed,

By His MAJESTY's Special Command.

APPOINTED TO BE READ IN CHURCHES.

CAMBRIDGE,

Printed by *JOHN BASKERVILLE*, Printer to the UNIVERSITY.
MDCCLXIII.

CUM PRIVILEGIO.

Title-page of the 1763 Bible *(reduced from 315 × 495 mm)*

FIGURE 4.9   Sample of type designed and printed by John Baskerville. The title page of his 1763 bible, much reduced, is shown. (Title page of the 1763 Bible reproduced from F. E. Pardoe, *John Baskerville of Birmingham,* © 1975, Frederick Muller, Ltd., an imprint of Century Hutchinson Ltd.)

FIGURE 4.10 Effects of ink spreading, embossing of the paper, and of paper texture, in an early letterpress print sample.

shape the shape of the type, or of the resulting impression? Similarly, nearly all early print samples were printed on soft paper, causing the type to emboss the paper and print, at least in part, with the beveled side of the type. Should the image of this edge be part of a digital image? Was it anticipated by the designer? Baskerville for one was certainly that thoughtful. Figure 4.10 shows some of these effects.

Since metal type wears out as it is used, an early impression may be quite different from a later one made with the same piece of metal. In terms of the ideal shape, what was the intended design point? We have to take some sort of position on this issue to know how to treat the sample. Other effects requiring compensation involve the texture of the paper, the stiffness of the ink used, and the sharpness of the particular impression. Master designers and craftsmen such as Baskerville did take these effects into consideration, and thus the samples we have may express the intended letter shapes more accurately than one might expect. However, correction and adjustment will always be necessary [Pardoe 1975:48].

In truth, good, sharp examples are available from phototypesetting masters, transfer letter sheets, sample books, and other sources. Although these typefaces do not necessarily portray accurately the original designs whose names they bear, they avoid some of the vagaries of working from early examples. Even so, it is productive to analyze a design to try to understand the reasons for its particular characteristics: A font created at lower resolution must preserve the essential features of the design in order to achieve family membership.

Remembering our musical analogy, the goal of top-down font design is to create shapes that create the desired perception of the design despite imperfections in the presentation. Therefore understanding the graphic intent of the design helps in creating fonts at different sizes and resolutions. Just as earlier designers such as Baskerville and Caslon managed to create a good overall perception in spite of variations from letter to letter and printing to printing, a top-down font designer seeks the same overall perception despite variations in output-device characteristics.

Thus top-down design presents the problem of determining the ideal shape for the letterforms. It is also necessary to compare letters to understand the logic of the entire design. For example, are the 'h', 'n', and 'm' letters the same basic shape, sharing a common width of the counter (interior space), or is there a systematic variation? A good eye and no small amount of experience in discovering and reinforcing the logic of particular designs are needed to perform this analysis and impose the required relationships.

Having achieved good outlines for a typeface, the next problem in top-down design is to create bitmap versions at the required resolutions. A new problem appears: The dimensions of the original design are not multiples of the pixel spacing at the required resolution.

Figure 4.11(a) shows a letter 'h' on a grid. Not only is it difficult to capture the subtle characteristics of the letter at the grid resolution (the curve of the serifs and the slender join between the horizontal and vertical strokes), it is hard to decide what choices to make for the larger features. Should the verticals be two pixels wide? The left-stroke vertical is wider than the right, even though both are about two units wide. This subtlety would be lost. If we make the main stroke wider than the other, the difference would be exaggerated. Similarly, the interior space, the space between the vertical strokes, bears yet a different relationship to the widths of the black parts. There just is not enough resolution to keep these characteristics in the rasterized image. Should the resulting digitized form be as in Fig. 4.11(b), or maybe as in (c)?

Perhaps the problem in the preceding example was only insufficient resolution to give a good rendering of the original typeface design.

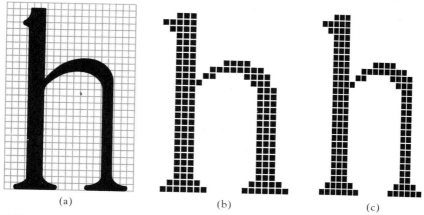

(a)   (b)   (c)

FIGURE 4.11 Possible ways to digitize a letter. The 'h' in (a) does not have features that are integral multiples of the grid. Depending on the intent, various interpretations of the design are possible, such as those in (b) and (c).

Ultimately this must be true because some fineness of resolution would be sufficient to capture all of the visible features of the letter. As long as the output devices employed do not provide this degree of fineness, however, the issue remains. In fact, some typefaces are particularly resistant to digitizing because of their subtle characteristics. Figure 4.12 shows a sample of the typeface Optima, designed by Hermann Zapf. It is characterized by delicate curves and, especially, by near-

abcdefgh
ijklmnopqrstuvwxyz
1234567890

ABCDEFGH
IJKLMNOPQRSTUV
WXYZ&

FIGURE 4.12 Optima, a typeface that is difficult to represent digitally, even at moderately high resolutions. Designed by Hermann Zapf, Optima is characterized by subtle changes in line width and near-vertical edges.

FIGURE 4.13   Four sizes of a screen typeface. Note that the design for the letter 'w' is different in each size.

vertical lines that are difficult to capture at resolutions sufficient for more rectilinear designs.

If one is tempted to make different compromises for different letters, uniformity of style may also be difficult to maintain. For example, the typeface shown in Fig. 4.13 uses different shapes for the letter 'w' at different sizes, simply because a larger size affords the opportunity to make a nicer letter. Designers must constantly make decisions like this. Is the overall result preferable with consistency or with better individual designs?

Can variations in size or resolution be created automatically? Programs now exist to adjust high-resolution letterforms to the lower-resolution raster in a way that preserves important letterform properties [Sauvain and Wayman 1987; Hersch 1987]. The process is heuristic, which is to say that a particular, acceptable result is not guaranteed. Automatic adjustment of letterforms is a real step forward in making the top-down method more routine and less labor intensive. The procedure implemented by such programs attempts to discover the relative natural dimensions of the design: stroke width, stroke spacing, bowl and counter space, interletter spacing, ascender and descender relationships, and so on. Then the raster is distorted both vertically and horizontally to optimize the fit of the design features to the raster units. Finally, individual letters are distorted to fit the new raster.

Another approach used by researchers at IBM [Casey, Friedman, and Wong 1980] uses pattern-processing methods to scale bitmap fonts both up and down. These researchers found that the conventional

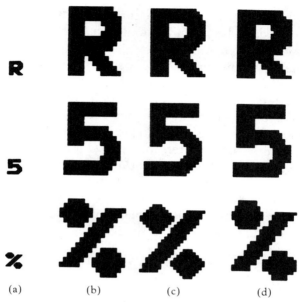

FIGURE 4.14   Results obtained by Casey, Friedman, and Wong [1980], who rescaled bitmap fonts using a feature-sensitive algorithm. The leftmost columns contain the original 24x18 characters to be rescaled, shown actual size (a) and enlarged (b). The third column (c) shows the rescaled characters at 40x24, using the algorithm. In comparison, the rightmost column (d) shows the same rescaling, but with a conventional interpolation algorithm. (Figures reprinted by permission from R. G. Casey, T. D. Friedman, and K. Y. Wong, "Use of Pattern Processing Techniques to Scale Digital Print Fonts." *Proceedings of the Fifth International Conference on Pattern Recognition,* © 1980 IEEE.)

spatial-filtering techniques used for scaling grayscale pictures did not work for letterforms; they produced substantial distortions. They developed alternative techniques that use such properties as symmetry, separateness of pieces, smoothness of contours, and presence of corners to guide the rescaling operation. Figure 4.14 shows an example of their results.

When a system requires presenting the same typeface at more than one resolution, the top-down method generates noticeable differences in design, in proportion to the difference in resolution. For example, in a typesetting system with a screen resolution of 80 dots per inch and a typeset resolution of 2000 dots per inch, substantial differences in the designs must appear. The print resolution in this case is high enough to reproduce the original design, but the screen resolution requires substantial compromise.

Or consider a system with 300-dpi paper output used for proofs of 2000-dpi typesetter output. Here good presentations of the shapes and positions of letters can be made at the proof resolution, but fine details such as the shape and weight of thin joins may not match at all.

Some systems, such as the Apple Macintosh computer and LaserWriter (PostScript) printer, incorporate a top-down strategy directly into the system's operation. Outlines form the basis for printing at whatever size or orientation is requested. Bitmaps are generated at printing time from the outlines as needed and cached (stored temporarily) to the extent that available memory allows. Screen fonts are generated and hand tuned based on the outlines, not generated on the fly.

Bottom-Up Font Design

The bottom-up approach, on the other hand, seeks to optimize the appearance and quality of low-resolution presentations. Thus what can be done at low resolution influences letter shape at higher resolutions. To carry out bottom-up design, a designer creates a font tuned to the low-resolution device. The source font may well be based on a traditional design, but compromises for the device and resolution will have been made to optimize its appearance. Basic shapes and spaces can be designed as multiples of the raster unit. By working with the available resolution, a designer can create a better design, with no need to accurately match a particular external model.

Of course, bottom-up designs must result in letterforms of reasonable legibility that respect people's investment in reading traditionally shaped letters. Freedom from the requirement of matching a specific analog design can result in exceptionally good designs, given the resolution. These designs avoid some of the problems that afflict top-down designs—difficult features such as hairline joins, near-vertical lines, and subtle variations in line thickness.

If bottom-up design is applied at each resolution required in a system, substantially different designs result; the designer cannot reasonably say that the designs are the same typeface. If a good match is necessary, the designer creates higher-resolution versions based on the units and design ideas used in the low-resolution font. This is a substantial

The quick brown fox jumped over the lazy dog. 9 pt.—computed

The quick brown fox jumped over the lazy dog. 10 pt.—stored

The quick brown fox jumped over the lazy dog. 12 pt.—stored

The quick brown fox jumped over the lazy dog. 14 pt.—computed

The quick brown fox jumpe
24 pt.—stored

The quick brown b
36 pt.—computed

FIGURE 4.15   Automatic scaling used to create intermediate sizes of screen fonts that match good fonts in the print output device. In the example, (the New York family from the Macintosh) only 10-, 12-, and 24-point screen fonts are available; other requested values are computed from the available fonts.

handicap. A higher-resolution output device, which is capable of greater subtlety and refinement, will be limited by the relatively coarse features of the design.

The first step of the process of translating the original typeface design to a higher resolution is to enlarge the small design to the higher resolution algorithmically, and then to tune the new images to match the rest of the family. If gross features are changed, the higher-resolution design will not resemble the low one as strongly as otherwise. If features are not changed, a "clunkier," coarser design results at the higher resolution.

The Macintosh also incorporates a bottom-up font strategy directly into its system. When screen fonts are not available at a given size, they are created algorithmically as needed. Although this approach gives lower-quality screen fonts for generated sizes, it does provide coverage without the memory necessary to store intermediate sizes. Figure 4.15 shows the difference in quality between stored and generated screen fonts for the Macintosh.

Collateral Font Design

Top-down design thus has the problem of producing low-resolution fonts of lower quality, while bottom-up design forces compromises in the high-resolution fonts. The third method, collateral design, combines the top-down and bottom-up methods, attempting to solve the problems inherent in the other methods. Instead of creating a reference design at either high or low resolution, the collateral method creates the required range of high- and low-resolution designs simultaneously. This allows the designer to trade off quality and detail at each level in such a way as to create a design of relatively uniform quality and typographic features. In effect, one larger design problem replaces two or more smaller ones. It is harder to design this way, but the payoff can be a greater unity of font design, better quality, and a better match between designs at each resolution.

In collateral design, the designer invents a design idea for the font family that generally avoids features that cannot be represented well at the lower resolutions involved, but that uses some of the finer detail possible at higher resolution. A good designer can strike a balance, building into the basic design a visual tolerance for some of the low-resolution coarseness and at the same time making good use of higher resolutions. Typographically, the best possible design cannot be achieved in either high- or low-resolution design, but the overall level of quality may be higher than in either the bottom-up or top-down approaches. Figure 4.16 shows a pair of fonts designed by the collateral method.

In summary, the three design approaches allow for quality of the resulting fonts to be distributed differently, depending on what compromise between resolution and features the designer chooses. These approaches also represent different trade-offs between using fonts that match at different sizes and resolutions versus providing the most readable letterforms in each situation.

Top-down design is the method of choice when high-resolution design quality is paramount, as with a production typesetting system. Bottom-up is ideal when the low-resolution font is the most important—for example, terminal- or workstation-based systems intended primarily for on-line access to text, when hard-copy output at a higher resolution is secondary. Finally, collateral designs are best when the quality at each resolution is equally important. Collateral designs are suited to desktop-publishing applications, for example, because users of such systems spend hours working with screen versions of their documents, but the printed documents, the useful result of the on-line work, are then read by others.

Excellence in typography is the result of nothing more
Its appeal comes from the understanding used in its pl;
must care. In contemporary advertising the perfect int
elements often demands unorthodox typography. It m;
Compact Spacing, Minus Leading, Unusual Sizes, Weigh
whatever is needed to improve appearance and impact.
of human event's: 'one true people politic' daily dissol
swept blackout; necessary odd because illicit navy craf

(a)

Excellence in typography is the result of nothing mor
Its appeal comes from the understanding used in its]
must care. In contemporary advertising the perfect in
elements often demands unorthodox typography. It n
Compact Spacing, Minus Leading, Unusual Sizes, Weig
whatever is needed to improve appearance and impa(
of human event's: 'one true people politic' daily disso
swept blackout; necessary odd because illicit navy cr;

(b)

FIGURE 4.16 A collateral design, resulting in good quality in both the low-resolution (a) and high-resolution (b) versions. The typeface shown is Lucida. (Courtesy of Bigelow & Holmes.)

Grayscale and Color in Fonts

On some kinds of output device, CRT displays in particular, there is the possibility of using *grayscale*—varying intensities between white and black—for minimizing jaggies and creating more subtle shapes. This technique works because of the eye's ability to enhance edges when viewing shapes. Instead of seeing a soft edge, as actually displayed, a sharper one in an intermediate position is perceived (see Fig. 4.17). This useful ability allows intensity information to be substituted for spatial information. Indeed, conventional television cameras are designed to provide gray transitions around sharp boundaries by averaging the image. The television receiver then displays this relatively gradual transition. Thus, by careful design, television transmission avoids high frequencies during sampling that could cause aliasing, and avoids reconstruction errors during display.

Note that there are limits to the visual angle for which this substitution will work. Just as viewing a TV image from very close reveals

(a)   (b)

FIGURE 4.17   Intensity variations used in fonts (a) make letterforms appear sharper and smoother when displayed at text size on a CRT (b). (From the thesis of Avi C. Naiman, *High-Quality Text for Raster Displays*, © 1985. Reprinted with permission of the author.)

indistinct boundaries, viewing a computer display on which the intensity changes are spread over too large a visual angle results in fuzzy boundaries for text and graphics. As was shown in Chapter 2, the spatial frequency sensitivity of the eye depends on contrast. At high frequencies, high contrast is required to allow the eye to distinguish edges. A low-contrast edge of small dimension (high spatial frequency) is not perceived as such, but it does help us perceive the location of the larger object of which it is part.

As few as two levels of gray, in addition to white and black, may be enough to improve appearance [Schmandt 1980], but three or four bits (8 to 16 levels, including black and white) give better results [Warnock 1980:306]. Gray levels are particularly useful on displays with very limited spatial resolution, such as conventional TV sets used to display text. They have the additional benefit of diminishing text flicker resulting from interleaving, because grayscale equalizes the intensity between adjacent parts of letters in different fields.

Designing grayscale fonts manually is difficult because of the amount of information that must be specified for each bit. It is difficult for people to invent consistent gray values that create the right effects, although incremental improvements can be made to an existing design. A pragmatic way to create fonts with grayscale is to digitize them via a TV camera[2] and then make modest editorial changes via a font editor.

Good results can be attained computationally from rasterized high-resolution fonts [Warnock 1980]. A computational approach is more practical than manual design because it allows new fonts to be created automatically for various needs and situations. Computing grayscale fonts gives better control than does generating values directly by means of a TV camera or digitizer.

The following method is used to compute grayscale fonts: A master, high-resolution black-and-white image provides the source data. It may be a bitmap, or an outline or other representation that can be sampled at various points as required. For purposes of discussion, assume it is a bitmap. The resolution of the master image must be much greater than that of the grayscale font to be created.

First a low-pass filter is applied to the master image. This suppresses high-spatial-frequency components that would otherwise result in digitization artifacts, that is, aliasing. Then the filtered image is sampled to acquire the grayscale values for the desired font.

Conceptually, this process is similar to that of a TV camera (see Fig. 4.18). At any point in its scan, the camera generates a gray level that corresponds to a weighted average of the intensities of the image within some radius of the sampling point. For the filtering and sampling, overlapping regions are considered in turn, and a weighted average of the image within each circle is calculated.

One possible weighting is nothing more than the average intensity within the sampling region. This approach, while simple, does not give results as good as with functions that give more weight to the part of the image at the center of each sampling region. Various weighting functions are described in the computer graphics literature. (See [Warnock 1980], [Kajiya and Ullner 1981], and [Leler 1980].) The best results are obtained only when the characteristics of the output device and the eye are taken into consideration in the filtering function [Kajiya and Ullner 1981]. For example, the gaussian-intensity contour of pixels on CRT displays must be considered.

---

[2] Schmandt has done some of this work at MIT.

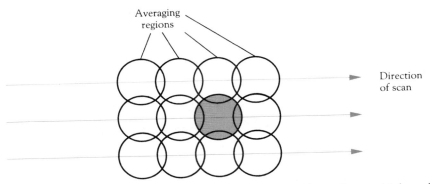

FIGURE 4.18   TV scan of a character, giving grayscale rendering. (Adapted from [Warnock 1980].)

Using such a grayscale approach allows finer letter positioning than the pixel resolution of the output device. The sampling grid can be positioned arbitrarily with respect to the symbol, creating a sampled letter that is positioned as desired relative to the pixel coordinates. Several such samplings can be created at intervals, resulting in the same number of complete fonts with differing positions relative to the output grid. For example, if four such fonts are created, this would amount to having two extra bits of spatial positioning available. This technique is called *subpixel addressing*.

When laying down letters in grayscale fonts, the edges usually overlap. In other words, there are nonwhite pixel values at the edges of adjacent symbols that must be combined. A simple approach is to add these values, so that two overlapping gray values result in a darker gray or black. But this only approximates the values that would result from sampling the letter combinations.

Another virtue of automatic creation of grayscale fonts is that they can be computed for angles other than horizontal, with good results. When text is not aligned to the output device axes, it may not be practical to have predetermined fonts—too many would be required.

Grayscale techniques are particularly relevant for text on a color display. Not only is there the added dimension of color, but variations in intensity are intrinsic to displays that can show a continuous range of colors. A strategy is necessary to ensure that text looks good and does not interact objectionably with color.

If text can obliterate its background, filling in a background color around itself, then it is easier to choose suitable color combinations for foreground and background so as to achieve good visibility and readability (see Chapter 3). When colored text must be laid on top of a colored background without changing the background, however, the problem is much more difficult.

One approach is to use the grayscale values at each point to interpolate between the foreground and background color. In other words, gray levels are interpreted as the degree of mixing of foreground and background colors. This interpolation can be made in many ways, which do not necessarily yield the same results. In particular, if the colors are described as combinations of red, blue, and green the results will be different than if described by hue, saturation, and value [Naiman 1985:99–109).

Another approach due to Naiman [1985] is to adjust the color of the text at each pixel to contrast with the background. At each pixel, choose a color of high contrast by changing the green component to an opposite extreme. If the green value is less than 50%, set it to 100%; if greater than 50%, set it to 0%. This method ensures a color at each foreground pixel that contrasts in both hue and intensity with the background color it replaces. One shortcoming: On a noisy or complicated background the letters may be affected so greatly by the background as to be illegible. Further, the method cannot guarantee that a foreground pixel will contrast with adjacent background pixels, since these pixels are independent of the choice of foreground color. Nonetheless, this algorithm has merit when the background is uncomplicated, or when the text moves relative to the background, as in animation or cursor movement.

Spacing of Letters

Properly spacing letters of low resolution is difficult, consuming much of a font designer's time. Overly tight spacing, the temptation when resolution and horizontal space are at a premium, results in uneven, blotchy text when letters are viewed as a block (Fig. 4.19). Combinations such as 'll' might be placed as close as one pixel between the stems in a sans serif face, but other combinations—for example, 'wy'—cannot support such close spacing. Wider interletter spacing is neces-

She likes lilliputian lilies.

(a)

She likes lilliputian lilies.

(b)

She likes lilliputian lilies.

(c)

FIGURE 4.19   Text that is too-tightly spaced is blotchy (a) compared with widely, more rhythmically spaced letters (b) and (c). The letterforms in all three examples are identical.

sary to achieve balance and to avoid disturbing the underlying rhythm of vertical strokes.

One resource for adjusting interletter spacing is *sidebearings*, the empty space at the right and left of each symbol that is part of its design (see Fig. 4.20). Sidebearings correspond to the shoulders of letterpress type, space that is built into the design of each letter. Using sidebearings to adjust spacing for the whole alphabet is time consuming but important. Each combination of letters must be examined. It is a combinatorial problem because sidebearings adjust the individual letters, not the combinations. Any change to a letter's sidebearings must be checked against its combination with all other letters, some of which may then require adjustments as well.

A simple way of checking is to generate all combinations of letters

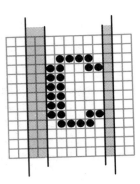

FIGURE 4.20   Sidebearings.

```
aabacadaeafagahaiajakalamanaoapaqarasatauavawaxayaz
abbbcbdbebfbgbhbibjbkblbmbnbobpbqbrbsbtbubvbwbxbybz
acbcccdcecfcgchcicjckclcmcncocpcqcrcsctcucvcwcxcycz
adbdcdddedfdgdhdidjdkdldmdndodpdqdrdsdtdudvdwdxdydz
aebecedeeefegeheiejekelemeneoepeqereseteuevewexeyez
afbfcfdfefffgfhfifjfkflfmfnfofpfqfrfsftfufvfwfxfyfz
agbgcgdgegfgggghgigjgkglgmgngogpgqgrgsgtgugvgwgxgygz
ahbhchdhehfhghhhihjhkhlhmhnhohphqhrhshthuhvhwhxhyhz
aibicidieifigihiiijikiliminioipiqirisitiuiviwixiyiz
ajbjcjdjejfjgjhjijjjkjljmjnjojpjqjrjsjtjujvjwjxjyjz
akbkckdkekfkgkhkikjkkklkmknkokpkqkrksktkukvkwkxkykz
alblcldlelflglhliljlklllmlnlolplqlrlsltlulvlwlxlylz
ambmcmdmemfmgmhmimjmkmlmmmnmompmqmrmsmtmumvmwmxmymz
anbncndnenfngnhninjnknlnmnnnonpnqnrnsntnunvnwnxnynz
aobocodoeofogohoiojokolomonoooopoqorosotouovowoxoyoz
apbpcpdpepfpgphpipjpkplpmpnpopppqprpsptpupvpwpxpypz
aqbqcqdqeqfqgqhqiqjqkqlqmqnqoqpqqqrqsqtquqvqwqxqyqz
arbrcrdrerfrgrhrirjrkrlrmrnrorprqrrrsrtrurvrwrxryrz
asbscsdsesfsgshsisjskslsmsnsospsqsrssstsusvswsxsysz
atbtctdtetftgthtitjtktltmtntotptqtrtstttutvtwtxtytz
aubucudueufuguhuiujukulumunuoupuqurusutuuuvuwuxuyuz
avbvcvdvevfvgvhvivjvkvlvmvnvovpvqvrvsvtvuvvvwvxvyvz
awbwcwdwewfwgwhwiwjwkwlwmwnwowpwqwrwswtwuwvwwwxwywz
axbxcxdxexfxgxhxixjxkxlxmxnxoxpxqxrxsxtxuxvxwxxxyxz
aybycydyeyfygyhyiyjykylymynyoypyqyrysytyuyvywyxyyyz
azbzczdzezfzgzhzizjzkzlzmznzozpzqzrzsztzuzvzwzxzyzz
```

FIGURE 4.21 Combinations used to discover spacing irregularities—an aid to adjusting character sidebearings. Here the font has already been pretty well adjusted, but the 'ha' combination is a bit too far apart. Note also how the 'w' stands out as too bold when the font is presented this way. Another interesting feature of this test is that the number of distinct line lengths is the number of distinct lowercase character widths, six in this case.

and examine them for spacing anomalies. Then examine ordinary running text of some length as a check. (See Fig. 4.21.) A variation is to generate nonsense words based on digraph letter-frequency data (the likelihood of occurrence of each letter combination) for the languages to be printed with the typeface.[3] "Reading" nonsense words makes it easier to find spacing problems because there is no content to distract from the examination.

Unfortunately, the process of adjusting sidebearings may not con-

---

[3] Digraph frequencies are published in the cryptographic literature. For data on English, German, French, Italian, Spanish, and Portuguese, see [Gaines 1939:218–223].

ANACHRONISM
(a)

ANACHRONISM
(b)

FIGURE 4.22 Spacing adjustment for sequences of uppercase letters is required even in metal type. Here (a) shows the text set solid, without spacing adjustment, while (b) shows it with thin spaces added to equalize visual space between the letters. (Courtesy of The Anachronism Press.)

verge on an acceptable set of values that makes all combinations of letters look good. A more sophisticated solution to the problem may be needed.

How was this problem solved in traditional printing? With movable type, a *kern* is a piece of one letter that sticks out over onto the shoulder of another letter, thus printing within its horizontal space, as determined by the metal body it sits on. Figure 2.2 (page 12) shows how this works. No actual adjustment of spacing for pairs of letters happens automatically; spacing is usually handled by sidebearings. But kerns allow the design to vertically overlap parts of adjacent letters. When necessary, the printer can add space between letters by placing thin shims of metal between the individual pieces of type; however, the space cannot be reduced so easily. (Sometimes printers miter individual letters to get them closer, cutting or filing away some of the body metal.)

Kerning in digital typography is the process of adjusting the spacing of letters pairwise. Each combination of letters needs to be considered for proper spacing relative to the rest of a font. Spacing must be visually equal, which implies unequal geometrical distance between letters. Kerning is thus a misnomer in the digital world; more accurately, this spacing correction would be called "digraph spacing adjustment," but the term kerning is in common use.

Uppercase letters do not space well in most traditional typefaces (Fig. 4.22). This is because the sidebearings are tuned to combinations

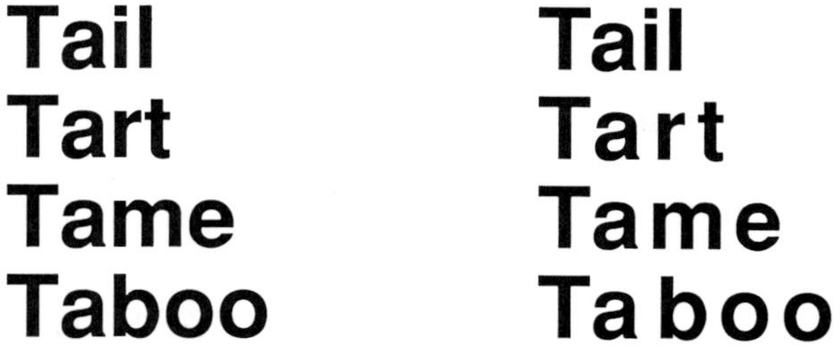

Tail   **Tail**

Tart   **Tart**

Tame   **Tame**

Taboo   **Taboo**

(a)   (b)

FIGURE 4.23   The best-quality letterspacing requires adjustments based on the larger context of each letter pair. In this example from Naiman [1985:78], compare the spacing of the letters 'Ta' using pairwise kerning (a) with using kerning based on the whole word (b). (From the thesis of Avi C. Naiman, *High-Quality Text for Raster Displays*, © 1985. Reprinted with permission of the author.)

with lowercase letters, not other capitals. Thus kerning is particularly important for text set in all uppercase.

The relationship between kerning and sidebearings is worth noting. If kerning were done for all possible combinations of letters, sidebearings would in effect be incorporated into the kerning table. The correct spacing of every pair could be looked up. As a practical matter, this is inconvenient. Sidebearings provide a default spacing that is adjusted by kerning for only those combinations that require it. Kerning tables are in fact sparse arrays of numbers. Most combinations have an adjustment of zero because their natural widths (sidebearings) give the correct spacing.

In fact, ideal letterspacing depends on more than just pairs of letters [Naiman 1985:77–78; Kindersley and Wiseman 1979]. The best-possible kerning must consider a broader context of several letters. For example, uppercase words must sometimes be spread out to achieve equal visual spacing because of a single awkward combination of letters. Consider 'ANACHRONISM' versus 'ANACHRONISM'. Because of the openness of the 'AN' and 'NA' combinations, spacing elsewhere in the word must be looser to achieve evenness. This idea is further illustrated in Fig. 4.23.

Certain combinations of letters require the adjustment in most typeface designs. Figure 4.24(a) shows the pairs that usually require kerning. Incidentally, these pairs are the ones to check first when

AT	AV	AW	AY		
KO	KY				
LO	LT	LV	LW	LY	
PA	P,	P.			
TA	Ta	Te	To	T,	T.
VA	Va	Ve	Vo	V,	V.
WA	Wa	We	Wo	W,	W.
YA	Ya	Ye	Yo	Y,	Y.
fi	ffi	fl	ffl	ft	

(a)

DAWN   DAWN

Want We Won't   Want We Won't

FLY firefly   FLY firefly

(b)   (c)

FIGURE 4.24 Some letter combinations that usually require kerning (a). Some of these combinations, particularly 'fi', 'fl', 'ffi', and 'ffl', are handled with ligatures in fonts that have them. Also, the table ignores combinations that do not usually occur in English, though such combinations are common in acronyms and thus deserve attention. Without kerning, some typeface designs are uneven in spacing (b). Kerning solves the problem (c). Some combinations, such as the 'WN' in 'DAWN', are hard to fix with pairwise kerning. A broader consideration of context is necessary.

evaluating a typeface design for the quality of fit between letters. Figure 4.24(b) shows a print sample with no kerning, while Fig. 4.24(c) shows the same letterforms with pairwise kerning.

Kerning values depend on resolution if they are expressed in raster units. One approach is to use a new table for each font at each resolution. However, generic kerning tables are sometimes used, based on the general shape of the letters in the alphabet. An alternative is to store kerning data at very high resolution for each style, independent of size or resolution, and round the value to the nearest value for the resolution being printed. This top-down approach works less well at lower resolutions.

Another approach to automatic kerning is to calculate the kerning table based on the shapes of the letters themselves. One method is called *sector kerning*. Letters are divided into a number of horizontal bands or sectors. For each letter and each sector, the designer of the typeface can specify how deeply an adjacent letter can penetrate. For each pair of letters, a value is found that provides the closest spacing that does not violate the penetration constraint for any band [Naiman 1985:78–82].

Research on the problem of correct optical spacing suggests that it is possible to model what people do when they make spacing adjustments visually [Kindersley and Wiseman 1979; Kindersley 1987], but with the current hardware the calculations may be too expensive to do on the fly. Nonetheless, such algorithms may allow kerning tables to be calculated for new fonts. Algorithms such as those of Kindersley take into consideration the larger context in which the letters appear, but further work on algorithms for calculating correct optical spacing is needed. Better spacing algorithms would adjust an entire word or line at a time to achieve the best appearance.

Proper spacing of letters also requires attention to *ligatures*, those special letterform designs that incorporate two or more letters, such as 'fi' and 'fl'. Many typeface designs include ligatures, which must be substituted for their constituent letters before letterspacing is attempted.

Representation of Fonts

There are several methods of storing, representing, and reproducing fonts inside a computer. They differ in their economy, efficiency, and typographic utility, as shown in Fig. 4.25. The simplest method is to store the glyphs as arrays of bits—that is, as bitmaps—the identical way that fonts are used in most output devices. Figure 4.26 shows an array of bits that as might be used to store all the symbols in a font.

While bitmap form is most immediately useful for outputting bits to a printer or screen, it has many shortcomings. First, it consumes a sizable amount of computer memory. For example, a 12-point font,

Representation Method	Storage Growth Factor	Easy to Scale	
		Up	Down
Bitmap	n^2		
Run-length code	$\approx n$		
Vector	n		√
Arc and vector	k		√
Spline	1	√	√

FIGURE 4.25   Storage scaling requirements for various font-representation methods.

```
00000000000000000000000000000000000000000000000 ...
00000000000000000000000000000000000000000000000 ...
000000011000000000000000000000000000000000000 ...
00000001111000000000001111111111111110000000 ...
000000111011100000000111000000000011100000 ...
000001110001110000000111000000000011100000 ...
000011100000011100000111000000000011100000 ...
000111000000001110000111000000000111000000 ...
001110000000000111000111000000000111000000 ...
001110000000001110001111111111111110000000 ...
001111111111111111000111111111111110000000 ...
001111111111111111000111000000000111000000 ...
001110000000001110001110000000000111100000 ...
001110000000001110001110000000000111100000 ...
001110000000001110001110000000000111000000 ...
001110000000001110001111111111111110000000 ...
00000000000000000000000000000000000000000000000 ...
00000000000000000000000000000000000000000000000 ...
00000000000000000000000000000000000000000000000 ...
00000000000000000000000000000000000000000000000 ...
```

FIGURE 4.26   Font data in bitmap form.

which might be used for book text, stored as a bitmap at 75 dpi, might occupy about 1.5K bytes. The storage required increases as the square of the change in size, and also as the square of the resolution. Twenty-four-point type stored this way consumes four times the space at the same resolution, or 6K bytes in this example. Similarly, 1200-dpi 12-point type would require $1.5 \cdot (1200/75)^2$ or 384K bytes—256 times the storage of the original font. While one such font may not burden a particular system, the price will be high if fonts of many different styles, sizes, and variations must be available, or if large sizes or high resolutions are involved.

As always in data-representation problems, speed may be sacrificed to save space, and vice versa. One mechanism for reducing the size of bitmap data is *run-length encoding.* Using this technique, the computer calculates and stores counts of ones and zeros, rather than the actual bits themselves. To encode the marked column in Fig. 4.26, start counting from the top. There are two zeros, then two ones, then six zeros, then two ones, and so on. Thus the information in the line can be condensed to a sequence of these counts, 2,2,6,2,8 in this case. This form may use less memory space, but it necessitates some computation to create and then reconstitute the data when needed.

Even paying this computational price, run-length codes still grow larger as font size and resolution increase. With a larger font, the same number of black-to-white and white-to-black transitions occur in each column (or row), so the number of counts required increases linearly with the number of scan lines. In addition, as the numbers become larger, it takes more bits of information to represent each one. If the number of bits used to store the counts is varied to economize on storage, then run-length-coded fonts grow at a rate slightly greater than n, where n is the ratio of sizes.

A third way to store fonts is as a list of lines that, when drawn, create the desired form. This technique originated in an earlier display and plotter technology in which the output devices drew only lines and points—they were not raster oriented. For example, the Hershey fonts [Hershey 1972; Wolcott and Hilsenrath 1976] are a public-domain collection of typefaces represented this way. To use these fonts with a bitmap output device, they must be *rasterized,* that is, the lines must be drawn into a bitmap array and the resulting array presented on a screen or on paper (see Fig. 4.27).

A better way to encode the shape of letters is to store a description

COMPLEX ITALIC

A B C D E F G H I J K L M N O P Q R S T U V W X Y Z
a b c d e f g h i j k l m n o p q r s t u v w x y z
1 2 3 4 5 6 7 8 9 0 , . ( ) − + * / = $ @

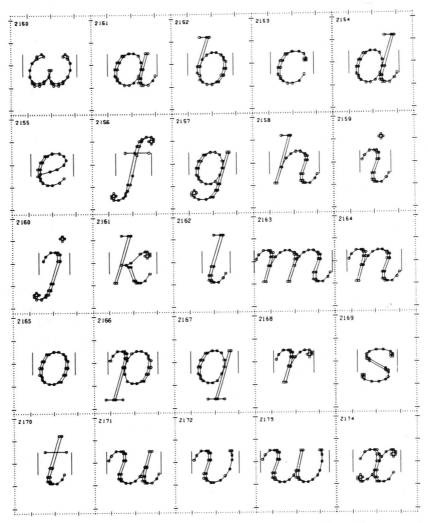

FIGURE 4.27 Hershey fonts are stored as overlapping strokes. The pen path and the resulting inked letterform are shown. (Reproduced from [Wolcott 1976].)

FIGURE 4.28 Character shape stored as a polygonal outline (shown enlarged).

of their *outlines*. Frequently, analog fonts that are digitized for high-resolution computer output are stored this way. Because only points on the periphery of letterforms are recorded, fewer data are required to encode shapes accurately. Figure 4.28 shows how an outline font might be described.

Using points on the outline of a shape to store it, and assuming that straight segments connect the points, letterform shapes are encoded as polygons. This requires a great many data points to approximate curves accurately. Most letterforms include curves, often of some complexity. Stored with polygonal outlines, even more data are required to encode larger fonts, though the increase is only linear with size, and is little affected by resolution.

A method that embodies curves intrinsically gives better results. One such encoding is circular arcs and straight lines (also termed the arc-and-vector form). (See Fig. 4.29.) Although still an approximation, with this method fewer arcs can do the work of many line segments at capturing a given shape.

One issue in choosing curves to describe letters is the number of segments required to describe the shapes involved. As a practical matter, just about any kind of curve can be used to describe a given shape if enough segments are used. The arc-and-vector method, for example, is sufficient in this respect. The consequences of a poor choice, though, are using large amounts of storage to represent the letter shapes, and requiring the designer to provide a great many data points in specifying the shape. For this reason, researchers have investigated various alternatives.

The most compact representation results from the use of *splines* to

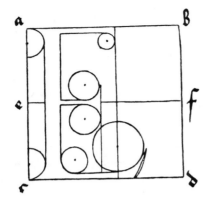

THE LETTER E.

FIGURE 4.29   Letterform shape can be analyzed and stored as straight lines and circular arcs. This is an old idea, as demonstrated by this 1535 illustration by Albrecht Dürer.

record and regenerate the shape of curves. Splines are curves that are controlled by a small set of given points, tangents, or other data. The origin of the term spline is in boat building, in which long strips of wood called splines are attached to a frame at a number of points. The strips assume a smooth curve that goes through each attachment point on the hull frame.

Mathematically, splines are piecewise polynomial parametric curves, generated by varying a parameter over a specified range, that have certain constraints on their continuity. For example, $x(t)$ and $y(t)$ might be two functions that supply points $(x(t), y(t))$ along a curve as t is varied (Fig. 4.30).

To approximate a particular desired curve, it is necessary to break the curve into segments that meet at their endpoints. The meeting points are called *joints*. Each segment can then be specified by a parametric formula. The formulas are polynomials, which is to say that they have the general form

$$x(t) = a_0 + a_1t + a_2t^2 + \ldots + a_{n-1}t^{n-1} + a_nt^n$$

$$y(t) = b_0 + b_1t + b_2t^2 + \ldots + b_{n-1}t^{n-1} + b_nt^n$$

where a_i and b_i are cooefficients and n is the order of the polynomials.

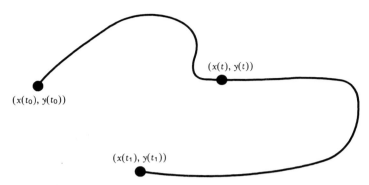

FIGURE 4.30　As the parameter t ranges from t_0 to t_1, the curve $(x(t), y(t))$ is traced out.

When n is 2, the polynomials are called conic; when n is 3, they are cubics. A pair of formulas defines each segment in the spline. The constants are not chosen arbitrarily, but rather so as to achieve smoothness at the joints. In general, splines of order n have continuity in the $(n − 1)$ derivative at each joint. Thus a conic spline has a continuous first derivative (slope), and a cubic spline has continuous first and second derivatives at the joints.

When defining the shapes of letters, it is sometimes necessary to create a discontinuity in the slope of the curve at a given point, as with a corner in a letterform. This information can be used to specify the shape of the curve, via the derivatives, at the endpoints of the spline curve.

In addition to saving data, spline curves have the virtue of allowing complex or subtle curves to be expressed in a simple way—interactively, for example, by moving the control points with a graphic mouse. One possible reason for choosing a certain kind of spline over another is that the graphic result of positioning the control points may be more or less intuitive and easily controlled with different splines. Of course, the ability of the splines to express useful and beautiful shapes for letterforms is also essential.

The many kinds of parametric curves that can be used for describing letterforms fall into two categories: those for which the curve is constrained to pass through the control points, called *interpolating curves*, and those without this constraint. The significance of this distinction for human interface is that it may be harder for the user of a design system to specify points not on the desired outline correctly.

Noninterpolating curves may have control points both on and off the curves. The on-curve points at the joints provide one kind of specification, the curve's location, while the off-curve points determine the slope and shape of the curve as it passes through and between these points. The off-curve control points are both a plus and a minus for a user trying to define a shape. On the one hand, the user need not manipulate them at all, leaving the computer to supply values. On the other hand, adjusting the off-curve control points may not provide an intuitively useful way to create a desired shape.

Bézier splines are one imporant class of cubic splines. Because Bézier curves provide useful shapes for letterforms, are relatively fast computationally, and offer both kinds of user interaction—on-curve and off-curve control points—they have become very popular in design systems.[4] The basic behavior of the curves can be described by a set of constructions [Knuth 1986:13]—see Fig. 4.31. In Fig. 4.31(a), the four points (A,B,C,D) are connected by straight lines. Then the midpoints of the lines are connected in sequence (Fig. 4.31(b)). This process continues, connecting adjacent midpoints, until at the limit a curve is formed (Fig. 4.31(c)). This curve is the spline curve defined by the four original control points. One of the curve's properties is that it goes through the endpoints, A and D. Also, the curve goes from A in the direction of B, and from C in the direction of D. Finally, the curve is well behaved, staying within the convex hull of the four points, that is, within the convex region between the points.

Knuth gives a simple formula, in complex-number notation, for these cubic splines in terms of the four control points shown in Fig. 4.31 [Knuth 1986:14]:

$$z(t) = (1 - t)^3 z_1 + 3(1 - t)^2 tz_2 + 3(1 - t)t^2 z_3 + t^3 z_4.$$

where z_i are the control points (x_i, y_i) and t is the parameter ranging between 0 and 1.

The use of outlines results in compact storage at the price of substantial computation to reconstitute the raster forms. One attraction of storage in this form is that it is easily scaled: Letters of varying size with the same design can be created from the same data. Similarly,

---

[4] Bézier splines are used in METAFONT and PostScript.

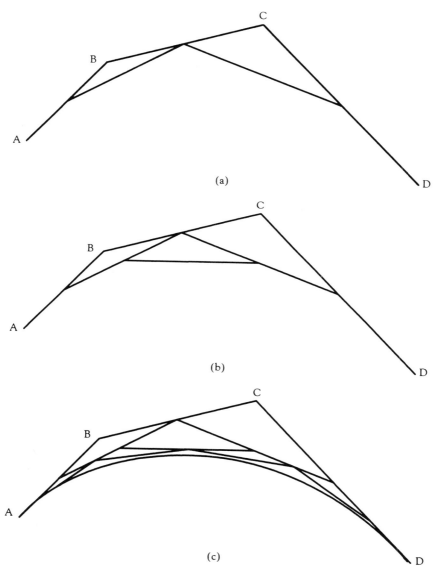

(a)

(b)

(c)

FIGURE 4.31   A graphical interpretation of the shape of Bézier spline curves.

. . . *lazy dog's back.*

(a)

. . . *lazy dog's back.*

(b)

FIGURE 4.32   A slanted roman (a) is not an italic (b). Note the different shapes of the letters, especially the 'a'.

condensed and expanded versions can be calculated by compression or expansion in the x dimension.

Oblique forms can also be created from an original upright outline form, but at the expense of constraining the shapes to those of the roman forms. Algorithmic slanting works better with some fonts than with others, as Fig. 4.32 shows. A coordinate transformation creates the slanted form by shifting the top of the letter to the right relative to the bottom. Compare the joins in the 'd' and 'a' in Fig. 4.32.

A relative of outline font encoding is *inlines*. Using inlines requires fewer data, but may result in lower-quality images. Only a pen path and pen shape are stored (Fig. 4.33). Inlines work best for sans serif designs. As with outlines, slanted forms can be generated from roman, as can bold ones if a broader pen is used. Unfortunately, bold typefaces generated this way tend to lose important detail—for example, the

FIGURE 4.33   Inline representation of a character uses a pen path and pen shape to encode the way to draw the character.

```
The quick brown fox jumped over the lazy dog's back.
The quick brown fox jumped over the lazy dog's back.
The quick brown fox jumped over the dog's back.
The quick brown fox jumped over the dog's back.
```
(a)

the lazy dog's back.
the lazy dog's back.
the lazy dog's back.
the lazy dog's back.

(b)

FIGURE 4.34   Four fonts generated from one inline representation (a), enlarged in (b).

joins between strokes tend to be filled in by the broader pen. Figure 4.34 shows a font encoded with an inline and used to generate slanted, bold, and bold slanted versions. Note how detail is lost, for example in the lowercase 'a' at the joins in the bold and bold italic versions.

A potential method of encoding fonts deserves mention: storing the font as a program that generates the required shape. Such a program would be run whenever the corresponding font (or a symbol from it) was required. It might be an even more space-efficient storage mechanism than the other methods discussed, and even slower to retrieve. However, it could more sensitively adjust the design to the size and variation required in each situation.

Font-Design Tools

Many tools have been developed for designing fonts. Some are research vehicles, while others are available commercially. These tools can be grouped into general types, corresponding to three forms in which typefaces are manipulated:

1. Bitmap type. Fonts are described and manipulated as explicit bitmaps.
2. Outline type. Typefaces are described and manipulated as outlines composed of curves, splines, and so forth. When bitmaps

are required for output, they must be generated from the outlines.
3. Algorithmic type. Typefaces or even families of typefaces are
described as programs that generate them. The algorithms may
be parametric, allowing varying designs to be generated by
changing values in the program.

These types might be combined into a single tool—for example, one
that allowed work with bitmaps and outlines. Or a program-based tool
might create outlines that could be edited interactively.

Another difference among design tools is how extensional or intentional they are. An *extensional* design specification describes in great
detail the exact shape of the letters; the design is expressed concretely.
This expression can take the form of explicit pixels, numeric values,
or points on the outline. For example, bitmap tools are strongly extensional. In contrast, a shape described by a formula is *intentional* because
the exact shape arises from the description; it is an emergent property
implicit in the description. Intentional descriptions provide the properties, goals, or procedures that define what is being described. In the
case of font design, extensional information might include explicit
points on the outline of letters, while intentional data might include
the desired weight and contrast. Most letterform design tools inhabit
the middle ground, exhibiting both intentional and extensional characteristics.

Additional characterizations are whether the design tool is interactive or not, and whether it provides facilities for creating original letter
designs, or just transcribing and editing designs from some other
source. Figure 4.35 provides examples of systems with these different
properties.

A further description of each kind of design tool, along with a
description of a representative system, is given next.

Bitmap Tools

The bit-map editor is the primary bitmap-manipulation tool. Bitmap
editing is useful for all methods of typeface design—top down, bottom
up, and collateral—because ultimately most designs must be realized
as bitmaps in the printer or display device. These editors provide the
basic facility for bottom-up design. Of necessity, they focus the user's

User Representation

	Bitmap	Outline	Program
Extensional	Fontastic	Fontographer	METAFONT
Intentional	————	Ikarus Typefounder	METAFONT

FIGURE 4.35 Some examples of font-design tools, categorized by intentionality and representation. METAFONT appears twice, indicating that it can be used both intentionally and extensionally.

attention on the details of a particular font at a specific size and resolution.

Many bitmap editors are in existence; for example, Fontastic, developed for the Macintosh computer. Editing bitmaps is always tedious because of the level of detail involved. Not only must each pixel of each element of a font be determined, but all symbols must be made to match each other and also to match similar symbols in related fonts.

Enforcing this similarity is difficult, and most bitmap editors provide some facilities to make it easier. One useful feature in this respect is reference markers for the x-height, the heights of ascenders, descenders and capitals, and the width of the side bearings. These markers make it easier to design all letters to the same specifications. Similarly, it is helpful to be able to see a selected letter "under" the letter being edited, and thus be able to use it as a template and reference.

A bitmap editor must allow a certain amount of global information to be specified for each font. Because of the way most systems work, fonts are normally constrained to a single vertical size for all symbols. Therefore, overall height—the point size—is a global parameter.

Specification information that is useful to the system can also be altered via the editor. Examples of this information are the font name, the family to which it belongs, characteristics such as whether it is the bold or italic member of a family, and internal parameters such as the font number and the output devices for which it is intended.

Various operations on symbols allow specification and editing, and facilitate design work. A useful set follows.

COPYING
- Copy a symbol or set of symbols.
- Copy a whole font.
- Copy certain symbols from one font to another.
- Merge two symbols ("logical OR").
- Copy a region or picture into a symbol.

EDITING
- Erase a symbol.
- Change a pixel.
- Change a rectangular region of pixels.
- Draw a line between two points.
- Draw a circle, given the center and radius or three points on the circle.
- Draw a curve, as specified by control points.
- Fill a closed region.
- Adjust sidebearings.

GLOBAL OPERATIONS
- Scale a font up or down.
- Create and adjust guide marks.
- Set a background symbol or image.
- Algorithmically change the weight of a font.
- Slant a font to obtain an oblique version.
- Set sample text.

To see the effect of editing, a text sample must be displayed. It is desirable that this text be updated whenever a change is made, and that the user be able to specify the content of the test text. Figure 4.36 shows the screen layout for the Fontastic bitmap editor.

Outline Tools

Working on outlines is particularly helpful in top-down typeface design. An outline is a good way to represent an idealized design at high resolution, expressing the shape independent of size and resolution. For collateral design, working with outlines is also helpful because they provide a basis for similar designs across the required variations.

In addition to interactive editors, various outline manipulation tools

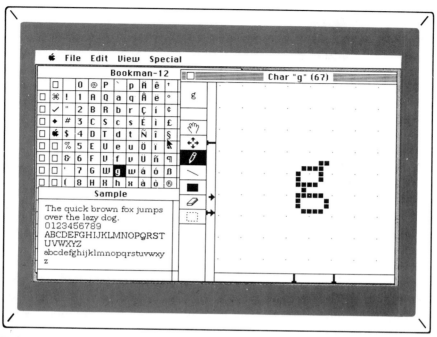

FIGURE 4.36　A bitmap editor screen (Fontastic on the Macintosh computer).

exist. Early systems such as Karow's Ikarus [Karow:1979] created out-lines from digitizer input, performing a primarily data-formatting job. Another kind of specialized tool converts outlines from one represen-tation to another (for example, from vectors to splines), with a certain degree of approximation to the input data. This kind of tool is very helpful in reducing the amount of data contained in a design represen-tation. There are also rasterizing programs that convert outlines to equivalent bit-map forms for output to a bit-map device, and scanned bit-maps to outlines [Sauvain and Wayman 1987].

Working interactively with outlines necessitates a somewhat differ-ent editing tool. Many features of bitmap design tools are relevant. All the operations that identify a font, specify its use, or allow global transformations make sense for outlines. For example, as a symbol is manipulated interactively, it is useful to have a reference symbol or image in the background.

Operations specific to outline editors relate to manipulating the

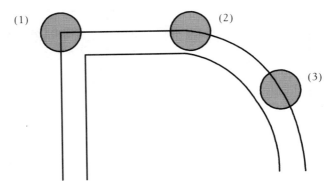

FIGURE 4.37   Different joins useful in outline specification. Case (1) is a vertex where two straight lines join. Case (2) joins a straight segment with a curved one. The tangent may have a discontinuity, depending on the curve. Finally, Case (3) joins to curves with the constraint that the tangent be continuous.

outlines themselves. Depending on the representation used, outlines are specified via various points on the desired curve, control points, and tangents or directions. While batch-oriented tools are useful when large numbers of letters are digitized and converted to outlines, it is always necessary to adjust the resulting outlines. These changes are best made interactively.

It is useful to be able to specify various kinds of points on a curve: straight line segments, circular arcs, general curves, and vertices where lines and curves join. Figure 4.37 shows the three ways in which segments might be joined: (1) with a discontinuity in the slope, creating a vertex or abrupt change in direction of the line, (2) with no discontinuity in the slope, constraining one segment to be straight, and (3) with no discontinuity in the slope, allowing adjustment in both segments as they approach the join.

When inlines are used, that is, when a letterform is created by inking along a penpath, the further question arises of how to join the lines formed. In this case, the path creates a black image with thickness and shape, instead of filling a region determined by an outline. There are three cases, as shown in Fig. 4.38:

- Continuous stroke. The strokes are joined with no discontinuity in the slope of a tangent line. The junction is determined entirely by the pen path (Fig. 4.38a).

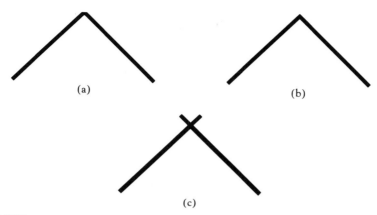

FIGURE 4.38   Three possible relationships between two pen paths. In case (a), the shape of the pen used to draw the lines determines the shape of the join. Alternatively, the lines can be mitered, as shown in (b). Case (c) shows the two strokes not interacting at all.

- Mitered joint. The lines are fitted together with a discontinuity in the tangent. The angle of the corner created is determined by the angle of the lines at their intersection (Fig. 4.38b).
- Disjoint strokes. The lines are not modified to mesh (Fig. 4.38c). The shape at the end of each stroke is determined by a defined curve, brush shape, and so forth.

Another issue is how an outline should be filled. Conceptually it is straightforward to fill the space within a closed curve or between closed curves, but computationally this is not necessarily easy [Shani 1980]. Further, filling a closed curve is not always what is desired. There are in fact several cases, as shown in Fig. 4.39. First, the outline can be filled between two closed curves, one containing the other. Second, regions enclosed by a single curve can be filled. Finally, it is possible to fill the concave region determined by an open curve.

In each case, the curves may overlap or a curve may loop on top of itself. Here are two possible ways to fill an outline in these situations. In the even-odd method, a region is filled if it is reached from the outside by crossing an odd number of boundaries. The second approach uses a *winding number* to determine fill. In this algorithm, the direction n which the curve was drawn is remembered and used. As with the

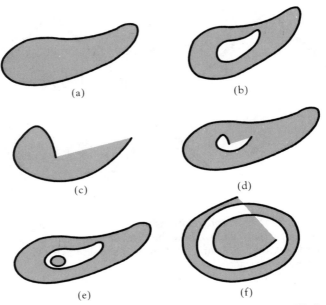

(a)

(b)

(c)

(d)

(e)

(f)

FIGURE 4.39   Various ways to fill a curve. A simple curve is filled in (a). A region contained within another is not filled in (b). Curves that are not closed represent a problem. The usual solution is to treat the curve as if the end points were connected (c). This can be complicated by inclusion of one curve within another (d). A curve within a curve within a curve requires further consideration of what is intended (e). Finally, complex open curves, in which connecting the endpoints causes a crossing of the curve itself, may lead to surprising results (f).

other method, follow a path from outside the figure to the region in question. The direction of the first boundary is defined as plus one. Add or subtract one from the total as each subsequent line is crossed, depending on its direction, until the inside point is reached. If the total is zero or negative, fill the region.

A typical screen setup for an outline editor is shown in Fig. 4.40. Ikarus provides another example. Although Ikarus input is based on digitized letters and the program is rather limited for creating original designs interactively, it does include typographically significant parameters such as slant, serif type, and expansion and contraction. It is also capable of interpolating between two designs. Thus if a roman version

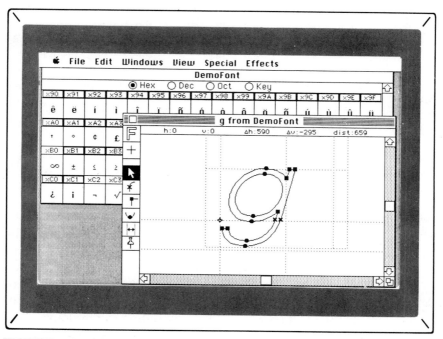

FIGURE 4.40 An outline-editor screen setup (Fontographer on the Macintosh computer).

and a bold version of the same (or different) faces are entered, Ikarus can generate hybrid versions.

A more recent and sophisticated product of similar concept is the Camex Letter Input Processor (LIP), which in addition to the capabilities of Ikarus can line up points within a specified region; this is called channelization. LIP includes a library of letter parts that can be used to construct letters interactively. These parts can be referenced in a recursive structure that defines each letterform. For example, an ascender can be defined in terms of a vertical stem plus serifs. Then this compound object can be used as part of a larger letter definition. However, the meaning of these letter parts is not known to the system; that is the user's responsibility. LIP does not know how to combine parts of letters sensibly to form letters.

One difficulty with editing outlines is that inside and outside boundaries must be coordinated. Although inside and outside curves are

T

FIGURE 4.41   In many typefaces, serifs are not symmetrical, as shown by this Garamond 'T'. This is but one example of the requirements that demonstrate the need for flexibility and richness in letterform-design tools.

parallel in many parts of letters, this is not always true. Thus it is desirable that the design tool provide some way to relate the shapes without forcing equality.

Another problem is that shapes used in letters may be hard to copy from letter to letter. Of course, a letter design can be copied exactly, but consider the problem of making all the serifs in a design similar. Since the serif is part of a larger figure, a given tool may provide no natural way to copy the shape of a segment of one letter to a segment of another. Further, the designer may not wish to make all the serifs identical; it is common for serifs to vary according to the shape of the individual letter, as shown in the letter 'T' in Fig. 4.41. An approach to this problem is to allow portions of letters to be treated as independent objects that can be combined to form the various letters and symbols.

Algorithmic Design Tools

The third general approach to letterform design and specification is to write programs that specify how the letters look. The output of an algorithmic tool is one or more fonts represented in a useful manner, such as via bitmaps or outlines. Such an approach offers the possibility of changing a design via parameters that are supplied each time the program is executed. It is used primarily for top-down design, but programs can also take into account the actual size, resolution, and output device characteristics when producing particular fonts. Therefore algorithmic description of typefaces may make automated collateral design possible.

Programming letterforms also helps ensure that the characteristics of a design are expressed in each letterform, that is, common design characteristics are propagated. As applied to letterform parts, the programming idea of the subroutine creates an environment in which pieces of different letters can be created by the same code in the program. When variations are required, parameters can be passed with each invocation of the subroutine to make the necessary variations within the constraints of the overall design.

An early design program by Philippe Coueignoux [1975] tried to provide a design structure for programs that specify typeface designs. His language, CSD (Character Simulated Design), used the set of primitives shown in Fig. 4.42. Ghosh and Bigelow [1983] tried a similar idea. They created a syntactic description of letterforms consisting of various strokes, serifs, curves, and so on. Individual letters are specified as combinations of these constituent elements.

One result of this kind of work is that it is difficult to know just how to parameterize the programs so as to achieve typographically good results.

METAFONT, an interesting and useful algorithmic design tool, was developed at Stanford University by Donald Knuth [1986]. It embodies a number of good, fresh ideas that have advanced the art of digital typeface design. The language is based on Bézier curves and a well-conceived vector geometry for specifying points, paths, distances, and other geometric relationships.

Even though METAFONT is a specialized programming language, it still has the problems (and benefits) of such languages. In particular, it has great expressive power of the intentional sort, but requires its user to express ideas in a mathematical, analytic form that is foreign to most artists and typographers. Knuth [1986:1] explains the basic idea behind METAFONT as follows:

> Why is the system called METAFONT? The '-FONT' part is easy to understand, because sets of related symbols that are used in typesetting are traditionally known as fonts of type. The 'META-' part is more interesting: It indicates that we are interested in making high-level descriptions that transcend any of the individual fonts being described.

Metadesign is much more difficult than design; it is easier to draw something than to explain how to draw it. One problem is that different sets of potential specifications cannot easily be envisioned all at once. Another is that a computer has to be told absolutely everything. However, once we have successfully explained how to draw something

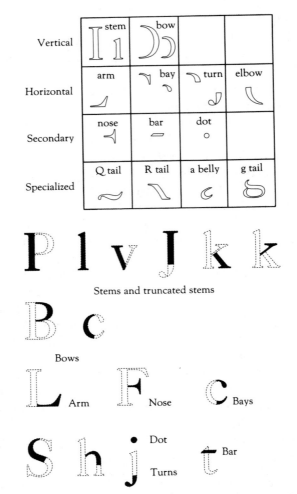

FIGURE 4.42   Primitives in Philippe Coueignoux's Character Simulated Design language. (From Philippe J. M. Coueignoux, "Generation of Roman Printed Fonts." Ph.D. Thesis, June 1975. Reprinted with permission of Massachusetts Institute of Technology.)

in a sufficiently general manner, the same explanation will work for related shapes, in different circumstances; so the time spent in formulating a precise explanation turns out to be worth it.

Figure 4.43 shows a METAFONT program and the resulting output. The description is inescapably a program, hard to understand if one is unfamiliar with the language. Fortunately, the language was crafted by a master, and thus is relatively easy to learn by those who know how to program. Users of METAFONT enjoy the power it gives them to describe graphic forms. Nonetheless, even an experienced METAFONT programmer will be unable to visualize the exact shape of the ampersand that results from the program in Fig. 4.43 because its detailed shape is implicit; it is an emergent property.

Another idea fundamental to METAFONT is that of describing shape via pen paths. Letters are described as a number of strokes with pens of varying sizes and shapes. Mathematically, this model is very powerful, allowing a large class of lines and shapes to be described. It also seems, at first consideration, to be a natural representation for letters. After all, letterforms evolved from pen and brush strokes.

In practice, however, both traditional artists and computer scientists have had great difficulty in creating high-quality typefaces with ME-TAFONT. A few good original designs have been created (see Fig. 4.44 for some samples) [Siegel 1985:27; Tobin 1985]. Knuth himself expended great effort on his Computer Modern typeface. As another example, Siegel [1985] describes a project that used METAFONT to create the Euler typeface for the American Mathematical Society. The typeface was designed by Hermann Zapf and programmed by a team at Stanford. According to Siegel, 484 symbols were created in less than 484 working days. Zapf designed the letterforms on paper, and measurements were taken from his drawings and entered as METAFONT programs. While type design is extraordinarily tedious and timeconsuming using conventional means, this example hardly suggests that automation made it much faster. Compare this effort with Frederic Goudy's account of completing most of a new typeface design by conventional means in 82 days [Goudy 1940:53]. This time included drawings and making patterns for production, and amounts to roughly two man-days per symbol.

The Euler project did not make much creative use of METAFONT for design, and some workers such as Flowers [1984] have suggested that METAFONT is not useful for production or for guiding an amateur

cmchar "Ampersand";
beginchar("&", $14u^\#$, $asc\_height^\#$, 0);
italcorr $x\_height^\# * slant - serif\_fit^\# -$ **if** *serifs*: $.4u^\#$ **else**: $1.5u^\#$ **fi**;
adjust_fit(0, $serif\_fit^\#$);
pickup *tiny.nib*; $pos_2(slab, -90)$; $x_2 = 4u$; *bot* $y_{2r} = -o$;
if not *hefty*: $(x, y_{2l}) = whatever[z_{2r}, (w - 5u, x\_height)]$; $x_{2l} := x$; **fi**
if *serifs*: $pos_0(fudged.hair, 0)$; .
   rt $x_{0r} + jut = \text{hround}(w - .9u)$; *top* $y_0 = x\_height$;
   $pos_1(fudged.hair, 0)$; $z_1 = whatever[z_0, (.6[x_0, x_2], 0)]$;
   $y_1 = \max(y_0 - 1.5bracket - .2x\_height, {}^2/_3x\_height)$;
   filldraw stroke z_{0e} --- z_{1e} ... $\{left\}z_{2e}$;   % short diagonal
else: pickup *fine.nib*; $pos_1(.25[slab, flare], -15)$; *rt* $x_{1r} = \text{hround}(w - 2u)$;
   $y_{1r} = good.y\ .75[bar\_height, x\_height]$; $x_{1l} := good.x\ x_{1l}$; $y_{1l} := good.y\ y_{1l}$;
   top $z_{2'l} = (x_{2l}, tiny.top\ y_{2l})$; *bot* $z_{2'r} = (x_{2r}, tiny.bot\ y_{2r})$;
   filldraw stroke $term.e(2', 1, right, 1, 4)$; **fi**   % short diagonal and terminal
pickup *tiny.nib*; **numeric** *slope, theta, reduced_hair*;
$slope = (h - 2vair - slab)/10.5u$; $theta = \text{angle}(-slope, 1)$;
$reduced\_hair = \max(tiny.breadth, \text{hround}(fudged.hair$ **if** *hefty*: $-2stem\_corr$ **fi**$))$;
lft $x_{3r} = \text{hround}\ .75u$; $x_5 = .5[x_{3r}, x_{6l}]$; *lft* $x_{6r} = \text{hround}\ .5(w - u)$;
$x_{3l} - x_{3r} = curve - tiny$; $pos_6(reduced\_hair, 180)$;
$pos_5(vair, theta)$; $y_5 = .5h$;
$ellipse\_set(2l, 3l, 4l, 5l)$; $ellipse\_set(2r, 3r, 4r, 5r)$;
$pos_7(vair, 270)$; *top* $y_{7l} = h + o$; $x_7 = .45[x_{6r}, x_{8r}]$;
$pos_8(fudged.stem, 30)$; $x_{8l} = good.x(x_{8l} + 3.5u - x_8)$; $y_{8r} = y_6$;
$ellipse\_set(7l, 6l, 5', 5l)$;
filldraw stroke $z_{2e}\{left\}$ ... $z_{3e}\{up\}$ ... z_{4e} --- z_{5e} ... $\{up\}z_{6e}$
   ... $z_{7e}\{left\}$ ... $z_{8e}\{down\}$;   % bowls
$pos_{10}(slab, 90)$; $x_{10} = w - 3.5u$; *bot* $y_{10l} = -o$;
$pos_9(fudged.stem, \text{angle}(z_8 - z_{10}) - 90)$;
$z_9 = .5[z_8, z_{10}] + (1.75u, 0)$ rotated $(\text{angle}(z_8 - z_{10}) + 90)$;
filldraw stroke $z_{8e}\{down\}$ ... $z_{9e}\{z_{10} - z_8\}$ ... $\{right\}z_{10e}$;   % long diagonal
if *serifs*: **pickup** *crisp.nib*; $pos_{10'}(slab, 90)$; $z_{10'} = z_{10}$;
   $pos_{11}(fudged.hair, 180)$; *rt* $x_{11l} = \text{hround}(w - u)$; $y_{11} = .5bar\_height$;
   filldraw stroke $z_{10'e}\{right\}$ ... $\{up\}z_{11e}$;   % terminal
   numeric *inner_jut*; **if** *rt* $x_{6l} + .5u < lft\ x_{0l} - 1.5jut$: $inner\_jut = 1.5jut$;
   else: *rt* $x_{6l} + .5u = lft\ x_{0l} - inner\_jut$; **fi**
   $dish\_serif(0, 1, a, .6, inner\_jut, b, .5, jut)(dark)$;   % serif
else: pickup *fine.nib*; $pos_{10'}(slab, 90)$; $z_{10'} = z_{10}$;
   $pos_{11}(\text{Vround}\ .5[slab, flare], 90)$;
   rt $x_{11} = \text{hround}(r - letter\_fit - u)$; *bot* $y_{11l} = \text{vround}\ .07bar\_height - o$;
   filldraw stroke $term.e(10', 11, right, 1, 4)$; **fi**   % terminal
penlabels(0, 1, 2, 3, 4, 5, 6, 7, 8, 9, 10, 11); **endchar**;

(a)

FIGURE 4.43 A METAFONT program that generates a continuum of ampersands, depending on the settings of parameters (a). Three possible outputs are shown in (b). (Donald E. Knuth, *Computers and Typesetting*, © 1985, Addison-Wesley Publishing Company, Inc., Reading, MA. Pps 362 & 363. Reprinted with permission.)

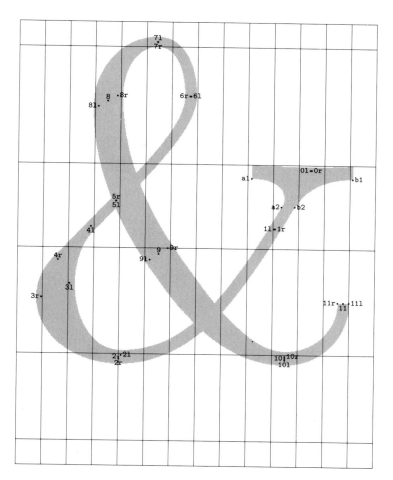

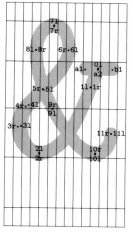

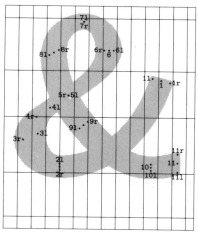

(b)

ABCDEFGHIJKLMNOPQRSTUVWXYZ
abcdefghijklmnopqrstuvwxyz
ΓΔΘΛΞΠΣΥΦΨΩ
αβγδεζηθικλμνξπρστυφχψωεϑῶφ
01 1234567890

ABCDEFGHIJKLMNOPQRSTUVWXYZ
abcdefghijklmnopqrstuvwxyz
ΓΔΘΛΞΠΣΥΦΨΩ
αβγδεζηθικλμνξπρστυφχψωεϑῶφ
0123456789 01

ABCDEFGHIJKLMNOPQRSTUVWXYZ
ðöffgttu abcdefghijklmnopqrstuvwxyz
ðøyℓ ("!&''+-/:;?=[]^~)
111 1234567890

ABCDEFGHIJKLMNOPQRSTUVWXYZ
abcdefghijklmnopqrstuvwxyz ffgttꞇ3
{ . ,‹/›`\§¬∧∨}¦ ðøyℓ
0123456789 111

ʃ *ABCDEFGHIJKLMNOPQRSTUVWXYZ*

ABCDEFGHIJKLMNOPQRSTUVWXYZ 1U ℵ

DIGITAL TYPOGRAPHY AT STANFORD
HAMBURGEFONSTIV   HAMBURGEFONSTIV

Art Begins Cunningly Disenfranchising Eskimos From Ghastly Horors In Juxtaposed Kashmir Lounges
Meanwhile Neo Pragmatists Quell Rembrandts Stored Temporarily Uptown Vexing Wild
Xebras Yellow Zylophones

(a)

Старик рыбачил совсем один на своей лодке в Гольфстриме. Вот уже восемьдесят четыре дня он ходил в море и не поймал ни одной рыбы. Первые сорок дней с ним был мальчик. . . Мальчику тяжело было смотреть, как старик каждый день возвращался ни с чем, и он выходил на берег, чтобы помочь ему отнести домой снасти или багор, гарпун и обёрнутый вокруг мачты парус. Парус был весь в заплатах из мешковины и, свёрнутый, напоминал знамя наголову разбитого полка.
--Эрнест Хемингуэй, СТАРИК И МОРЕ

(b)

FIGURE 4.44 Some typeface designs created using METAFONT: Euler (a), a Cyrillic face (b), and a version of Helvetica (c). (Samples courtesy of David R. Siegel (a), and Georgia K. M. Tobin, The Metafoundry™ (b) and (c)).

designer toward good designs. The design ideas in the Euler project appeared first on paper.

What is needed is design tools that provide systematic ways to express graphic design ideas and to apply these ideas to each letter. For artists and traditional typographers, at least, computers are not yet a significant aid.

What might help? Typeface design might best be described as a form of computer art; the use of a computer to express artistic ideas. With this perspective, the usual computer-aided design (CAD) approach is only marginally appropriate. Artistic ideas are expressed graphically and verbally, as are engineering ideas, but the interesting part of a result may be an æsthetic property, not the literal description of the

Once the characteristics of a style of type are defined in METAFONT's declarative algebraic language, *certain critical style-pervasive values – stem and hairline widths, the angle between the y-axis and the x-axis, and so on –* can be varied so that a stylistically consistent progression from one typeface to another within the same family can be achieved. *The different styles in this paragraph were all produced from a single set of letter definitions with four different sets of values provided at run time to account for the distinctions among the four type styles.*

Similarly, once a letter is defined, this parameterization gives enough flexibility so that the same definition can be used to produce a letter at different point sizes or at different resolutions. The different point sizes in this paragraph were all produced from a single set of letter definitions, and not by simple proportional scaling. Rather, each design is drawn by METAFONT 'from scratch' at run time for each new point size; the designer's task is to ensure that the initial definition is sufficiently flexible.

(c)

design. Experiments with teaching computer art to engineers and artists show that it is the deep consequences, not the surface details, that must be manipulated to achieve good artistic results [Rubinstein 1974:143–149].

Nonetheless, the terms that type designers use to describe designs should also be understood by automated type-design tools. Typographers talk about strokes, weight, sparkle, x-height, bowl shape, serifs, and so on. A good interactive design tool should allow these properties to be adjusted dynamically, with the result immediately visible. This suggests a more object-oriented approach in the operations performed by the computer system. Letters are things that the system user needs to manipulate. They have identities and interrelationships. Clearly, there is much room for further development in adapting design tools to the needs of type designers.

Conclusion

Frederic Goudy said of type design that "a design devoid of emotion, rhythm, and expression, yet technically excellent, merely betrays the fact that it has been produced by one who has nothing of value to express" [Goudy 1940:69]. This statement is quite an indictment of amateur type design, albeit from a master. It represents two kinds of challenge for computer-based design. On the one hand, it demands that the user of a design system have some artistic sense and some graphic ideas to express, lest the result be of little value. On the other, it demands that the makers of design programs allow the graphic ideas to be expressed in a facile and productive way. None of the commercial design packages yet produced has made type design easy for the designer who has good graphical ideas to express. The universal comment is that it is a great struggle to design good typefaces with computer-based design systems. This is clearly an area for innovative ideas about user interface and for productive models of the artistic content of the design process.

Chapter Summary

There are three general approaches to the design of digital fonts. Top-down design starts with the ideal external appearance for the font and renders it at the sizes and resolutions required by the system. Bottom-up design uses a reference design optimized to the characteristics of the system, creating other versions to match. Collateral design seeks a broader optimization over the whole range of system needs.

Any family of typefaces must have consistent properties, including weight, contrast, cap-height, x-height, ascenders, and descenders. At lower resolutions, the small number of choices makes it hard to match fonts of different size or resolution.

Grayscale fonts are one way to achieve better designs at lower resolutions. If presented properly, intensity information can substitute for spatial information. Grayscale fonts are also important for color displays.

A major part of any font design is the spacing of the letters. Intrinsic spacing, in the form of sidebearings, provides default spaces that work for most lowercase letter combinations. Exceptions, and adjustments to many uppercase combinations, are handled with kerning. Kerning information can be stored generically, or by individual handling of each font. Kerning is accomplished by storing kerning values in a sparse table, by calculating kerning on the fly with sector kerning, or by calculating optical spacing based on how people perceive interletter space.

Fonts can be represented as bitmaps, outlines, or programs. Bitmaps are ultimately needed by most output systems, but are awkward to store and manipulate. Outlines provide a better working representation. To minimize the data stored for outlines, and to aid manipulation, parametric representations are used. Splines are used to represent segments of the desired curves.

Various tools exist for manipulating font designs. Bitmap tools allow the most detailed editing, and are especially useful for tuning screen fonts (or other low-resolution fonts). Outline tools are more flexible. Bitmaps can be generated automatically from outlines. Finally, algorithmic design tools allow uniform specification of fonts, thus achieving controlled uniformity of features across a whole design or family.

PART TWO

Lines, Blocks, and Pages ❧

__5
Space and Putting Things in It

Readability is not wholly built in the letterforms as such. One half of it is in the spacing between the words, the lines, the columns; in the geometry of the text and the margins *i.e.* in the visual editing.
— *Fernand Baudin*

LIKE other artists, typographers frequently focus their attention on the space occupied by the objects that they create, what is normally background; this is a useful exercise in graphic design. This chapter considers the space occupied by text and pictures. The objective is to understand the relationship of the images to each other and to the pages on which they appear. The chapter also considers how text is distributed over space when document pages are prepared.

Earlier chapters dealt with the space between individual letters, including the fine adjustments of kerning. This chapter considers the placement of letterforms at three higher levels: as words, as lines, and as full pages. In addition, at the page-composition level, other graphic objects enter the picture, including line drawings, tables, and photographic images.

It takes some visual skill and mental flexibility to see the space rather than the letters on a page because of well-developed, generally useful habits to the contrary. Anyone familiar with the work of M. C. Escher will understand how interesting such alternate views can be when they are seen in relation to each other. Figure 5.1 shows the unfamiliarity of the space around letters when it is presented as the focus of attention instead of the background.

Documents that contain graphics, images, or other nontextual components in addition to text are called *compound documents*. Two-

FIGURE 5.1   A figure-ground reversal allows the space around a letter to be viewed.

dimensional placement presents interesting problems for digital type-setting systems. Good placement of words, lines, paragraphs, and graphics improves the appearance and thus the quality of the document. What are the correct relationships among these objects? How can useful variables be specified by system users? Can placement be controlled automatically to good effect?

What hangs in the balance with page layout is nothing less than the quality of the document being prepared. Will it be easy to read and understand, apart from its content? When people read continuous text, when they are reading *for comprehension* rather than just recognizing letters and words, certain characteristics of the text assume greater and lesser importance. When text is considered at this higher level, new cognitive processes—the full complexity of the reading process—come into play.

Views of Space

What is a good way to allocate space within a line when typesetting a line of text? When *justifying* lines so that the right and left edges of a block of text are straight, this simple question actually has a simple answer: The "extra" space can be distributed evenly between the words.

Extra space between letters within the words can degrade the legibility of print.

Typographers know this from experience, and vision experiments demonstrate that it takes longer to read letter-spaced (spaced-out) words than to read tightly spaced ones [Mewhort 1966]. It is not very hard to demonstrate to oneself that this effect is real, as shown by this sentence, which has just two extra points of space between each pair of letters. This presents no surprise; it is yet another way that the optimal spatial frequencies of letters might be disturbed. In contrast, interword spacing is less critical because the eye is not decoding shape information in the spaces between words, only recognizing breaks between the words themselves.

Some interesting work by Kindersley, however, suggests that if interletter spacing is determined properly, legibility is not impaired by adjusting letterspaces [Kindersley and Wiseman 1979; Kindersley 1987]. Kindersley's method involves kerning of a higher order (described in the previous chapter), considering the shape of individual letters in the larger context of a word or group of words.

A typographer's rule of thumb is that interword spaces no bigger than the interline white space are accommodated readily, and do not hamper reading [Dair 1985:36]. One justification for this rule is æsthetic: Limitations on spacing improve the texture and appearance of the page. In addition, overly large word spaces decrease reading speed. There are two reasons. Loose lines contain fewer words, with the result that readers must fixate the eye more times to read a given number of words. Also, larger spaces may be confused with the interline space itself, causing the eye to get lost momentarily while scanning the line. One improvement when lines must be loose—that is, when they will contain much white space between words—is to increase the interline spacing. Narrow columns are one such situation requiring greater line spacing, such columns are often loose because words cannot be hyphenated arbitrarily in order to pack each line tightly. Figure 5.2 illustrates the same text set both poorly and well in terms of the relationship of interline and interword spacing.

The usual typographic nomenclature for expressing leading is to give the type size and the interline spacing in points, for example 12/13 ("12 on 13"). This means 12-point type set in lines spaced 13 points

America was discovered accidentally by a great seaman who
was looking for something else;
when discovered it was not
wanted; and most of the exploration for the next fifty years was
done in the hope of getting
through or around it. America
was named after a man who
discovered no part of the New
World. History is like that, very
chancy.

(a)

America was discovered acci-

dentally by a great seaman who

was looking for something else;

when discovered it was not

wanted; and most of the explor-

ation for the next fifty years was

done in the hope of getting

through or around it. America

was named after a man who

discovered no part of the New

World. History is like that, very

chancy.

(b)

FIGURE 5.2   Text with large interword spaces needs more leading. Large
interword spaces often result when text is justified in narrow columns. In (a),
the lines have less space between them than the largest interword spaces. Sample (b) shows the identical text with enough leading.

apart. In other words, 12-point type is set with one point of extra
leading added between lines. Because type designs incorporate some
intrinsic interline spacing, settings like 6/6 and 11/11 usually have
some white space between the lines.

The term *color* is also used by typographers to describe the overall
tone of gray that text presents on a page (see Chapter 4). Interline

spacing affects the look of a block of text, its texture and typographic color, and is an important component of a typographer's design for a book or other printed work. Without extra leading, blocks of text may be very economical of space. Depending on the typeface design, however, such print may look too dense on the page, and may be harder to read than type spaced slightly more loosely. Conversely, widely spaced type may look too sparse, and may be hard to read because the eye is unaccustomed to finding the next line at such a vertical distance. In the middle is text that ranges from economical to opulent. Figure 5.3 shows how the same text can give different overall impressions depending on the leading used.

Typographers choose spacing with great care. The addition of a half point, less than 0.007 inches, can change the feel of a page from, say, very businesslike to somewhat freer and more airy. Note how subjective these descriptions sound. Impressions and feelings are not usually the stuff of engineering decisions, but people make these choices in order to create print that looks right and meets their specific needs. The success of a book or advertisement could depend on such judgments.

Typographers also deal with whole pages. Figure 5.4 shows a page layout viewed both as a collection of dark objects—paragraphs, pictures, captions—and as the blank space that surrounds these objects. In this view, blank space is a thing to be described, be it a margin, the space between paragraphs, or an indentation.

Margins are particularly important in page design. They must be viewed in relation to each other, and to the size and shape of the page and text on the page. An æsthetically pleasing page is one in which all elements, both objects and spaces, are in harmony. For example, it is usually desirable to have the text on a page, considered as a unit, have the same general orientation and shape as the page itself, as Fig. 5.5 shows. Although rules of thumb exist for the proportions of text and margins on the page of a book, designers use these rules as starting points, not as absolute specifications. However, it is useful to use ratios to express relationships between text and space dimensions. Unfortunately formatting programs require absolute measurements, leaving the user to do the arithmetic.

Again, none of this information seems concrete enough to put in a computer program for designing pages, allocating margins, or even spacing lines. For some time to come, these choices will remain the prerogative of people because they cannot be dealt with easily via

As quick as thought is an old mode of expression, used to convey an idea of the greatest rapidity: but no one, until lately, ever dreamed that a thought could be sent hundreds of miles in a few seconds; and that a person standing in London might hold a conversation with another in Edinburgh, put questions and receive answers, just as if they were seated together in one room, instead of being three hundred miles apart.

(a)

As quick as thought is an old mode of expression, used to convey an idea of the greatest rapidity: but no one, until lately, ever dreamed that a thought could be sent hundreds of miles in a few seconds; and that a person standing in London might hold a conversation with another in Edinburgh, put questions and receive answers, just as if they were seated together in one room, instead of being three hundred miles apart.

(b)

As quick as thought is an old mode of expression, used to convey an idea of the greatest rapidity: but no one, until lately, ever dreamed that a thought could be sent hundreds of miles in a few seconds; and that a person standing in London might hold a conversation with another in Edinburgh, put questions and receive answers, just as if they were seated together in one room, instead of being three hundred miles apart.

(c)

As quick as thought is an old mode of expression, used to convey an idea of the greatest rapidity: but no one, until lately, ever dreamed that a thought could be sent hundreds of miles in a few seconds; and that a person standing in London might hold a conversation with another in Edinburgh, put questions and receive answers, just as if they were seated together in one room, instead of being three hundred miles apart.

(d)

FIGURE 5.3   The mood of text varies with the leading. The top sample (a) might be appropriate for a scholarly monograph, economical of paper and tightly reasoned. Sample (b) might suit a trade book, still economical, but not extremely so. A text book might be leaded as in (c), and a sumptuous art book, as in (d).

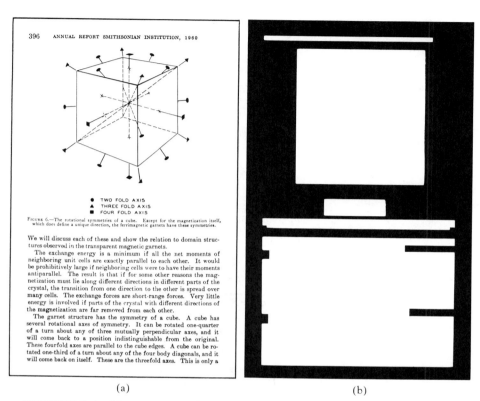

FIGURE 5.4   The same page layout, viewed normally (a), and with black and white reversed to emphasize the space as figure (b). (Page reproduced from *The Annual Report of the Board of Regents of the Smithsonian Institution*, Publication 4435, 1960.)

automatic layouts chosen by programs. Perhaps some typographic principles of space and layout could be captured in an expert system, an artificial intelligence program that stores and uses a large set of rules to create behavior that humans consider sensible.

Psychologists have a different view of space, though the similarities to the view of typographers are interesting. Gestalt psychology treats perception as the active creation of a division between figure and ground. Seeing is the process of sorting the image collected by the eyes into two semantically distinct sets: the thing being perceived, and everything else. Since seeing is active, the intelligent act of shifting

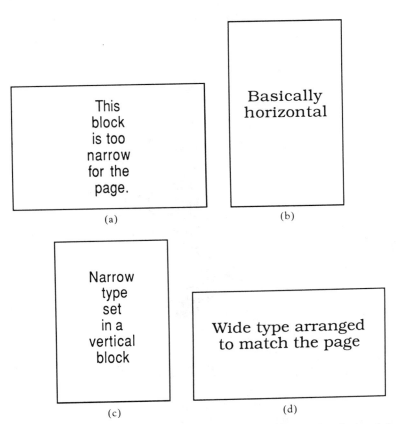

FIGURE 5.5   The shape of text on a page should relate to the shape of the page. It is not good typographic form to have a predominantly vertical form on a horizontal page (a) or a horizontal form on a vertical page (b). The examples in (c) and (d) are better matched. (After [Gress 1917:54–55].)

one's focus of attention may result in a different partitioning and in different objects' being resolved against a background. This shift of attention, called *figure-ground reversal,* is a perceptual phenomenon. People can interpret a picture in one way or another, but not in both ways simultaneously. An intentionally ambiguous picture in which figure-ground reversal is easy is shown in Fig. 5.6.

Cognitive psychologists might also speak of an object's being *parsed* in order to discover and apprehend its structure. Although such ter-

FIGURE 5.6 An ambiguous figure in which figure-ground reversal is easy. It is impossible to see the goblet and the faces simultaneously. (Adaptation of the illustration on p. 161 by Gabor Kiss in "The Interpretation of Visual Illusions" by Donald D. Hoffman, *Scientific American*, December 1983, courtesy of W. H. Greeman and Company.)

minology is usually applied to language, it is also appropriate to vision. It is certainly applicable to seeing a page of text in a book or magazine. There is a definite structure to any page; a well-designed page, like the pages reproduced in Fig. 5.7, has a readily apparent structure. Examining the pages, the reader sees text of different sizes. The smaller size text is understood to be captions. The captions are also indented slightly after the first line. It is unlikely that a reader, having read to the bottom of the main text on the first page, would continue with the caption at the top of the next page in the mistaken belief that it was the continuation of the text.

Only foveal vision, the central two-degree region of the field of view, collects enough detailed information to recognize letters and words. The information available in a number of fixations must be collected by the brain into an aggregate image. This collection process is tied intimately to the parsing of the page. Information collected initially, in conjunction with knowledge and expectations, is used to

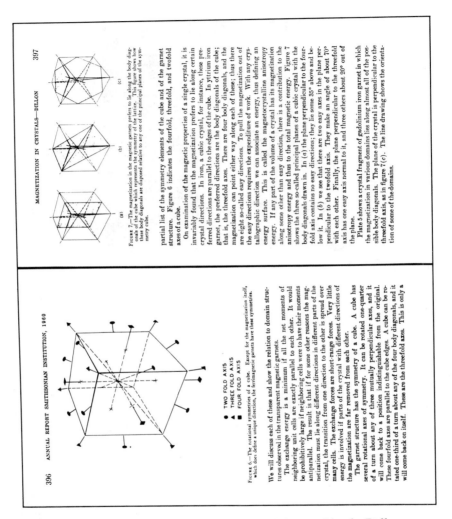

FIGURE 5.7 Two pages (reduced) from a well-designed book. Different kinds of information are present, but it is easy to parse. Figures are not confused with text; captions are not confused with main text. (Reproduced from *The Annual Report of the Board of Regents of the Smithsonian Institution*, Publication 4435, 1960.)

direct further data collection until a complete perception is created.[1] Seeing is an active process.

Parsing is aided by the presence of redundant information. This may seem counterintuitive, but one reason it is true is that people process information in parallel. A friend is recognized easily because many aspects of the person's appearance contribute simultaneously to the recognition. Similarly, understanding of speech is guided by a knowledge of the subject matter, by following the conversation, and by body language. Speech removed from its context is much harder to understand, even when the sound quality is equally good. It is the same with reading.

This is why the multiple differences between the caption and body text of Fig. 5.7 make sorting out the parts of the page quicker, easier, and less prone to error. A good book designer knows this, though perhaps not in psychological terms, and designs pages accordingly.

There is a great deal to know about the layout of pages, and substantial typographical literature exists on the subject.[2] In some publishing applications, it is the user's responsibility to specify layout and document design. In others, policy in the form of document design may be set by persons other than the nominal end user. In the second case, the policy makers must have the flexibility to achieve good designs. In either case, when systems impose policy that hurts the user's ability to achieve desired arrangements of the page, quality and user satisfaction suffer. As more and more people untrained in graphic design and typography become desktop publishers, their desktop-publishing software will have to make reasonable suggestions about document design. This knowledge must be embedded in software and in standard templates or specifications for documents of various kinds.

Book designers often use a *grid* as an aid to layout [Hurlburt 1978]. The grid is a rectilinear subdivision of the page that provides a template for the layout of each individual page. Figure 5.8 shows such a grid and several magazine pages laid out with its aid. Note that the space within the grid is used somewhat differently in each of the pages shown; sometimes two or three grid columns are combined into a text or picture area. The underlying structure provided by the grid is the basis

---

[1] In fact, expectations—at least in the form of the focus of attention—also affect data collection [Downing and Pinker 1985].
[2] See, for example, [Wilson 1974] and [McLean 1980].

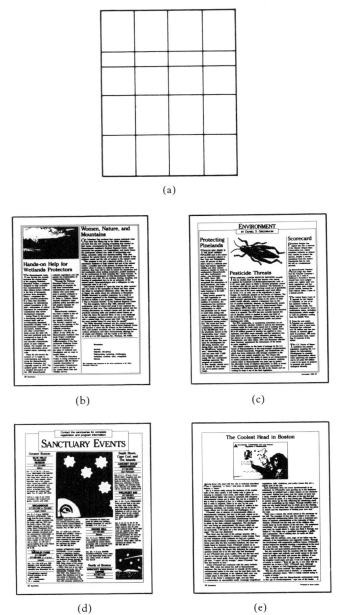

(a)

(b)   (c)

(d)   (e)

FIGURE 5.8 Example of a grid (a) and several pages laid out with its aid (b–e) (much reduced). (Reprinted from *Sanctuary: Journal of the Massachusetts Audubon Society.*)

for the reader's conceptual model of the structure of the page. People learn easily by example. By seeing a few combinations of the basic spaces on the page, readers absorb the plan of the book. They parse subsequent pages using this "grammatical" information.

Justification of Lines

Justification of lines of print is an essential function of typesetting. Justification is simply placing lines of text in some specified relation to the margins. Given a sequence of symbols that are to appear on a particular line, the system must decide where to place them. Since their order is fixed, and spacing between letters within words is generally not open to modification, justification comes down to deciding how much space should be placed between the words and at the left and right sides.

Several kinds of justification are possible:

- *Flush left, also called ragged-right.* Text abuts the left margin; all unneeded space is to the right.
- *Flush right.* Text abuts the right margin; all unneeded space is to the left.
- *Centered.* Text is centered; unneeded space is divided equally to the right and left.
- *Justified.* Text abuts both margins; space is distributed within the line.

There are several possible variations in justifying text. Sometimes it is desired to put the available space in the middle of a line, dividing the line in a specified place and pushing words on either side of the division to the margin. In typesetting, this is called *middle quadding*, which simply means putting the space (quads were large spaces in metal type) in the middle of the line. Another issue is how to treat the last lines of justified paragraphs. Should these lines remain flush left, or should they be justified like the others? The decision depends on how close to the right margin the end of the line would come. If it is close enough to allow word spacing no wider than in the rest of the paragraph, then justification may be preferred. Otherwise the line is set flush left.

Unfortunately, small matters such as how to treat the last line in justified paragraphs can not be dealt with identically in all typesetting jobs. The design of a particular document may call for one choice or another. Therefore professional typesetting systems must be able to accommodate varying rules, as well as individual exceptions, in order to meet the needs and expectations of system users.

Of course, type can be set ragged right instead of justified. This permits interword spacing to remain constant, although interword space can still be adjusted to even out the raggedness of the right-hand column. Studies and opinions disagree on whether text is more or less legible when set ragged right or justified [Fabrizio, Kaplan, and Teal 1967; Trollip and Sales 1986]. Some typographers prefer ragged right for narrow columns to avoid overly large word spaces [Lee 1979:4b], but the practice in most newspapers, magazines, and journals is the opposite. Until clearer evidence is available, whether to set text ragged right or justified remains a matter of document design, style, and .personal preference.

Some Layout Guidelines

Here are some general principles and guidelines that apply to document layout. They come primarily from typographic practice, but are consistent with psychological evidence and the nature of automatic typesetting.

Don't Impose Typewriter Habits   Typewriter habits, intended for a monospaced environment, should not be followed when typesetting with proportionally spaced typefaces. Several typing conventions in particular are not appropriate:

- Do not double space or add extra space after periods or other punctuation. The usual typesetting practice is to use the same spacing as between words, although there are differences of opinion here, and some book designers specify slightly more space after periods [Williamson 1956:113]. However, putting two space characters in the text may add far too much space, and the period itself creates some extra visual space because of its size and position. Adding space after punctuation encourages the formation of rivers of white within the text. This point is discussed further later in this chapter.
- Most punctuation belongs inside quotation marks. Not only is this good style, but it also avoids odd spacing.

"The greatest difficulty with typewriter habits is the extra   spaces
inserted after punctuation. They tend
to accentuate rivers in text. <u>Another
typing convention is to use underlining
to add emphasis:</u> when this is done
in typesetting, a visual distraction is
created, one that does not appear when
italics are used instead".   A period
terminates the previous sentence.   It
should be within the quotation mark.

FIGURE 5.9   What typewriter practices do to typeset material. Extra spaces
after punctuation tend to create rivers, as do misplaced punctuation marks.
Underlining within text interferes with interline spacing, creating an object of
unnatural dimensions within the text.

- Do not set very wide lines with narrow interline spaces, as is the
  norm in business letters. (More on this topic later.)
- Do not add extra space between paragraphs unless that is the
  specific style of the document design. Most books are set with
  indentations to indicate a new paragraph, but without extra vertical space except after headings.
- Underlining is used with typewriters to indicate emphasis. In
  typesetting, use italics for inline textual emphasis and bold for
  greater emphasis, such as headings.

Figure 5.9 shows the effects of some of these typewriter habits on
typeset material.

Typesetting "Typed" Material   When a "typed" look is required
by a document, consider using a proportionally spaced typeface reminiscent of typewriter styles, such as ITC Typewriter, or simply a typeface that contrasts with the other faces used. A distinction such as
this is frequently necessary for material containing computer programs
or other computer input or output (see Fig. 5.10). Sometimes, however, monospaced setting is indeed required because of the expected
alignment of individual character positions in the original computer
output.

Next, enter your retrieval request:

>Survey Chinese soup recipes.

      45   Won ton
      98   Hot and sour
    103   Sizzling rice

Note that the result is sorted by record
number, rather than alphabetically. If

FIGURE 5.10   Achieving a "typed" look without using monospaced type. A
sans-serif face provides adequate contrast to serifed running text to indicate
program input or output, as in this example.

Set Narrow Lines Ragged Right   When indented itemized lines are
set, the resulting lines may be very narrow. If such lines are justified,
large interword spaces are inevitable. The style of many typeset documents is, therefore, to set these narrow lines ragged right, even when
the surrounding text is justified.

Margins   Ample margins may facilitate reading by helping the
reader avoid distractions from objects near the text, and by preventing
a crowded look on the page. Bear in mind that books, folders, reports,
and other documents that open to reveal two pages have a double
margin at the center. Frequently, somewhat less space is used in this
"gutter." As a guide, compute the ratio of the area of the text body to
the area of the whole page. Surprisingly, for most books the main body
of the text occupies only 50% to 60% of the page. Thus the ratio of
text area to page area is about 1:2. A visual illusion creates the impression of greater coverage of the text. People shown pages with 50% text
coverage estimated that about 75% of the pages was actually text
[Tinker 1963b:111].
      Note that wide margins are almost never used on screens. Windows
on displays frequently have text right up to the edge, an undesirable
situation for printed output.

Use a Grid   The value of gridding for electronic publishing is
that it can provide a useful user-interface specification for layout. Only

a few current desktop-publishing systems offer grids (PageMaker is one). Automated grids provide a professional tool that is useful to even the typographical novice. It is easier to change standard designs expressed in part as a grid graphically than with numeric specifications. Designing new layouts graphically seems only sensible in an interactive, screen-oriented personal-computing environment.

The best guide for typographically inexperienced users is a standard layout that is designated as appropriate for their particular purposes. A library of such designs, created by experienced graphic designers and labeled according to use and connotation, would put most users on the right track from the beginning. For example, business-letter designs could be designated as appropriate for formal business, informal business, or personal correspondence. Some formatting programs—L^{A}T$_E$X [Lamport 1986], Scribe [Reid 1980], and DECpage [Digital 1984] are examples—currently provide document types, but do not necessarily identify the connotations clearly.

Provide Redundant Parsing Clues   As noted previously, multiple differences in page design make it easier for people to understand information. For example, footnotes can be smaller, at the bottom of the page, and more narrowly spaced. Quotations can be indented and in smaller type than the rest of the text. Figure captions can be italicized and smaller than the text. One advantage of multiple differences is that they allow smaller distinctions within each dimension than if a single kind of differentiation were used. Thus a slight decrease in type size, plus indentation, makes a quotation or figure caption visually distinct without a loss of legibility due to the substantial reduction in type size that might otherwise be required. Note that using a grid also provides redundant information—it sets visual expectations that the reader quickly learns and uses throughout the work.

Leading, Line Width, and Type

Formatting programs frequently take as givens the type size and line width, which depend greatly on the kind of document the user wants to produce, the size of the paper, and the sizes of type available on the printer. If good values for leading could be computed from a formula or algorithm, then formatting programs could produce results that would require little or no adjustment by the user. Better still, the user

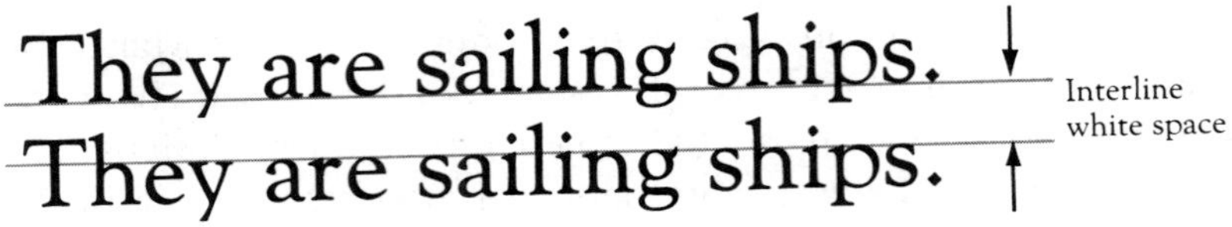

They are sailing ships. ↓
                                         Interline
They are sailing ships. ↑   white space

FIGURE 5.11   Interline white space as defined in the author's empirical studies. The definition ignores ascenders and descenders, which do not much affect the bulk of the white space between lines of text.

of such a system would need less typographical knowledge and experience in order to get good results. Unfortunately, conventional methods of choosing the "right" amount of space depend on human judgment. What information is the judgment based on? In fact, a number of typographic elements seem to bear on the choice of appropriate line space:

- Size of the type;
- The design of the type, especially the x-height and set;
- Amount of interline space intrinsic to the type design;
- Length of the line;
- Interword spacing for the loosest lines;
- Intended mood—scholarly, economical, open, and so on.

Interline white space is defined here as the space between the baseline and the x-height on the line below—that is, the white space between two adjacent lines of lowercase 'x's. This is an appropriate measure because ascenders and descenders fill little of the interline space, and in general the amount of overall white space present depends only on the interline space and the x-height. Figure 5.11 shows the situation.

Leading in Some Real Texts

Fifty examples of running text, in a diverse set of books and magazines, were measured. All the samples were commercially published works, presumably the result of at least modest attention by a book designer or printer. The group of samples represents common practice in the printing of running text. Because we seek a prescription for interline white space, it is interesting to look at that variable as a function of

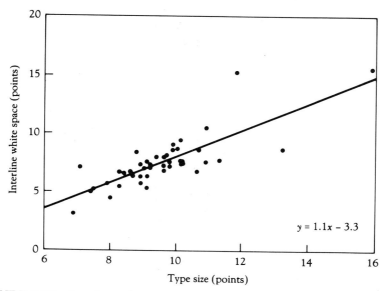

FIGURE 5.12   Interline white space as a function of measured point size. For this purpose, point size was defined as the distance between the top of the ascenders to the bottom of the descenders.

other measurable values. Figures 5.12 through 5.15 show interline white space in the 50 samples as a function of type size, x-height, set, and line width.

The increase of interline white space with type size is no surprise (Fig. 5.12). If the space did not grow with type size, lines of large type would be set so close together that ascenders and descenders would overlap between adjacent lines. One interesting question is whether larger sizes require proportionately more added space than smaller sizes. If type size is doubled, should more than twice the added leading be used? Figure 5.12 shows that this is indeed the case in the sample: The slope of the line fit to the data in that graph is 1.1.

For digital type the situation may be somewhat more complex, since some traditional typefaces have proportionately shorter ascenders and descenders in larger sizes. If, contrary to traditional practice, fonts are scaled linearly instead of being adjusted in design for size, in itself this will create additional white space, perhaps negating the requirement for proportionately more leading.

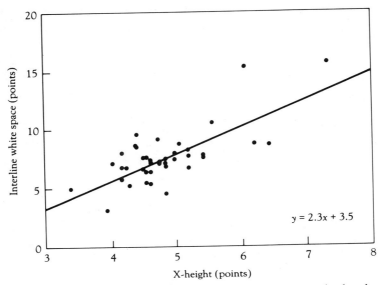

FIGURE 5.13   Interline white space as a function of measured x-height.

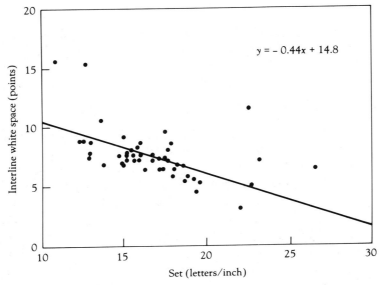

FIGURE 5.14   Interline white space as a function of measured average width of characters.

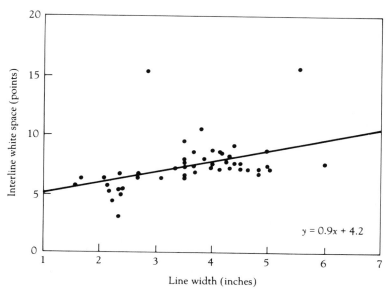

FIGURE 5.15   Interline white space as a function of line width.

The relationship between interline white space and x-height appears to be less well defined (Fig. 5.13). White space does increase with x-height, as predicted by the typographers, but again this partly reflects the increasing overall size of the type.

Figures 5.14 and 5.15 show white space in terms of set, the average number of letters per inch within the typeface (Fig. 5.14), and of line width (Fig. 5.15). These charts show clear relationships, again as predicted by the typography books. It's good to know that typographers and printers do as they say one should do.

The two outlying points on these charts, at about 15 points of interline white space, are of interest because they are far from the main sequence of values. One point represents a children's book, and the other an expensive art book. Each was designed with a great deal of additional white space for a reason. Another interesting item, a scholarly book on the history of technology, has the least white space. Again the white space is consistent with design. Scholarly books generally are economical of paper, and have a denser look about them than do other books.

Figure 5.16 portrays the same data expressed in terms of space added between lines of text, assuming that the typeface allowed intrinsically for no extra space between lines beyond the extent of ascenders and descenders. In Fig. 5.16(a), it appears that one group of items has about two or three points of leading for type about eight points and larger. Similarly, as a function of line width, Fig. 5.16(b), the amount of leading added settles down to about two or three points for lines longer than about three inches.

Do not take the trend lines in these graphs as absolute prescriptions. The graphs do not so much say what to do as what designers and printers do. But the graphs do indicate that there is both a structure to choices of leading, and a range of acceptable values.

Experimental Data

Most typographic issues affecting continuous reading have been neglected by psychologists, but good experimental data from some years ago bears directly on choices of column width, leading, and the like. It is important to distinguish two kinds of experimental measures: *visibility* and *legibility*. Visibility is the degree to which a letter or word can be seen, that is, how easily it can be decoded. Legibility, on the other hand, measures the ease with which text can be read and understood in normal reading. Road signs must have high visibility to ensure that they can be seen at some distance and in various lighting conditions. But legibility is the right metric for the quality of text that is intended to be read continuously, over a period of time, like a book. The term *readability* is also used to mean legibility.

Much experimental work in vision and reading concerns visibility. Because the primary need of electronic publishing is running text, this work applies only marginally to that field. Nonetheless visibility is relevant to advertising layout, map design, and other tasks in which isolated bits of text are used.

The difference between visibility and legibility is illustrated in Fig. 5.17. In Fig. 5.17(a) visibility is shown as a function of visual angle. Visibility rises steadily with visual angle, though the rate of rise diminishes with larger angles [Robinson 1952:44–46]. Legibility (Fig. 5.17(b)), however, shows marked decreases for type larger than some optimum size, at a given reading distance. To paraphrase the difference, letters become more and more visible the larger they are (within

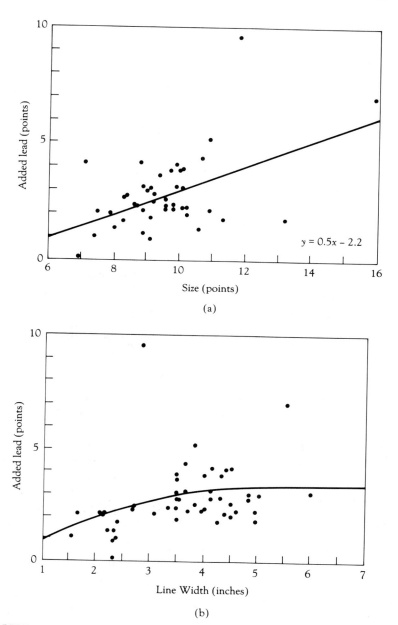

FIGURE 5.16   Added interline white space as a function of measured point size (a) and line width (b).

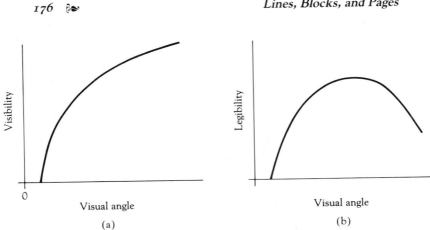

FIGURE 5.17   Visibility (a) and legibility (b) as a function of text size. Legibility is the more useful measure when considering the quality of running text.

reason). Visibility increases steadily with the angle subtended by the object. If a word must be seen easily, make it big. But for continuous reading, larger sizes reduce reading performance because less can be seen in each eye fixation [Morrison and Inhoff 1981]. The eyes must do more work to read the same number of words. Keeping the difference between these two measures in mind helps avoid apparent contradictions and paradoxes in reporting the quality of text.

Several difficulties plague any attempt to perform careful experiments on legibility. Clearly typography has a great many variables. It is difficult to devise an experiment that evaluates only one variable, unaffected by other factors. For example, it is hard to know how to produce two texts that differ only in line width. Should fewer words be placed on each of the short lines? Or should a font with a narrower set be chosen, so that the same number of words fits on the narrow lines? Either way, another variable is introduced that must be accounted for in the experimental design and in the analysis of the resulting data. Few experiments yield definitive statements about single variables.

Another problem is that variables that bear on typographic quality appear to behave differently in the aggregate than in isolation. Legibility may be little affected by degrading a single component of type, but may change entirely when several modest factors apply simultaneously.

Any useful psychological experiment to evaluate legibility must be based on an operational definition of legibility. A common, useful definition is stated in terms of reading speed and comprehension. If a text is read faster with the same level of understanding, or if a reading task (such as proofreading) is performed faster with the same level of accuracy, then legibility is said to be better in the faster case. All results of the form "thus-and-so decreases legibility so-many percent" are of necessity based on a performance measurement of some sort. This is as close as we can get to an objective measure of quality for text used in continuous reading.

One study by Wiggins [1967] provides some interesting data about legibility and line length. Wiggins found that the reduction of column width (on paper) from about 2 inches to about 1.67 inches, in two steps, resulted in a significant reduction in reading speed. This result suggests that column widths can be too short for optimum legibility.

Wiggins also found that holding column width constant and using narrower letters *increased* reading speed. Apparently the more letters one sees in a fixation, the fewer fixations are required. Certainly there is a lower limit to this effect. Letters that are too narrow are distorted and harder to read. Within the range of choices provided by normal typefaces, however, speed and economy of space are compatible. To put numbers on the widths involved, the narrower typeface averaged about one-and-a-half lowercase alphabets to fill a line (39 letters), and the wider one about one alphabet (26 letters). In contrast, only a slight effect of x-height on reading speed was found.

In fact, the earlier, very extensive work of Tinker [1963b;1965] supports the idea that individual parameters can be varied within ranges without great detriment to legibility, but that severe degradation sets in outside this range. For example, Tinker found no significant difference in legibility of type size in the range from 9 points to 12 points, when other factors affecting legibility were optimized for each size. However, larger type (14 points and up) was generally less legible. Smaller type (6 points) was much less legible, reducing reading speed 5% to 8%.

Tinker also found that long lines slow reading because more eye fixations are lost to tracking errors and to undershooting the beginning of the next line. Combined with Wiggins's observation, this suggests an optimum range of line width, above or below which reading performance drops off. Again note that the parameters interact. Tinker

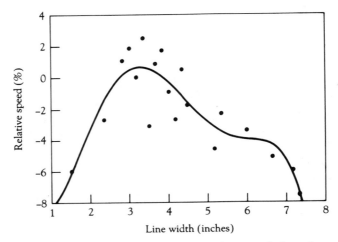

FIGURE 5.18   The effect of line width on reading speed, from four of Tinker's studies with 10-point type combined. (Data a composite from four studies by Tinker [1940:42–45].)

found that increased leading improves the legibility of long lines, increasing the scope of the acceptable range of line lengths.

Figure 5.18 shows the average relative reading rates over four of Tinker's studies, in which subjects read 10-point type at various line lengths. Leading was fixed (none was added in this case). Although the points are spread out, the results are typical: good performance within a central range, and sharp degradation outside the range.

In a study involving almost six thousand subjects, Tinker [1963b:94–102] was able to determine optimal line widths and leading for each type size he used (Table 5.1). His data are somewhat hard to use prescriptively, however, because he quotes the amount of leading *added* to the interline white space intrinsic to the typeface. The typeface used was Excelsior, a Linotype newspaper face [Tinker 1963a].

Despite its traditional use, added interline space is a poor way to specify leading. The right amount of lead to add depends on the details of the typeface design, and thus varies from typeface to typeface. The consistency of metal type for book and newspaper printing that made Tinker's data useful resulted from type designers' choosing generally similar amounts of interline space for their designs. Electronic type,

10-Point Type	Line Width	Set Solid	1-Point Leading	2-Point Leading	4-Point Leading
	9	−9.3	−6.0	−5.3	−7.1
	14	−4.5	−0.6	−0.3	−1.7
	19	−5.0	−5.1	0.0	−2.0
	31	−3.7	−3.8	−2.4	−3.6
	43	−9.1	−9.0	−5.9	−8.8
11-Point Type	Line Width	Set Solid	1-Point Leading	2-Point Leading	4-Point Leading
	7	−11.2	−9.0	−12.2	−10.2
	16	−4.7	−0.6	−0.8	−3.3
	25	−0.7	+0.7	0.0	−1.4
	34	−2.5	−0.1	−1.6	−2.6
	43	−6.4	−4.7	−3.5	−2.8
12-Point Type	Line Width	Set Solid	1-Point Leading	2-Point Leading	4-Point Leading
	9	−7.4	−6.0	−5.8	−5.0
	17	−2.6	−0.9	+0.8	−0.9
	25	−0.8	−2.5	0.0	+2.4
	33	−2.7	−0.7	0.0	+2.1
	41	−8.1	−3.7	−3.5	−3.5

TABLE 5.1 Optimal combinations of line widths (in picas) and leading for various text type sizes [Tinker 1963b:95,97,98]. (A pica is approximately 1/6 inch.) Figures are the percent reduction in speed relative to a chosen setting (shown in **bold face**). "Set solid" indicates no added leading. (Miles A. Tinker, *Legibility of Print.* ©1963. Reprinted courtesy of Iowa State University Press.)

free from the constraints of a metal substrate, varies more widely in the amount of intrinsic space provided. Interline white space, as defined and used here, provides a better measure for calculating and reporting leading.

The fundamental lesson for digital typesetting from the work of Wiggins and Tinker is that substantial variation of page designs is a legitimate choice for the system user or document designer. Within a range of values that provides good quality, choices of line length and leading will affect the feel and tone of a document without reducing its overall legibility. On the other hand, it would be very helpful if the standard values and range of choices offered by layout programs were based on these high-legibility ranges of the variables, guiding users to good choices.

Current Formatting Practice in Desktop Publishing

Most current desktop-publishing systems do not pay much attention to relationships among typeface, line width, and leading. Commercial typesetting equipment has long been operated by typographically sophisticated users who have the knowledge and experience to specify these variables. When a novice sits down with a publishing system, the defaults provided by that system strongly affect the quality of the results. Default values and relationships are in effect typographic recommendations built into the system, for better or worse.

The default layout values provided by many office-publishing systems fail to achieve good legibility. In particular, current desktop systems do not necessarily adjust interline spacing according to line length or typeface characteristics. They might provide "automatic" spacing based on the typeface size alone, or a specification included in a predefined document type or document template. For example, one formatting program, under the guise of "automatic" spacing adjustment, corrects for superscripts and subscripts on a line-by-line basis— usefully avoiding collisions between lines, but also creating disturbingly unequal overall line spacing. Programs such as MacWrite provide only limited choices for spacing, such as single, one-and-a-half, or double spacing. Such coarse divisions of spacing, a holdover from typewriters and word processors, do not give enough choices to achieve the best legibility for most line widths.

Some degree of typographic sophistication can be introduced into systems by providing formats, document designs, skeletons, and the like that incorporate good typographic and perceptual principles, as discussed earlier. Or automatic settings can be provided for parameters such as interline spacing, based on other values the user provides (such as type size and line width).

Hyphenation and Line Breaking

When typesetting a block of text, the system must decide where to break each line, that is, when to stop adding text to one line and begin another. The simplest algorithm, used by many word-processing systems, adds words to a line until one more would overflow into the margin. The entire overflow word then begins the next line. When justifying lines, this computationally easy scheme can produce very loose type, blocks of text with excessive white space between words—in short, terrible line breaking. The method works most poorly when columns are narrow compared with the length of the words. If the break word is long, much space is left to distribute across the line. Even when paragraphs are ragged right, this method yields unacceptably uneven lines.

An obvious way to improve line breaking is to allow the computer to hyphenate words. Human typesetters use hyphenation routinely, though sparingly, to break words across lines, to the benefit of the resulting paragraph and page; a modest amount of hyphenation makes a great difference in the appearance of a paragraph. Hyphenation requires skill and knowledge, and cannot be described as "mechanical" when done by people. Expressing the judgments that people make in the form of a program is a challenge, but one met by some current typesetting systems. Note that the rules of hyphenation differ from language to language.[3]

Consider the simplest-possible line-breaking and hyphenation scheme, denoted here as Level I. Text is assembled tentatively into a line, assuming average word spaces, until some word would not fit. Then there are four possible cases and resulting actions:

1. The line fits exactly without the overflow word. Set it that way, and bring the overflow word to the next line.
2. The overflow word can be fit on the line without hyphenation by shrinking the word spaces uniformly, without reducing them beyond the thinnest acceptable space. Set the line with the overflow word.
3. The overflow word has a possible hyphenation that meets the same criterion as either Case 1 or Case 2—it can be placed on the end of the line (with an added hyphen) without reducing the interword space unacceptably. The first section of the overflow word (with a hyphen) is added to the line, and the remainder is placed on the next line.
4. None of the above cases applies. Remaining space is split

---

[3] For example, compare Liang [1983] on rules of English hyphenation with Mañas [1987] on Spanish.

equally between words, and the entire overflow word is placed on the next line.

After the text for a particular line has been determined, it can be right justified by distributing the space remaining on the right equally across the word spaces. For flush-left text, this last step is not performed.

This algorithm, while it certainly will format a paragraph, suffers from several deficiencies. First, the algorithm can frequently produce lines with large interword spaces because the next indivisible chunk at any given point may be large. Second, if the minimum space value is at all low, the algorithm will frequently produce very tight lines. With no control of tightness from line to line, lines might alternate tight and loose within the otherwise acceptable constraints of reasonable interword spacing. Finally, many lines in a given paragraph might be hyphenated. Conceivably every line in a paragraph set this way, except the last, could be hyphenated. None of these faults would be tolerated in a traditional print shop. When a very loose or tight line would be set, or when more than two lines in a row would be hyphenated, a human typesetter adjusts a previous line slightly so the line breaks work out better. When a paragraph is set, it is examined as an entity to detect any global faults, and repaired as necessary. In extreme cases, the author is even called in to change the wording slightly and thus avoid an ugly paragraph!

Rivers

The even distribution of type across the space occupied by the print is a global property of paragraphs that affects their overall quality. Sometimes *rivers* appear in a paragraph as white rifts running between the words from line to line. Fig. 5.19 shows a paragraph containing bad rivers. A human typesetter avoids rivers by watching for them as the paragraph is set, and also checks by viewing the printed text at a sharp angle, which accentuates the problem if it exists. In careful printing work, many a paragraph is reset because of rivers.

Can a program eliminate rivers automatically? Yes. Level II line breaking includes paragraph-level optimization, allowing different breaking possibilities to be considered in terms of the quality of the entire paragraph in which they are contained. Level II line breaking resolves many of the problems encountered in Level I. First, the

As quick as thought is an old
mode of expression, used to
convey an idea of the greatest
rapidity: but no one, until
lately, ever dreamed that a
thought could be sent
hundreds of miles in a few
seconds; and that a person
standing in London might
hold a conversation with
another in Edinburgh, put
questions and receive answers,
just as if they were seated
together in one room, instead
of being three hundred miles
apart.

FIGURE 5.19   A paragraph with bad rivers. The eye can follow a path of
white from line to line. Space that should not be part of the perceived figure
catches the reader's attention and disturbs the continuity of reading.

method defines a line-breaking-quality metric. For example, the typesetting language T_EX adds up various "badness" scores, which Knuth
calls *demerits*, to rate a paragraph. Compressed or expanded interword
spaces contribute demerits as the square of their difference from the
nominal space. Hyphenated words result in demerits. Adjacent lines
of substantially different tightness, or series of hyphenated lines add to
the badness score. The rule for Level II line breaking is as follows:

> For a given badness function **B** that gives a badness score for a
> particular breaking of the paragraph, find the set of line breaks
> that minimizes **B**(P) over all possible breakings of the paragraph.

What goes into badness function **B**? Structurally, **B** contains two
parts, one local to each line, and one global to the entire paragraph:

$$\mathbf{B}(P) = \boldsymbol{\beta}(P) + \sum_{i=1}^{k} \mathbf{b}(l_i),$$

where P is a particular breaking of the paragraph, k is the number of
lines in that particular breaking of the paragraph, l_i are the individual
lines in the paragraph, **b** is the badness function that applies to a single
line in isolation, and $\boldsymbol{\beta}$ is the global badness function that looks at the
paragraph as a whole.

Lines have badness scores **b**(l) derived from tightness, compared
with ideal word spacing; looseness, compared with ideal word spacing;

and hyphenation. Similarly, paragraphs can be rated globally by the number of hyphenations, the number of consecutive hyphenations, alternating loose and tight lines, rivers, and whether there is a single word on the last line.

The numeric values for these components of badness functions is a matter of tuning based on experience. After all, the demerit method is an attempt to quantify for computer evaluation what would be judgment if performed by people. Though only a model, the method works quite well. Knuth and Plass [1981] provide the details of experiments, algorithms, formulas, and workable settings. Figure 5.20 shows a paragraph hyphenated by a Level I hyphenator, and the same paragraph hyphenated with TeX.

Rivers are not considered in the TeX algorithms. Knuth and Plass claim that their optimum-fit algorithm, used in TeX, rarely forms rivers because the algorithm usually achieves tight spacing. Pathological cases, such as very narrow columns or text with repeating patterns of words (for example, the attendees at a wedding as printed in the society column of a newspaper), will still result in rivers. Note also that rivers can arise in flush-left, ragged-right text. Although word spaces can be acceptably small in this case, the spaces may still align from line to line in the text. Thus checking for rivers would be a useful feature of any formatter designed to produce the highest-quality results.

Faster Line Breaking

Level II line breaking is implemented by a search procedure that compares the quality scores of different breakings of the paragraph, and chooses the best one. Various algorithms exist for searching the space of possibilities. It is necessary to avoid checking every conceivable break, however, since much too much time would be spent. A paragraph of 93 words, the length of the paragraph you are now reading, can be broken in about $5 \cdot 10^{27}$ ways, without counting possible hyphenations. In fact, the number of possible breakings of a paragraph with n words is just:

$$2^{n-1}$$

Most possible breakings of the paragraph would be extraordinarily bad. For example, one word could be placed on each line. Fortunately, good breakings can be found with relatively little searching. The possible methods include dynamic programming and variations upon it. The literature provides detailed algorithms [Achugbue 1981; Knuth and

The express train rushes along. It has already traversed nearly one hundred miles in two hours; another hour, and he will be in London; and at the thought, he clutches the booty with delight—for he knows not that just at that moment tidings of the robbery has reached the railway station he had left so far behind; that he had been seen in the neighbourhood where the robbery was committed; and that a messenger, with the rapidity of lightning, was travelling along those wires, that had already rung a little bell in the telegraph office in London, and was now telling the London policemen what had been stolen, describing also his very person, and the carriage in which he was riding. And all this immense distance had been traversed by the messenger, and the tidings delivered, in the space of a few seconds—even while the express train, with all its speed, had advanced but little more than a mile.

(a)

The express train rushes along. It has already traversed nearly one hundred miles in two hours; another hour, and he will be in London; and at the thought, he clutches the booty with delight–for he knows not that just at that moment tidings of the robbery has reached the railway station he had left so far behind; that he had been seen in the neighbourhood where the robbery was committed; and that a messenger, with the rapidity of lightning, was travelling along those wires, that had already rung a little bell in the telegraph office in London, and was now telling the London policemen what had been stolen, describing also his very person, and the carriage in which he was riding. And all this immense distance had been traversed by the messenger, and the tidings delivered, in the space of a few seconds–even while the express train, with all its speed, had advanced but little more than a mile.

(b)

FIGURE 5.20   Comparison of hyphenation by a Type I algorithm (a), and by T$_E$X (b). The Type I algorithm breaks anywhere it is possible according to its hyphenation dictionary, resulting in more hyphenations, but nonetheless some relatively loose lines. The hyphenations themselves are poor, inhibiting easy reading. T$_E$X, on the other hand, creates a more uniformly spaced paragraph with fewer and better hyphenations. However, it was unable to find a suitable break at line 3, leaving an overly long line and thus notifying the user of the problem.

Plass 1981; Plass 1981; Witten 1985]. Dynamic programming gets the number of breakings that must be considered down to

$$\frac{n(n+1)}{2}.$$

This is a vast improvement. For a 93-word paragraph, this comes out to 4371 breakings to be considered, a much more practicable quantity. Witten [1985:651] describes the dynamic programming approach to line breaking this way:

> To find the best way of breaking words 1 through k, find the best
> way of breaking words 1 through j for all $j<k$ and then consider,
> for each of these possibilities, the effect of adding the remaining
> words.

In other words, the optimal solution can be found by considering combinations of optimal partial solutions, eliminating the consideration of most possible breaks. Other search methods also make further dramatic reductions in the amount of computation required [Witten 1985:647–658; Knuth and Plass 1981].

Hyphenation Quality

One determinant of hyphenation quality is the method by which possible hyphenations of words are obtained. All methods use some form of dictionary. If a complete hyphenation dictionary were available, only correct hyphenations would be found and inserted in the typeset text. Unfortunately, a complete dictionary is not the answer. A complete dictionary would be very large indeed: It would have to contain not only all the root words of the language (English or whatever), but all of the inflected forms with their prefixes and suffixes. Thus in addition to 'happy' appearing in the complete dictionary, so would 'unhappy', 'happily', 'happiness', 'unhappily', and so on. Even on an extremely large computer, the space requirement would probably be unsatisfactory.

Another problem with the large-dictionary approach is that the dictionary can never be complete. Words come into the language constantly; people write documents containing nonstandard words; and most proper names are not contained in any dictionary. Therefore some better scheme is required.

One alternative is to develop a set of rules that hyphenates most words correctly, and also use an exception dictionary to correct any errors committed by the rules. This is a workable scheme, and is the basis of most hyphenation programs. Spelling patterns are identified that usually indicate acceptable hyphenation points. Then other rules are devised that eliminate potentially invalid hyphenations. For example, 're' at the beginning of a word might indicate the presence of a prefix, as in 'redecorate'. However, short words should never be hyphenated, so 'red' and 'read' could be screened out as inappropriate to hyphenate. Rules may look for more general patterns, such as

$$vowel + consonant - consonant + vowel,$$

which, in this case, allows for a hyphen between the consonants. Systems of rules improve with successive testing and tuning. Sometimes statistical rules are developed based on studies of the dictionary, resulting in ad hoc solutions of good quality for the particular language and dictionary used.

The quality of rule-based hyphenation depends critically on the balance between the quality of the rules and the size of the exception dictionary. Hyphenation algorithms are subject to two possible errors:

- *Type I hyphenation error.* A word is hyphenated in an unacceptable place.
- *Type II hyphenation error.* A valid hyphenation is not found.

Unfortunately there is some degree of trade-off between the two types of error. Attempts to provide all valid hyphenations will result in more invalid ones' being generated, and conservatism about offering possibilities will cause many valid choices to be missed. Good hyphenators strongly prefer Type II errors over Type I; they find fewer possibilities, but they rarely mishyphenate a word. One excellent hyphenator finds about 90% of the possible hyphenations for English, with "essentially no error" [Liang 1983].

It is also worth noting that no hyphenation scheme can provide 100% correct hyphenation unless it understands the text being hyphenated. Short of using artificial intelligence programs to provide better answers—a thoroughly impracticable approach for the foreseeable future—some provision will always be required for users to provide hyphenation information by adding acceptable hyphenations and disallowing unacceptable ones. This is not just a matter of preference or of words unknown to the system: The sense of some words determines where they can be hyphenated. Consider a phonograph 'rec-ord' that is to be 're-corded'. Figure 5.21 lists a number of such words whose senses determine the correct hyphenation.

Correctness of hyphenation according to one's favorite dictionary is not in fact the highest goal for a hyphenation program. Badness scores and global paragraph optimization will eliminate the use of too many hyphenations, but some valid hyphenations (according to the diction-

as·so·ci·ate	as·so·ciate
arith·me·tic	ar·ith·met·ic
even·ing	eve·ning
in·val·id	in·va·lid
prog·ress	pro·gress
re·cord	rec·ord
rep·re·sent	re·pre·sent

FIGURE 5.21 Some words whose hyphenation depends on use (see Liang [1983:3], from which part of this list is taken).

ary) are better than others. Hyphenation that is correct by the dictionary can change the meaning of a word. Consider the sentence 'Dr. Smith researched the old building'. If hyphenated as 'Dr. Smith re-searched the old building', it might mean that an additional search was conducted, rather than that Dr. Smith studied the building itself. This situation, not so farfetched as it may sound, has actually happened to ill effect in computer-typeset material.

Good hyphenation also depends on avoiding halves of words that mislead the reader because of meaning, spelling, or pronunciation. Dictionaries offer many potentially confusing breaks. Consider 'restrictive'. By the dictionary, it can be hyphenated as 're-strictive' [Merriam-Webster 1983:1006]. But the prefix 're-' suggests repetition, which is not part of the sense of the word. Or try 'European'. Hyphenating it as 'Europe-an' is confusing. Or consider 'an-timerger' and 'apart-heid', words rendered almost unreadable by hyphenation. When the spelling of the prehyphen part of a word suggests a different phonetic sound than is correct for the whole word, confusion can result from the hyphenation. Because of nonstandard spelling, proper names are particularly subject to misreading when hyphenated: Consider 'Mauchley.' A cautious approach to hyphenation is best. If paragraphs are optimized so as to do a minimum of hyphenation, a few awkward hyphenations may make little difference to the overall quality of the text. Nonetheless it is appropriate to limit hyphenation to those breaks that do not disrupt the flow of reading.

Another problem that plagues automatic hyphenation programs is speed of execution. If a large dictionary must be queried for each word to be hyphenated, failure to optimize data accesses results in unacceptably slow execution.[4] Rule-based systems can be much faster, but the more sophisticated the rules, the more computation is probably required to analyze and hyphenate a word. The problem is compounded manyfold by the need to consider hyphenating many different words when optimizing a paragraph globally. Depending on the search algorithm used, most of the words in a paragraph may have to be checked for possible hyphenation. Some scheme to remember recent hyphenations is required to avoid constantly rehyphenating the same words during the search for a good set of breaks for a particular paragraph. For example, potential breaks can be inserted into the running text as it is processed.

The overall speed of typesetting equipment may depend critically on the hyphenation algorithm. If a rule-and-exception-dictionary hyphenator took 1/100 second to do each hyphenation, and if the rest of the processing were infinitely fast (which it is not), then the whole system might process only a couple of hundred words per second, depending on what percentage of the words in a paragraph had to be considered for hyphenation. This rate would be unacceptably slow for many systems, especially real-time systems that keep the user waiting. Partly for this reason, the best optimizing typesetting programs currently operate in a batch mode, in which careful paragraph optimization is done while the user goes out for coffee. The speed of hyphenation is an area for development aimed at improving the quality of typesetting systems.

Reading from Screens versus Reading from Paper

An important psychological issue for the design of typographic computer systems is the speed and effectiveness of reading from screens as compared with paper. Reading from paper provides the baseline for human performance. Print on paper has been around for some time; it utilizes the human visual system well. We have nothing better to compare with.

A basic observation, reported by several experimenters, is that people read 20% to 30% slower from CRT displays than from paper [Gould 1987; Gould and Grischkowsky 1984; Gould and Grischkowsky 1986;

---

[4] Turba's [1981] article on detecting spelling errors includes information on building efficient large dictionaries.

Heppner *et al.* 1985; Kak 1981]. Research is under way to try to understand why this is the case [Gould 1987]. A large number of variables could be responsible for the difference in speed, including the following:

- Light letters on a dark background on a CRT differ from black on white on paper.
- CRT screens emit light rather than reflect it.
- Resolution on screens is coarser than on paper.
- CRTs flicker; paper does not.
- Screens are usually viewed when they are vertical; paper, when it is horizontal.
- Screens are more subject to glare than is paper.
- The intensity-contrast ratio of screens is usually lower than that of paper.
- Screen fonts are generally of lower quality than are paper fonts.
- Paper is more familiar to most people than are computer screens.
- Paper is more readily adjusted for viewer comfort than are screens.
- The viewing distance for paper is generally closer than for screens.
- Text on screens fills a different span of the visual field than does text on paper.
- Color displays and certain kinds of monochrome displays present text in colors other than black and white.

No single difference explains all or even most of the large difference in reading speed. While most of the variables seem to make some difference, the effect appears to be cumulative: Many small differences that might be accommodated individually with little loss of speed combine to create a vast differential in speed.

It is enormously difficult to do an unassailable experiment that isolates just one of the variables. For example, obtaining exactly the same image on paper as appears on a screen, in order to compare reading speed, is nearly impossible. Thus inferences from single experiments may not be definitive. However, the variables that relate to letterform quality seem to have a larger effect than do the other variables [Gould 1986]. This preliminary result offers the possibility of constructing very high-quality screen displays that are just as effective and easy to read as paper. Although people today usually prefer paper over screens, this might change if typographic quality on screens were improved—and if reading were better understood.

Some of the parameters just listed do deserve comment from an experimental and perceptual point of view; the design of systems often requires making choices or setting defaults in these dimensions. Although trying to make images on screens more like those on paper may ultimately lead to better-quality screen text, current systems must be built with current technology.

Screen Polarity

Tinker's work showed a significant reduction in reading speed for white text on black on paper, compared with black on white. Gould's work, however, indicates that polarity on CRTs alone does not explain any of the differences in reading speed [Gould 1987].

Most CRT users prefer black letters on a light background, or vice versa. While user preference is extremely important, there are several reasons why black on white may become the dominant mode of text presentation. One is that black on white resembles the paper documents that are printed by publishing systems. Another is that eye fatigue is greater for white on dark when the user must look alternately from paper (perhaps on a desk or copy stand) to screen and back. The fatigue results from accommodating to the difference in overall intensity of the image.

CRT Screens Emit Light

This does not appear to be a major problem. Contrast and the related problem of glare are more significant.

CRTs Flicker

At refresh rates of less than 80 or 90 per second, CRTs do not appear to be as steady as images illuminated with incandescent or natural light. However, the flicker is probably not responsible for large differences in legibility [Gould 1986]. Flicker may nonetheless contribute to fatigue in reading.

Viewing Distance

Paper is more easily adjusted to suit the user's preference for viewing distance than is a screen, and it is easier to avoid glare with paper. Since legibility depends critically on the apparent size of text (that is, on the angle subtended by text at the eyes), fixed viewing distance can result in less than optimal legibility. One defense is to consider the

Color Combination Compared with Standard Black on White	Difference in Percent
Black on white (standard)	0.0
Green on white	−3.0
Blue on white	−3.4
Black on yellow	−3.8
Red on yellow	−4.8
Red on white	−8.9
Green on red	−10.6
Orange on black	−13.5
Orange on white	−20.9
Red on green	−39.5
Black on purple	−51.5

TABLE 5.2 Legibility of colored print on colored paper [Tinker 1963b:146]. Negative percentage values indicate decreases in reading rate (legibility) relative to the standard. (Reprinted by permission from *Legibility of Print* by Miles Tinker © 1963 by Iowa State University Press, 2121 So. State Ave., Ames, Iowa 50010.)

usual viewing distance when setting type size. Another is to make it possible for users to adjust text size or viewing distance to suit themselves.

Color Displays

The possibilities of displaying text in color and on colored backgrounds bear exploration. It is usually the intensity contrast more than color that determines legibility, as described in Chapter 3. For paper, black on white provides the highest legibility compared with other combinations, as shown in Table 5.2 [Tinker 1963:145–148].

Typography

Typefaces and layouts on screens are frequently inferior to those on paper. Gould's results suggest that better typefaces alone may significantly narrow the gap between reading speed for screens and paper. Similarly, screen layouts are seldom designed by graphic designers or book designers for clarity or æsthetic quality. Careful layout may also play a role in closing the gap.

Final Words on Layout

Certain specifications in the layout of a document cause problems for hyphenation and justification:

- Narrow columns;
- Itemized and enumerated lists (such as bulleted items);
- Long words;
- Monospaced typefaces;
- First lines of paragraphs.

These problems do not necessarily have good solutions from the point of view of a typesetting program. If the user specifies narrow, justified columns, and includes many long words that do not hyphenate well, the result will be poor typesetting. Interactive document preparation can help because the user can see what is happening and modify the document to counteract it. Another partial remedy is careful specification of the design of standard documents. For example, the standard design could leave bulleted and numbered lists as flush left, as a matter of style, to avoid those situations in which such lists would look bad.

Chapter Summary

Typographers attend to space, the part of the page *not* occupied by the image. The layout of text facilitates the visual parsing of pages by readers, helping them find information and avoid confusion in reading.

Typewriter habits are responsible for some defects in typeset material. Extra space after punctuation, wide lines with little interline space, and extra space between paragraphs are all contrary to good typesetting practice.

Good page design allocates about 50% of the space on the page to margins. This practice contrasts with the norm on screens of having negligible margins in windows.

The amount of space between lines affects the legibility and overall feel of text. Experiments show that interline space must be adjusted to reflect line width, set, and x-height. Guidance for users of desktop-publishing systems can be provided via standard layouts and algorithms that allocate enough interline space for the type and line width being used.

It is not well understood why reading rates differ so dramatically between CRTs and paper. Many variables distinguish the two situations, but typographic quality may prove to be the most significant.

Good hyphenation markedly improves the quality of typeset material by helping to control interword spaces in justified material. Linebreaking algorithms should consider the overall quality of paragraphs to achieve optimum presentation with a minimum of hyphenation, variations in interword spacing, rivers, and so forth.

— 6

Matching Screen, Paper, and Expectation

Oft expectation fails, and most oft there
Where most it promises.
　　　　— *William Shakespeare*
　　　　All's Well that Ends Well

MANY electronic publishing systems display on a screen a representation of what will later be printed on paper. Generally the paper output is the objective of the work: a letter, proposal, report, memo, article, plan, or book. Sometimes the paper is only a proof of more-finished printed material that will be typeset on fancier equipment. In either case, the screen image is supposed to match the final printed output. This matching of screen and paper goes by the name of WYSIWYG, pronounced wizzy-wig, which stands for What You See Is What You Get. Many typesetting and word-processing systems are advertised as having this property; it is a marketing virtue, perhaps a marketing necessity.

Unfortunately the term WYSIWYG does not mean the same thing to everyone. Some vendors use it to mean only that editing on the screen is by direct manipulation, that is, by pointing and hitting keys so as to change a screen image directly. An exact match between screen and printout is not claimed. Others suggest an absolute equality of appearance when they use the term. A system that previews the appearance of the printed document, in an operation separate from editing or formatting, might also be termed WYSIWYG.

In what dimensions might screen and paper images match? With WYSIWYG, the screen image is a facsimile of the page to be printed. To varying degrees, the two presentations can match or not match in these ways:

- Typeface design, size, weight, set, variation, and style;
- Position of text and graphics on the page;
- Line and page breaks;
- Line spacing;
- Margins and page layout;
- Quality of text and graphic images;
- General appearance—color, texture, and mood.

The degree to which a system can achieve a satisfactory screen and paper match depends on the details of the screen and print technologies, how much differences matter to the user, and the extent to which the software can achieve these ends. Many of the problems of producing high-quality text described in previous chapters bear on the matching problem: The different characteristics of screen and paper media result in differing methods and choices for optimizing quality. As a consequence, what comes out of the printer may or may not meet the user's expectations. This chapter discusses the problems that arise in trying to achieve an accurate match, and suggests how they can be solved.

Problem Areas

Resolution

Resolution is almost always different for screen and paper. The difference in resolution between the two output devices underlies many of the problems of WYSIWYG. Screen resolutions are usually lower than those of draft printers, and those of draft printers lower than those of typesetters. In order to achieve the greatest quality, it is appropriate to optimize output at different resolutions in different media. But other characteristics of the output device also matter. Screens allow dynamic and interactive presentations of text and graphics impossible on paper. Draft printers are less expensive and often faster than their higher-quality cousins. Within the confines of available technology and the inevitable trade-offs between features and cost, differences in resolution and quality are inescapable.

Some people find it surprising that much greater resolution is required on paper than on CRTs to achieve equivalent quality. In fact, it would cripple the paper-output part of a system to limit it to the resolution of the screen. Why? One significant reason is the user's expectations. People are used to reading typeset-quality printed materials on paper because of their lifelong experience with magazines, newspapers, and books. Even office typewriters, with their carbon ribbons, produce crisp letters with no noticeable roughness. Only recently have typewriter and computer vendors been passing off dot-matrix print as "near-letter quality." Following in those same footsteps, some companies advertise 300-dot-per-inch laser printers as providing "near-typeset quality." Clearly they know the standards by which they are judged.

Greater resolution is required on paper than on CRTs because human interaction with CRT images is more forgiving of low resolution than is human interaction with paper. Since CRT pixels are actually quite fuzzy and soft compared with the dots delivered by laser printers and typesetters, the spatial frequencies contained in a CRT image better approximate the frequencies at which the fonts and graphics are digitized, reducing the reconstruction artifact produced. In other words, the spatial frequencies of CRT output are bandwidth limited to a lower frequency, relative to their output resolution, than are most printing devices.

Laser printers and typesetters produce sharper-edged pixels. Higher resolution is required to prevent reconstruction artifact from being visible in the output. The same is true of any output device with pixels that have much sharper edges than the output resolution—for example, liquid crystal displays. A CRT will produce a text image of apparently higher text quality, at a given resolution, than that of an LCD. The LCD image will be sharper, but will have more visible jaggedness.

Font Differences

To the extent that resolutions differ between output devices, the actual fonts used at any given size will also differ. At the higher resolution, more information is available to express the letterform. Better letterforms are different letterforms. The problems of uniformity of font design discussed in Chapter 4 become apparent when output at two different resolutions is compared. If a bottom-up approach to design generated the fonts, the crudeness in form of low-resolution screen images will show on paper. Top-down design provides more satisfactory paper output, but is still a poor match to screen-letterform shapes.

Even collateral designs show substantial differences when the resolutions differ substantially.

An illustration of the differences that arise serves to demonstrate the problems of matching screen and paper typefaces. The Macintosh and Imagewriter present a well-designed low-end example of the bottom-up method. In this environment, in which the printer has twice the resolution of the screen, the screen fonts are used directly on the printer. In "high-quality" mode, a font of twice the screen size is actually used for printing—for example, the 24-point screen font is used to print 12-point text from the screen.

Figure 6.1 shows samples of one such font from this environment for use at two resolutions: 72 dpi (screen) and 144 dpi (paper). The samples are enlarged to show the design details. Both designs appear somewhat smoother than in the figure when either displayed or printed because of the edge-smoothing characteristics of the CRT and dot-matrix printer.

Some typographic problems do appear; the most obvious is spacing. At the lower screen resolution, spacing is necessarily coarser, for both letter-to-letter positioning and spacing between words. If the font is designed well, the lowercase will appear reasonably well spaced on the screen. But when printed, the font must be spaced either at the finer resolution (a good choice), or at the coarser resolution of the screen to better match its screen appearance. Either way, it is tempting to change the font design to utilize the higher resolution on the printer; the result is a divergence in style and in general appearance. The higher-resolution version tends to become a different, though better, font. Similarly, the difference between roman and italic letterforms may be dramatic. For example, the letter 'a' frequently has a very different shape in the italic: '*a*' rather than 'a'. If algorithmic slanting is used for "italic" or oblique screen fonts, these fonts will not match the high-resolution designs at this level of detail. These differences in letterform shape may have little effect on legibility, and be unnoticed by most readers, but they are philosophically troublesome under the strict WYSIWYG interpretation.

One way to improve paper output when using screen fonts directly on paper is *smoothing*, a spatial-filtering technique that interpolates the low-resolution font at the high resolution. Smoothing algorithms remove jaggies and may improve the output (Fig. 6.2) by reducing the noise content, but they cannot fix the degenerate shapes of the tran-exploration for the next fift

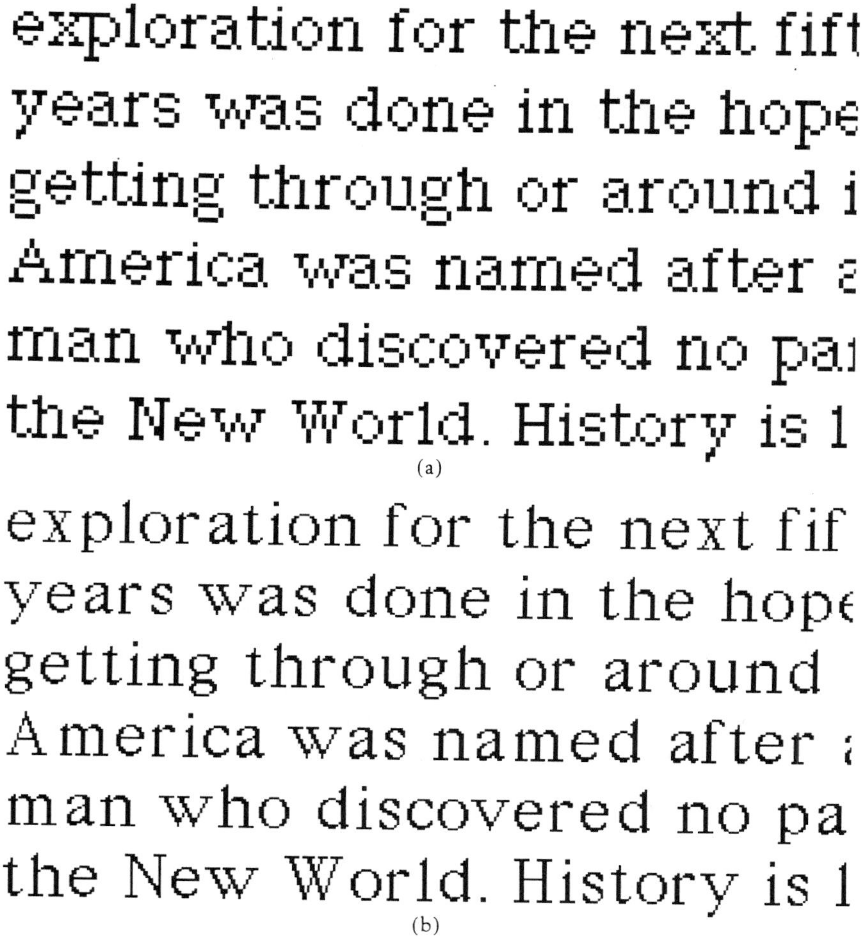

years was done in the hope

getting through or around i

America was named after a

man who discovered no pai

the New World. History is 1

(a)

exploration for the next fif

years was done in the hope

getting through or around

America was named after a

man who discovered no pa

the New World. History is 1

(b)

FIGURE 6.1 Two examples of Macintosh New York fonts, both intended to be printed at 12-point size. Note the differences in some letter shapes at the two resolutions, in particular 'W', 'w', 'f', and 'x'. Example (a) is a 12-pixel-high font for use at screen resolution of 72 dpi, and (b) is 24 pixels high for use at dot-matrix printer resolution, 144 dpi. Both fonts have been scaled to 24 points and printed with a 300 dpi laser printer to make it easier to compare details.

America was discovered accidentally
by a great seaman who was looking for
something else; when discovered it was
not wanted; and most of the exploration
for the next fifty years was done in the
hope of getting through or around it.
America was named after a man who
discovered no part of the New World.
History is like that, very chancy.

—Samuel Eliot Morison

(a)

America was discovered accidentally
by a great seaman who was looking for
something else; when discovered it was
not wanted; and most of the exploration
for the next fifty years was done in the
hope of getting through or around it.
America was named after a man who
discovered no part of the New World.
History is like that, very chancy.

—Samuel Eliot Morison

(b)

FIGURE 6.2   Results of smoothing the high-resolution version of a bottom-up font design. (a) shows the font at screen resolution; (b), as smoothed.

scribed letterforms. Spatial filtering in itself does not add any useful typographic information.

In the end, the best solution to matching typefaces between screen and paper is to increase the screen resolution substantially. CRTs with resolutions of 300 dpi or more can represent even typeset letterforms well enough to eliminate many surprises about the shape of letters. Such CRTs are now on the market.

America was discovered accidentally by a great seaman
(a)

America was discovered accidentally by a great seaman
(b)

FIGURE 6.3 Coarse letterspacing units, carried over from a lower-resolution presentation, result in unacceptably spaced letters (a). Compare the same text set with a finer spacing unit (b).

Letter Spacing

The even spacing of letters depends on the fineness of the resolution unit. Resolution is a resource for white space as well as for black image. At low resolutions, limited choices of interletter spacing can give text a rougher appearance. Figure 6.3 shows what happens if low-resolution spacing units are adopted for higher-resolution printing. The horizontal positioning of letters creates regular spacing of the strokes of the letters that is disturbed by coarseness in their exact positioning. In terms of spatial frequencies, the coherence of the low frequencies is disturbed by the low resolution of letter placement on the line, as shown in Fig. 6.4. This makes the text harder to read.

As a result, using screen-resolution letter spacing on paper actually runs counter to expectation, and does not support the WYSIWYG philosophy. Such letter spacing can make text noticeably different on paper, and certainly leads to less quality on paper than otherwise possible.

Fonts for low-resolution presentation can be designed to accommodate the coarser unit of interletter spacing without appearing too loose at higher resolution. This difficult font-design task works best with collateral design. The typeface shown in Fig. 6.5 achieves this end.

Since optimal sidebearings and kerning depend on resolution, such a design allows better use of the resolution at each level. However, it does constrain the choice of typeface. Only typefaces expressly designed for a digital environment can be expected to be this tolerant and forgiving. Transcriptions of traditional fonts will not fare as well.

Device characteristics

Screen and printer technologies are fundamentally different because of the different typographical properties of the devices. For the reasons

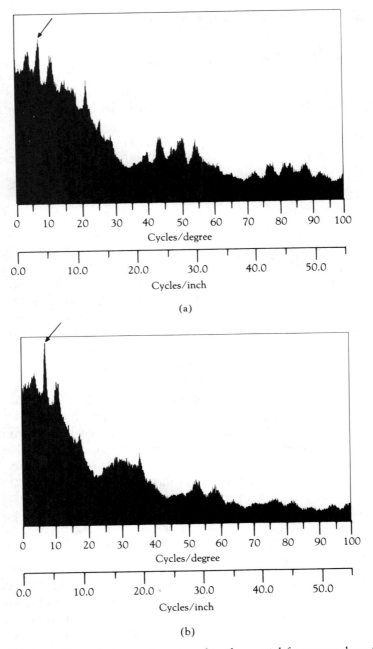

FIGURE 6.4 Coarse letterspacing viewed in the spatial-frequency domain. The coherence of the main stroke frequency is lost and harmonics of the spacing unit appear (a) compared with well-spaced text (b).

The graphic signs called letters are so completely blended with the stream of written thought that their presence therein is as unperceived as the ticking of a clock in the measurement of time. Only by an effort of attention does the layman discover that they exist

FIGURE 6.5 Lucida, a typeface design that tolerates coarseness in the horizontal placement of letters. Lucida is characterized by large x-height, short ascenders and descenders, and relatively open interletter spacing, all properties that improve its appearance on the screen. (Courtesy of Bigelow & Holmes.)

discussed in Chapter 3 (for example, the loss of contrast for black-on-white images on CRTs and the alteration of shapes by laser printers), different font designs for the two kinds of devices are necessary, even at the same resolution.

In some user environments, very little can be known about how a document will be printed at the time it is viewed on the screen. For example, when a user transmits a document over a communications network to other users, it may be printed on a number of different devices. Even if fonts are transmitted or agreed upon, in this situation it may be impossible to optimize screen presentation to the characteristics of the various output devices.

Because of the differences among devices, selection or creation of rasterized fonts (from stored outlines) can be postponed until the last moment, when the characteristics of the output device can be taken into account. For example, assumptions about resolution made before printing might constrain the quality of the printed result unnecessarily. Similarly, characteristics of the device itself, such as anisotropy, cannot be accommodated in fonts until the particular device is identified.

Line Breaks

Users are surprised when they discover that lines have broken at different places in the printed version of a document that was prepared and previewed on the screen. Such a disparity can arise easily if the formatting program uses the best fit of text at each resolution. If fonts are kerned and spaced optimally for each output device, more words may fit on some lines at one resolution than at another. This occurs because tighter spacing is possible at higher resolution. The choice appears to be between loose spacing at higher resolution, which impairs legibility, or disparities in line breaks and page breaks, which tend to surprise the user.

A better method may be a collateral one: Compromise screen or print appearance somewhat in order to accommodate word spacing and kerning at printer resolution. The procedure is first to determine where the line breaks would fall at printer resolution. Then the screen version is spaced as well as possible using these line breaks. If this can be done without unacceptably narrow word spaces, no other accommodation need be made. The letters in each word are spaced as usual for the screen resolution.

Some provision must be made, however, for the cases in which these line breaks create word spaces that are too narrow. A typographic criterion is that word spaces should be no narrower than 1/5 of the point size. This is referred to as a 1/5 em or five-to-the-em space. A space of 1/4 em is the preferred value. Figure 6.6 shows text with tight word spacing, at a screen resolution. At low resolutions, there are not many choices. For example, when type is 12 pixels high, 1/5 em is more than 2 pixels, but less than 3. In this case, 3 pixels is the narrowest word space consistent with good legibility.

Two choices are possible when not enough space is left to provide adequate word spaces. First, the print line can be loosened somewhat, by breaking it in a different place. This collateral approach to line breaking limits line length as a function of both screen- and print-line tightness. Alternatively, all the text lines on the screen display can be made longer than those on the paper. Slightly longer lines on the screen may be unnoticed by users, and are certainly preferable to illegible text. The disadvantage of longer screen lines is that they depart from WYSIWYG. The shape of paragraphs and of whole pages as presented on the screen will be distorted—another occasion for surprising users when they look at the paper output.

Other, more-global differences in appearance may appear between the presentations at the two resolutions. If the lower-resolution version has looser spacing, there may be more rivers in that presentation. Overall texture and typographic color will also differ. The specific application, and the types of user, will determine the degree to which such divergence should be addressed in design.

Size Expectations for Printed Materials

Another WYSIWYG issue—users' expectations about the size of type—affects the whole system. Normal reading distance for a large-screen

As quick as thought is an old mode of expression, used to convey an idea of the greatest rapidity: but no one, until lately, ever dreamed that a thought could be sent hundreds of miles in a few seconds; and that a person standing in London might hold a conversation with another in Edinburgh, put questions and receive answers, just as if they were seated together in one room, instead of being three hundred miles apart.

(a)

As quick as thought is an old mode of expression, used to convey an idea of the greatest rapidity: but no one, until lately, ever dreamed that a thought could be sent hundreds of miles in a few seconds; and that a person standing in London might hold a conversation with another in Edinburgh, put questions and receive answers, just as if they were seated together in one room, instead of being three hundred miles apart.

(b)

As quick as thought is an old mode of expression, used to convey an idea of the greatest rapidity: but no one, until lately, ever dreamed that a thought could be sent hundreds of miles in a few seconds; and that a person standing in London might hold a conversation with another in Edinburgh, put questions and receive answers, just as if they were seated together in one room, instead of being three hundred miles apart.

(c)

FIGURE 6.6   Tight word spacing is generally preferred in print, but difficulties arise at screen resolution. The typeface shown is 12-pixels high. In (a), 1/3-em spaces are used between words (1/3 of 12 pixels, or 4 pixels). In (b), 1/4-em, or 3 pixels, is used. Finally, (c) shows 2-pixel spacing, which is 1/6-em. 1/5-em spaces cannot be realized at this resolution.

display, typical of workstations, is greater than the reading distance for paper. Larger text is required on the screen than on paper to subtend the same visual angle. What appears the right size on a large screen, say for a business letter or report, will look as if it were intended for a children's book if printed the same size on paper. At workstation-viewing distances, 14-point type may look right for a letter or report, but 14-point type is definitely oversized for printing most such documents. Ten- or 11-point type is closer to the mark, as demonstrated in Fig. 6.7.

There are several possible solutions. Some personal computer systems—the Macintosh, for example—avoid the problem by having a small screen. People work close, minimizing the disparity between

As quick as thought is an old mode of expression,
used to convey an idea of the greatest rapidity:
but no one, until lately, ever dreamed that a
thought could be sent hundreds of miles in a few
seconds; and that a person standing in London
might hold a conversation with another in
Edinburgh, put questions and receive answers,
just as if they were seated together in one room,
instead of being three hundred miles apart.

(a)

As quick as thought is an old mode of expression,
used to convey an idea of the greatest rapidity:
but no one, until lately, ever dreamed that a
thought could be sent hundreds of miles in a few
seconds; and that a person standing in London
might hold a conversation with another in
Edinburgh, put questions and receive answers,
just as if they were seated together in one room,
instead of being three hundred miles apart.

(b)

FIGURE 6.7   The same text printed at different sizes has different connotations. The text here looked fine for a technical report at 14 points on a large screen (a) because the viewing distance was long compared with normal reading distance for paper. On paper (b), it looks more like a children's book. The difference is simulated here for viewing at reading distance.

reading distances to screen and paper. The inability to display a complete page, a deficiency, thus has one positive consequence in the design. Also, the entire page is never presented on a small screen, and thus expectations about the look of the page as a whole may be less strong (also a mixed blessing). It may also be possible to build systems that people use the way they use paper—an electronic notebook or a display built into a desktop, for example. Such systems would have no disparity because the reading distance would be similar.

Another approach is to make it clear to the user that the image on the screen is scaled, and is not the size of the corresponding paper image. Ironically, the "scaled" text may be the actual size it will appear on paper. (Using smaller text on the screen may also make for greater fatigue in reading.) Alternatively, reformatting the document when the paper copy is created allows both presentations to be of optimal size, but violates users' expectations of what is on each page and where it is.

A final possibility is a "virtual" representation. Why not present the page so that it looks right given the greater viewing distance? If 12-point type is intended on an 8.5 × 11 inch page, for example, and the viewing distance is such that an image 25% larger than paper is required to subtend the same angle, then we present 15-point text on a 10.625 × 12.5 inch page. There are two problems with this approach. First, people estimate size fairly well, independent of distance. Although the type will subtend the right angle, it and the page will probably look too large. The image would appear exactly the same only if viewed with one eye and without other distance clues. The virtual-display approach might nonetheless succeed if no attempt were made to present a whole page. Second, as a practical matter, large, high-resolution displays are expensive, and it may be hard to justify the cost of the extra "real estate" on the screen. System requirements may suggest using a large display to present several documents or windows rather than a single scaled page.

None of these approaches is entirely satisfactory. Better solutions are needed.

Margins

Margins, almost always present on paper documents, are rarely present in windows on computer screens. This basic disparity guarantees a different appearance for pages of text, and also creates incompatible expectations for users.

The reasons for this different treatment are not hard to find. Margins on paper documents shield the eye from distractions. They are also necessary to allow a book to be trimmed without cutting off part of the text. But screen "real estate" is more precious than paper, and many screens provide barely enough room to display a whole page without its margins. Considering the 50% rule—in books about half the area of pages is white space—the difference in presentation is all the more marked.

How important are margins? It has long been speculated that adequate margins improve reading performance by shielding the reader from the distractions of surrounding objects and images. Tinker's experiments, however, found only minor differences in reading speed with and without margins [Tinker 1940:97–98]. On the other hand, one function of gutter margins in books is to keep the printed part of the page relatively flat, not curving away from the reader as it would in a thick volume printed close to the edge of the paper. Such curvature does indeed reduce legibility [Tinker 1965:183–184]. The fact that books are conventionally printed with margins for historical and æsthetic reasons also means that printed documents without margins are unacceptable.

The differing expectations for margins on screen and paper present a hard problem. Since it is not sensible to remove margins from paper documents that require them, the only way to achieve equality is to incorporate margins on screens. For some time this will mean creating the perception of excess space on the screen for those used to more economical screen utilization. Also, less of the available resolution on screens will be committed to faithfully rendering letterforms and other images.

Relation of text to graphics

Another source of differences between what you see and what you get is that text and graphics have different properties, and thus behave differently at different resolutions. Desktop-publishing systems of necessity incorporate both text and graphics, usually allowing the two forms to be mixed somewhat. Some systems, in fact, employ two kinds of text: ordinary text and graphics text. Graphics text consists of letterforms created by graphical operations, and thus has the properties of graphics rather than text. For example, it may be composed of vectors, and thus be subject to arbitrary rotation (unlike bitmap fonts). It may not be possible to edit graphics text in the same way as ordinary text because it is represented as a graphical data structure.

Figure 6.8 shows how relationships that appear to hold on the screen may not hold in the corresponding paper image. Although the differences in absolute terms are small, small errors in graphical relationships can be quite visible. Lines may not join correctly, or may fail to show other properties such as being tangent to curves. The difficulty is really a result of having captured wrong information when creating the image

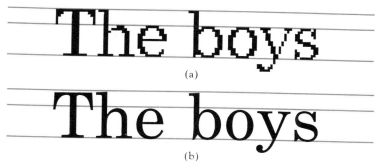

FIGURE 6.8 The detailed relationship between text and graphics can change from screen to paper presentations. In this case, the screen presentation (a) shows the center line at exactly the x-height. At higher paper resolution (b) the specified position does not result in exactly the same relationship.

on the screen. If the editor records the absolute position on the screen of each object, then the coarse resolution of the screen is incorporated into the data, and differences will result when the data is rerasterized at higher (or lower) resolution. On the other hand, if the semantic relationships are captured, for example as constraints, then the relationships can be enforced at the higher resolution. Thus recording the fact that a line is supposed to be tangent to a circle means that the line and circle will just touch at any resolution.

Complex Writing Systems

Script writing systems present special problems for typesetting systems, not the least of which is that keyboarding the symbols may not be natural. Some scripts are written right to left, and it is often necessary to mix text that reads in opposite directions. The result is difficulty in keying in the text, as well as frequent surprises for users because what the computer displays is not what was intended. Similarly, line-breaking rules for non-Latin writing systems can be complex, requiring judgments when performed by human beings. Such writing systems place a great burden on the designer, who must try to devise a natural way for users to express their documents. For an example of these difficulties and some of their solutions, see Becker's article on Arabic word processing [Becker 1987].

Physical Reality

The user reads screen and paper under different circumstances. All of the differences discussed in the previous chapter—emitted versus reflected light, flicker, and so on—can affect the appearance of text whether or not they affect the ease with which it is read. Physically an image on a screen simply is not a piece of paper, and thus can never be quite the same.

What You Got Is Not Exactly What You Saw

Because of all the problems just discussed, differences are bound to arise between the screen and printed versions. The strict WYSIWYG philosophy—that the text as it appears on a screen should be utterly identical when printed on paper—is unachievable. And, in fact, it is not desirable to reproduce the exact appearance of the screen if it has lower resolution; to do so would hobble the printing with the limitations of the screen device. Conversely, forcing the screen image to reflect the superficial appearance of paper would result in less-legible screens than otherwise.

A better overall goal is to try to balance the quality of screen and paper presentations. Although these presentations may not be equally important in all systems, for desktop publishing and general use they do matter equally. Users of office-publishing systems spend most of their system-contact time reading from screens, with paper output the result of their work. Often the paper is read by other people in addition to the user. The quality of the paper end product reflects on the user's status and ability. The paper presentation may positively or negatively bias how the content of the material is perceived.

Compromises, the essence of engineering, are the rule of thumb for WYSIWYG; a computer system represents one compromise or another among the constraints imposed by different output devices. The need to equalize the quality of presentation argues in favor of collateral design, or at least a great deal of attention to quality and matching appearance on each device. Compromise means accepting minor differences in the two presentations. The skill employed in choosing these differences will be reflected in the user's perceptions of the resulting system, and therefore in its quality.

A different standard of matching, WYGINS, describes output that matches user expectations. With WYGINS, What You Get Is No Surprise, the user should not be surprised by the appearance of his or her document. This standard can be achieved if designers understand the kinds of differences between screen and output that users can tolerate.

One way to help a user have accurate expectations, when, of necessity, the screen appearance and paper appearance differ, is to provide a proofing mechanism on the screen. When fine detail cannot be seen at screen resolution, an enlarged version makes it possible to check the detail and make corrections as necessary. For example, the version of TEX called TEXTURES provides a magnifier for examining a small portion of an output proof, making individual pixels visible. This feature is possible in TEX because the printer fonts are bitmaps and are available to the formatter for proofing. Proof versions at reduced scale allow overall layout and page appearance to be checked when the entire page is too large to appear on the screen. Although scaled previewing like this requires the user to go through separate steps, it does help match expectations to paper output.

A large component of human interface design consists of matching expectations. The conceptual model that users develop—how they think about the system and how it works—helps to determine what is surprising. Simply stated, if the behavior is predicted by the user, it is not surprising; and, the converse also applies. [1] To illustrate this point, consider the problem of matching sizes. If the user knows that the screen representation is different in size because of a scaling factor or another feature in the user interface, the size difference will not be surprising.

An Approach to General Office Typography

Thus the problem is to design an effective publishing system that meets users' expectations and needs with a minimum of surprises. At least two types of surprises relate to the complexity of systems. Very complex systems may exhibit surprising behavior, while very limited systems may demand surprising ingenuity to accomplish reasonable goals. By way of example, this section suggests a basic typeface strategy for office-publishing systems for nontypographers, people like architects, secretaries, and engineers who prepare documents as an adjunct to their work rather than as its focus.

The number of distinct typefaces required for a general office environment is far less than the number needed by a book designer, typog-

---

[1] For further discussion of conceptual models, see [Rubinstein and Hersh 1984].

rapher, or printer. Office users do not know typefaces by name—most don't know a serifed typeface from a sans serif one, much less the difference between two essentially similar faces. Therefore "name" faces are not appropriate in this environment, or at least users should not be expected to associate type designs with their names. Consider, for example, how people choose type for business cards, signs, and the like. They pick from a selection of samples that often differ in layout as well as typeface.

Notwithstanding their lack of nomenclature, office users do have varying needs for different type designs, determined by the kind of documents they produce. Letters of varying degrees of formality express varying moods beyond the words. For a system in which a typographer specifies the design of different types of documents, typeface specification is essential.

Economics, compatibility across systems, and overall simplicity dictate minimizing the number of type families supplied. The basic set should support the range of typographic distinctions that must be made in office documents, but need not offer further choices.

Bigelow [private communication] conducted an informal survey of typeface usage in offices. Studying the use of type balls for typewriters rented by office users, he discovered that six type balls account for most of the usage. Surprisingly, there are some definite but unusual requirements, such as a decorative typeface for party invitations, retirement announcements, and certificates. Thus one of the six more popular balls prints in script.

The trend in supplying printer fonts is toward scaled outline representations; it is not necessary to limit the number of distinct sizes of type that can be printed. On the other hand, screen fonts in small sizes must be carefully tuned to obtain high quality and a good match with print. Cost benefits accrue from limiting the number of sizes of screen fonts.

What distinctions do office users need? Typographic wisdom suggests that relatively few sizes, faces, and variations are required. Consider what one prominent typographer, Jan Tschichold [1967:50] had to say on the subject:

> Too many sizes in one job are unpractical and seldom give good results. The number used should generally be limited to three. Two will suffice for short jobs and four will be used in complicated matter.

Style	Renditions	Hand-tuned Screen Sizes	Printer Sizes[a]
Serif	roman italic bold (bold italic) decorative	{ 9, 10, (11), 12, 14, (16), 18, 24 points }	0–72 points
Sans serif	roman oblique bold (bold italic or oblique)	{ 9, 10, (11), 12, 14, (16), 18, 24 points }	0–72 points
Monospace	roman (italic or oblique) bold	{ 10, 12, 15 pitch[b] }	0–72 points
Symbols	roman bold (italic or oblique)	{ 9, 10, (11), 12, 14, (16), 18, 24 points }	0–72 points

[a] Six points is the smallest typographically useful size. Zero is specified for completeness when scaling large documents to fit within a particular paper size, etc.

[b] Characters per inch.

TABLE 6.1   Members of a generic face for office typography.

Tschichold goes on to suggest that one typeface family is sufficient for any single document, assuming that variations such as different weights are available. As noted in Chapter 2, print shops need many faces because different jobs have different requirements, even though a single job may call for only a few. But is one family sufficient for any significant portion of office typography?

The usual differentiation for emphasis provided by italic and bold is certainly important. A bold italic variation is also of some use, since occasionally the bold variation of a face is used for text, as in a figure caption, and the bold italic is useful to provide emphasis relative to the surrounding bold.

Table 6.1 shows a suggested set of typefaces that could provide a generic basis for office typesetting without being either too restrictive in what can be accomplished with variations or too liberal in the number of designs required. Included are serifed, sans serif, and monospaced faces and their variations. If instances of each are to be used in the same document, for example the serifed font for text and the

Helvetica
ABCDEFGHIJKLMNOPQRSTUVWXYZ
abcdefghijklmnopqrstuvwxyz .,:;!?"""
0123456789#$%@+-=<>^~_()[]{}/|*

Times
ABCDEFGHIJKLMNOPQRSTUVWXYZ
abcdefghijklmnopqrstuvwxyz .,:;!?""""
0123456789#$%@+-=<>^~_()[]{}/|*

Courier
ABCDEFGHIJKLMNOPQRSTUVWXYZ
abcdefghijklmnopqrstuvwxyz .,:;!?'`""
0123456789#$%@+-=<>^~_()[]{}/|*

FIGURE 6.9   The three most popular typefaces are Helvetica (a), Times New Roman (b), and Courier (c). The three faces do not match very well in terms of overall style, weight, or color.

sans serif for headings or captions, then the basic face designs should be compatible. That is, the designs of the faces should be related. Choosing faces independently, based on their individual popularity, is less desirable. For example, the three most popular faces are Times New Roman (serifed), Helvetica (sans serif), and Courier (monospaced)—see Fig. 6.9. Used alone, each face is fine, but these faces do not mix as well as other possible combinations. Some modern "super-families" include coordinated serifed and sans serif designs. Gill Sans (sans serif) and Perpetua were coordinated in this way by their designer, Eric Gill (Fig. 6.10). Similarly, the Lucida digital typeface family includes serifed, sans serif, and monospaced designs that mix and match well (Fig. 6.11).

Office-publishing systems should have sufficient typefaces, with variations and sizes, to allow creation of the vast majority of documents that users of the product want. What is needed is the ability to create the desired tone and the desired distinctions within the document. A serifed face is useful for running text, general correspondence, and the like. A sans serif face, more businesslike and modern, can be used for

QRST

(a)

QRST

(b)

FIGURE 6.10   A coordinated pair of faces, one serifed and the other sans serif. Monotype Gill Sans (a) and Monotype Perpetua (b) were both designed by Eric Gill.

business letters, signs, technical manuals, legends on diagrams, and so on. Finally, a monospaced face is useful when the distinction between commentary and output must be made—for example, for presenting computer output in a technical manual. Monospaced type is also useful when the look of typewritten material is desired, and sometimes when columnar material is being printed.

The collection of faces in Table 6.1 contains more variations than strictly necessary. The intention was to be complete, and to provide a maximum of symmetry consistent with typographic utility. The less necessary fonts and sizes (in parentheses) serve special purposes; most offices could do without them. Note that the decorative face is *not* listed as optional. Bold oblique variants (or bold italic, depending on the typeface design) are included for completeness and symmetry. Their typographic utility is limited, except as noted earlier.

Finally, an italic symbol font may be useful for emphasis in certain mathematical contexts. Many special symbols are also needed for setting mathematics, so this font alone does not solve the problem, but with the appropriate set of symbols it is useful for some kinds of material. It has little other typographic utility.

roman
ABCDEFGHIJKLMNOPQRSTUVWXYZ&
abcdefghijklmnopqrstuvwxyz .,:;!?'""
0123456789 #$%@+-=<>^~_()[]{}/|*

bold
ABCDEFGHIJKLMNOPQRSTUVWXYZ&
abcdefghijklmnopqrstuvwxyz .,:;!?'""
0123456789 #$%@+-=<>^~_()[]{}/|*

italic
ABCDEFGHIJKLMNOPQRSTUVWXYZ&
abcdefghijklmnopqrstuvwxyz .,:;!?'""
0123456789 #$%@+-=<>^~_()[]{}/|*

bold italic
ABCDEFGHIJKLMNOPQRSTUVWXYZ&
abcdefghijklmnopqrstuvwxyz .,:;!?'""
0123456789 #$%@+-=<>^~_()[]{}/|*

sans
ABCDEFGHIJKLMNOPQRSTUVWXYZ&
abcdefghijklmnopqrstuvwxyz .,:;!?'""
0123456789 #$%@+-=<>^~_()[]{}/|*

sans bold
ABCDEFGHIJKLMNOPQRSTUVWXYZ&
abcdefghijklmnopqrstuvwxyz .,:;!?'""
0123456789 #$%@+-=<>^~_()[]{}/|*

sans italic
ABCDEFGHIJKLMNOPQRSTUVWXYZ&
abcdefghijklmnopqrstuvwxyz .,:;!?'""
0123456789 #$%@+-=<>^~_()[]{}/|*

sans bold italic
ABCDEFGHIJKLMNOPQRSTUVWXYZ&
abcdefghijklmnopqrstuvwxyz .,:;!?'""
0123456789 #$%@+-=<>^~_()[]{}/|*

FIGURE 6.11   Samples of the Lucida family, a set of digital designs that includes serifed, sans serif, and monospaced designs that can be intermixed effectively with a single document. (Courtesy of Bigelow & Holmes.)

Communicating Typographic Information

Related to the problem of providing a single user with the output he or she expects is the problem of meeting expectations with transmitted documents. Few problems arise when typeset documents are communicated to systems of the same design as the originating system. If different configurations are in use, however, differences may arise from disparate device resolutions or characteristics. These differences are potentially within the control of the system designer, and can be dealt with in the course of design.

Any screen or printer that might be configured with a system should be able to present text sensibly for that system. Consider the situation in which two users of the same vendor's system have installed printers with very different characteristics. For example, one user has a laser printer with 300 dots-per-inch resolution, while the other has a 2400-dpi typesetter. Although the same file might have the same appearance on both of their screens, one or the another user may be surprised by the printed output. The compromises struck in the previous sections may fall apart. If the sender's document was formatted with the assumption of 300-dpi output, the typeset output will not make the best use of the available resolution. Should the trade-offs be made between the higher-resolution screen and output device? If so, the loser is the user with the lower-resolution device, the laser printer, whose output will be less than optimal.

The situation is far worse when communicating systems are not coordinated by a common design. Not only do device resolutions and other characteristics differ materially, but the document has to be expressed in some intermediate format that both systems can create and read. This cross-system communication problem is the motivation for standard protocols and languages for expressing formatted documents.

Batch-formatting systems such as TEX, Runoff, and Scribe have an advantage in environments that require cross-system communication: A document described by these formatters is essentially a program that, when executed, yields the formatted document. Fewer user expectations are set as to line breaks and the like because the document is prepared indirectly and is not necessarily previewed on a screen. In the absence of user expectations, differing but well-formatted printed documents are less likely to create surprise or confusion. Even when batch-formatted documents are previewed, expectations may be somewhat more abstract and functional—the user may expect only a well-formatted version of the material, not necessarily the exact one that was previewed.

What about the direct-manipulation, real-time formatting style of system that is (rightly) becoming so popular? One approach to document transmission is to include in the transmission protocol all the line- and page-break information, not to mention the fonts. Output is optimized for some intermediate resolution, perhaps 300 or 600 dpi, yielding reasonably good performance across the range of devices used to print documents. This works when there are agreed-upon fonts, but systems from different vendors usually embody vastly different assumptions and components, including different typefaces.

The font-matching problem can be addressed by employing a single family for general use, as described in the previous section. This reduces the number of requirements when a document moves across architectures, but does nothing at all to match the details of the fonts in each system. Inevitably, the generic faces chosen will differ in set, x-height, and other ways, resulting in substantial differences in presentation. Nonetheless, this approach is viable for some situations, and especially when no greater degree of commonality across systems is possible.

It is useful to describe typefaces by their characteristics and by their intent within a particular document. The role of the typefaces in the document is thus part of the document's style. Rather than specifying a specific typeface for each purpose, say Century Schoolbook, Century Schoolbook bold, and Century Schoolbook italic, specifications can indicate the change relative to a base font—for example, "Shift to the bold variation of the typeface in use." Similarly, when sizes are specified, relative sizes are easier to match than absolute ones. Footnote text can be described as one size smaller than body text, or chapter headings as two sizes larger and sans serif.

It is also possible to describe typefaces analytically to allow the remote system to attempt to match the characteristics that affect spacing and leading. The following characteristics might be transmitted:

- Point size;
- Variation (roman, italic, bold, outline, and so on);
- Serif type or stylistic category (modern, old style, and so on);
- X-height; ascender and descender length;
- Set, expressed as the width of the lowercase alphabet;
- Color;
- Weight;
- Typographic contrast.

These characteristics provide enough information to achieve a good match of typefaces, although they do not account for the subtle differences between similar typefaces of different design. Unfortunately, it is hard to know how best to match such a multidimensional description against a list of available typefaces. The point size and set are the most important components in matching line and page breaks. Of course, information on leading, line width, and so on also affect page formatting, and must be included in the document description. The other parameters affect the general appearance, and thus the texture, color, and mood of the typeset page. Figure 6.12 shows two documents set in similar laser-printer typefaces. Although differences are discernible, the overall match of the documents is quite good. Their characteristics are compared in Table 6.2.

Intentional Document Specification

Even when the characteristics just discussed are taken into account, matching may nonetheless be difficult—the best match in size, set, and variation may provide a poor match in the other dimensions. In this case, a more global approach to matching the style of documents is appropriate. The document style—that is, the description of the document design independent of content—provides the basic link for creating compatible presentations across systems.

Just as typefaces were specified in Chapter 4 extensionally or intentionally, so can documents be specified. If the details of a document—the typeface, size, margins, and so on—are given in detail, this is an extensional description. The document can be reconstructed accurately to the extent that these detailed specifications can be met. On the other hand, specifying the visual effect desired—what distinction a second typeface is required to make with respect to a first—allows some degree of flexibility in achieving the desired intent. This is intentional specification.

Consider, for example, a document that must have headings, footnotes, figure labels, and emphasis within the main text. An extensional specification might be as follows:

Use	Typeface	Size
Text	Century Schoolbook roman	12/14 points
Emphasis	Century Schoolbook italic	12/14 points
Headings	Century Schoolbook bold	16 points
Footnotes	Century Schoolbook roman	10/12 points
Figure legends	Century Schoolbook bold	9/12 points

INTRODUCTION

———————∞ • ∞————————

The introduction of the decimal system of weight, measure, and coins, is steadily progressing in most parts of the world, but when or wherever it is first proposed, it meets with many natural and reasonable objections. The inconvenience of the decimal arithmetic is well known, and better bases for the same have been frequently proposed, but there has not, that I am aware of, been made any earnest attempt, by proper authority, to introduce a system that would in all its bearings constitute the greatest possible simplicity and efficacy, nor to remove the principal objections to the decimal arithmetic. Questions may arise, *first,* what are the difficulties and objections? and *secondly,* how can they be removed and overcome?

The principal difficulty and objection to the decimal system is, that the base 10 does not permit of binary divisions, as required in the shop and the market. In attempting to introduce the decimal system in England, it met the said reasonable objections by Lord Overstone's observation that "the number 12 presents greater advantage than 10; a coinage founded on the first number is more convenient for the purpose of the shop and market." It is evident that 12 is a better number than 10 or 100 as a base, but it admits of only one more binary division than 10, and would, therefore, not come up to the general requirement.

(a)

FIGURE 6.12 Two documents printed with two similar laser-printer type-faces. Although different, the two versions might satisfy the same intent. (a) is set in New Century Schoolbook, and (b) in Palatino. The faces are stylistically distinct, but have roughly the same weight, set, and x-height.

INTRODUCTION

————∞ ● ∞————

The introduction of the decimal system of weight, measure, and coins, is steadily progressing in most parts of the world, but when or wherever it is first proposed, it meets with many natural and reasonable objections. The inconvenience of the decimal arithmetic is well known, and better bases for the same have been frequently proposed, but there has not, that I am aware of, been made any earnest attempt, by proper authority, to introduce a system that would in all its bearings constitute the greatest possible simplicity and efficacy, nor to remove the principal objections to the decimal arithmetic. Questions may arise, *first,* what are the difficulties and objections? and *secondly,* how can they be removed and overcome?

The principal difficulty and objection to the decimal system is, that the base 10 does not permit of binary divisions, as required in the shop and the market. In attempting to introduce the decimal system in England, it met the said reasonable objections by Lord Overstone's observation that "the number 12 presents greater advantage than 10; a coinage founded on the first number is more convenient for the purpose of the shop and market." It is evident that 12 is a better number than 10 or 100 as a base, but it admits of only one more binary division than 10, and would, therefore, not come up to the general requirement.

(b)

	New Century Schoolbook (Fig. 6.12a)	Palatino (Fig. 6.12b)
Point Size	12	12
Variation	roman and italic	roman and italic
Serif type	bracketed (straight)	bracketed (oblique)
X-height	5.7 points	5.7 points
Descender-height	2.2 points	3.2 points
Ascender-height	8.5 points	8.5 points
Set (lowercase alphabet)	59 mm	58.1 mm
Weight	.20	.20
Color	149	146
Contrast	2.4	3.0
Interline spacing	14 points	14 points

TABLE 6.2   A description of the typefaces used in Fig. 6.12.

A corresponding intentional specification that could meet the needs of the document creator, using any number of combinations of faces, could be the following:

Use	Typeface	Size
Text	Serif text roman	Large text
Emphasis	Serif text italic	Large text
Headings	Serif text bold	Heading
Footnotes	Serif text roman	Footnote
Figure legends	Serif text bold	Small footnote

Similarly, intentional specifications would identify a paragraph as a quotation, footnote, or figure caption; the document style specification would provide the details. There are also higher-level abstractions that relate to the structure of the document: footnotes, paragraphs, sections, chapters, headings, parts, addresses, cross-references, and so on. Describing a document in terms of these more abstract units might result in greater separation between the specification of a document's content and its ultimate appearance when formatted. More on this topic in the next chapter.

Transmitting a document becomes a matter of transmitting the document style in a standardized way, and sending the content keyed to that style. The document design takes care of setting margins, as well as of typeface differences and all other differences in presentation that might arise from different computing and output environments. Although details of documents described this way will not match, the style specification ensures that the content of the document will be presented well.

Documents as Images

A totally different approach to transmitting documents is to completely typeset the document locally and then transmit it as an image, that is, as a picture of the typeset page. This can be termed the facsimile approach. The virtue of such a system is that it can be integrated into an existing facsimile network, used for transmitting printed documents over phone lines or data networks. Also, paper documents from other sources can be mixed into the system. If the system is intended primarily for interoffice communication in a strongly paper-oriented environment, this approach may prove entirely satisfactory.

Not only WYSIWYG expectations and user surprises are affected by different presentations of a given document. Many business situations also require formats to be matched exactly. Consider a telephone conference call by three lawyers about a contract whose sections appear on different pages in the different copies they are looking at. Their communication would be improved if their copies matched; facsimile-based systems may perform well in such situations.

The primary difficulty in transmitting typeset documents by facsimile is that all the structural information contained in the documents is lost. At the receiving end, it is no longer possible to edit without reentering the text into a word processor or typesetting system. Automatic character recognition could alleviate this problem, but it places heavy computational loads on the system and demands the user's attention to resolve ambiguities. Furthermore, much information about document structure cannot be recovered in this way, or even by human inference. The fact that a title was centered explicitly rather than positioned absolutely, for example, or the fact that a number in a spread sheet is based on other numbers in other locations, are semantic relationships that are lost.

There are typographical issues of print quality, associated with resolution and digitizing, that relate to facsimile transmission of documents. What is an adequate resolution for capturing or expressing the typographic and graphic information on a page? Many current facsimile systems operate at about 300 dpi. At first consideration, this resolution seems adequate, since it matches the output resolution of many laser printers. It makes a substantial difference, however, whether the transmitted image is synthesized or instead scanned at such a resolution.

As explained in Chapter 4, scanning requires more resolution than does printing. In a typographic facsimile system, images created in a computer memory and printed can be redigitized adequately only at much higher resolution. The Nyquist sampling criterion, which dictates a sampling resolution of twice the highest frequency to be captured, describes the actual resolution requirement. The computer-printed document may have much higher spatial frequencies than the resolution of the output device. For example, a 300-dpi laser printer may produce edges with frequency components of 600 cycles per inch. To scan and reproduce such an image accurately, at least 1200 samples per inch scanning resolution is necessary. Thus the facts of information theory place a more stringent requirement on the scanners in facsimile systems than on the printers.

Interchange Formats

If a single standard existed for representing and transmitting formatted, compound documents, the world would be a simpler place. Within a company or community that uses similar systems throughout, documents can be moved easily from one location to another by transmitting them as files. A document can be created by one person, edited by another, reedited by the first, and then read by still others. But since everyone in the world does not have the same equipment or software, it would be sensible to develop a standard interface between document-preparation systems. Such a standard is called an *interchange format.*

Batch formatters such as TEX, Runoff or Scribe sidestep the problem. Programming languages in their own right, and largely independent of the details of the machines they run on, they serve as their own interchange formats. But using batch formats does not suit everyone or meet every need. Further, formatter languages usually require a great deal of computation to compile a document into printable form.

Moreover, the formatter-language approach begs the question of compatibility with other styles of document creation.

Consider creating a common, editable, compound-document format for use with various systems, both real time and batch. On the one hand, we require a method of representing a complex document inside the computer system. In a WYSIWYG system, the document is usually represented by a data structure in a disk file. This data structure may or may not correspond to the data structure used while the document is being edited, when the document is resident in the computer's memory. On the other hand, the data structures that represent the document are not usually in a form that allows them to be transmitted over a communications line. Rather, they contain internal pointers, flags, and the like that are meaningful only locally. The data structure used to represent a document is different for every system design, since it is intimately related to the specific features offered by the particular system and to the details of how these features are implemented. The various system manufacturers are unlikely to agree on a common set of internal representations for compound documents, given their independence and competitive stance, their differing needs and requirements, and the differences in the machines on which the systems run.

Therefore some standard way to communicate this information is desirable. This problem is the origin of *revisable formats.* If a language allows the structure of a document to be expressed independent of the implementation, then the document could be created in or translated into this language, transmitted to the other computer, and then modified and used there.

Currently no single, satisfactory standard exists. Although several languages are extant [Joloboff 1986], it is unclear which will come into wide use. SGML, which stands for Standard Generalized Markup Language, is a standard set by the International Organization for Standardization (ISO). Its virtues include moderate human readability and a well-defined syntax to ensure unambiguous machine parsing. ODA (Office Document Architecture) is a related standard proposed by the European Computer Manufacturers Association (ECMA) and adopted by ISO. It is intended for expressing compound documents in revisable, machine-readable form [ECMA 1985]. Finally, Interscript [Ayers *et al.* 1984], developed at Xerox Palo Alto Research Center, creates a more sophisticated processing model. This language provides a machine-parsable transmission format, and it has an internalized form that results from processing documents expressed in that format, in much the same way that computer languages are compiled and executed.

The problem is quite difficult, and not yet well-enough understood for a satisfactory standard to be adopted. One difficulty is that any communications language limits the scope of the documents for all systems. No capability or feature can be present in the document formatter that cannot be expressed in the language. However, most interchange formats do provide for passing uninterpreted information, outside the defined scope of the language. It then falls to the receiver of the document to interpret the embedded information. But this mechanism, which is used to get around the incompleteness of the format, also restricts compatible communication to compatible systems. Incompatibility thus creeps into the once-universal interchange format, which then ceases to be useful for interchange between incompatible systems.

Thus a revisable interchange language must be extremely complete, general, and powerful, which would allow it to express the same document in many ways. As a result, it is difficult to make the interchange language neutral about the terms in which documents are described. Because the same document can be described in different ways, the particular features on the sending system bias the expression of the document, and in a way that may make it awkward for the receiver.

Consider a sending system that stores information about formatting on a paragraph basis, as a property that can be modified as desired. The system codes this information for each paragraph in the interchange language, of course. Suppose that a series of paragraphs is declared as each having a blank line before its first line. This bit of document-style information is stored in the paragraph descriptions. If the receiving system does not have a special status for paragraphs, then it will generate an isolated blank line between paragraphs. Little harm is done; indeed, the document is correctly represented in the receiving system. But if the document is sent back to the originator (or to another system like the first), the original formatting information is lost. The blank lines will be intervening (empty) paragraphs.

Nonetheless, a common interchange format is much needed because it would allow documents to cross system and vendor boundaries usefully.

Page-Description Languages

A related problem is the transmission of compound documents in a noneditable form. The use of a common output format, referred to as a page description language (PDL), permits documents to be transmitted between dissimilar systems for viewing and printing only. The PDL approach has been successful in increasing the compatibility of dissimilar systems. Several proposed standards exist in this area.

The ideas intrinsic to today's PDLs were developed at Xerox Palo Alto Research Center and first described in the technical literature in 1982 [Warnock and Wyatt 1982]. The resulting Xerox PDL is called Interpress [Bhushan and Plass 1986]. Two other PDLs currently in use are Adobe's PostScript [Adobe 1985a and 1985b] and Imagen's DDL (Document Description Language) [Imagen 1986]. By way of example, Fig. 6.13 shows a PostScript program and its output.

Although fundamentally similar, these PDLs have some interesting differences.[2] Each PDL is a true programming language, with variables, routines, operators, control structures, and so forth. Each language includes graphical operations to facilitate creating images, and each has font facilities to handle multiple fonts and sizes flexibly.

All of the PDLs are raster oriented. Thus they focus on rasterizing images specified as lines, regions, outlines, and so on. They provide facilities for scaling and rotation of graphical objects, and for converting fonts in a storage format (usually outlines) into bitmaps of the required sizes. All allow fonts to be cached for efficiency, reducing the need to rasterize letters repeatedly. DDL even provides caching for objects other than characters.

The PDLs are differentiated by their emphasis on one part of the page description problem or another. Interpress implements a standalone environment that allows printing to occur without interaction with the computer that originated the document printing request. In contrast, PostScript maintains a somewhat closer relationship with the

---

[2] For comparisons of Interpress and PostScript, see [Mendelson, 1985] and [Reid 1986].

```
% ..................... Variables ....................
/MainFont
    /Helvetica-Bold findfont 15 scalefont def
/SloganFont
    /Helvetica-Oblique findfont 7 scalefont def
/OwnerFont
    /Helvetica findfont 10 scalefont def

% ..................... Procedures ....................
/rightshow        % stk: string
  { dup stringwidth pop      %get length of string
    120 exch sub %calc. white space
    0 rmoveto    %Move over that much
    show } def   %show string


/CardOutline      %Print card's outline
  { newpath
    90 90 moveto
    0 144 rlineto
    252 0 rlineto
    0 -144 rlineto
    closepath
    .5 setlinewidth
    stroke } def


/doBorder         %Print card's border
  { 99 99 moveto
    0 126 rlineto    %Border: 126 pts high
    234 0 rlineto    % & 234 points wide
    0 -126 rlineto
    closepath
    2 setlinewidth  %2-point-wide line
    stroke } def
```

```
/Diamond
  { newpath       % define & fill
    207 216 moveto       % a diamond-shaped
    36 -54 rlineto       % path
    -36 -54 rlineto
    -36 54 rlineto
    closepath
    .8 setgray fill } def

/doText           % Print card's text
  { 0 setgray 90 180 moveto
    MainFont setfont
    (Diamond Cafe) rightshow
    90 168 moveto
    SloganFont setfont
    ("The Club of Lonely Hearts") rightshow
    216 126 moveto
    OwnerFont setfont
    (Sam Spade) show
    216 111 moveto
    (Owner) show } def

% ................... Main Program ....................
CardOutline
doBorder
Diamond
doText


showpage
```

(a)

(b)

FIGURE 6.13 An example of a PostScript program (a) and its output (b). (Adobe Systems, Inc., *PostScript Language*, © 1985, Addison-Wesley Publishing Company, Inc., Reading, Massachusetts. Pps. 42–43. Reprinted with permission.)

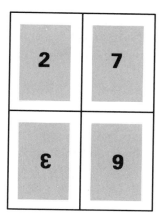 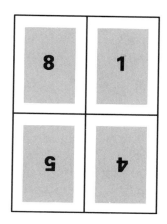

Side 1 of sheet   Side 2 of sheet

FIGURE 6.14   Signature printing is illustrated for a single sheet of paper that is printed with four pages of the finished document on each side. When folded and trimmed, the result is eight sequential pages. The pages are used in this order: 2,7,3,6,8,1,5,4. Half the pages must be inverted when printed.

originating system. All PDLs offer device independence—document descriptions do not include information specific to the output device.

Performance is hotly debated area. One distinction among the languages is *page independence.* If a PDL has this property, the processor is free to format each page independently, in any order, allowing for higher speed in the printer by use of parallelism in hardware. Thus separate processors can format many pages of a large document at the same time, raising the throughput of the printer. Interpress and DDL have intrinsic page independence, while PostScript does not.

Page independence has another virtue: increased ease of performance for some operations of production printing. In particular, two-up (two page images side-by-side on the same sheet), two-sided, and signature printing all use the access to pages in an order convenient to the printer, which is not necessarily the sequential order in which the document is described. (Signature printing is the printing of whole sheets that are later folded and cut to create a sequence of pages in a book, magazine, or pamphlet. It specifically requires access to pages out of sequential order—see Fig. 6.14.)

In fairness to PostScript, note that page independence is possible in that language by software convention. Some universal demarcation between pages is required, allowing the printer to pick out pages from a file to be printed in the order required, without rasterizing the whole file first.

A further interesting difference among PDLs lies in the intentional or extensional expression of documents. Since PDLs are programming languages, particular systems can operate at various points along the intentional-extensional spectrum if programmed differently. Both Interpress and PostScript are predominantly extensional in philosophy. A sequence of operations creates graphic objects or effects until a page is complete, without any explicit representation of the purpose or role of the results in the overall document.

DDL's claim to distinction, in contrast, is that it allows document layout to be expressed independent of content. This is an intentional form: The same content can be printed in different ways as a result of changes in a document-style specification.

What typographic properties do page description languages have? An important issue is the extent to which they can support WYSIWYG output, matching screen images with printed output, and matching printed output produced with different printers.

First it must be said that this is the *raison d'être* of PDLs, and all do a credible but not perfect job. How do they fall short of their goal?

Because of isomorphic scaling, all current PDLs degrade very large or very small type. Outlines are scaled linearly, rather than being adjusted in shape, as described in Chapter 2. Of course, this has nothing to do with the expression of documents in the PDL, but is rather a practical matter related to implementation. In theory, by using more than one outline, the languages do permit nonlinear variations with size. For example, three outlines of a given face and variations might be used: for sizes of 8 points or smaller, for those between 8 and 16 points, and for those larger than 16 points. In practice, however, because additional outlines and additional programming are needed, this is not done.

A similar typographic issue for PDLs is their ability to preserve the quality of letters when rounding off dimensions and positions during rasterization. In general, screen and print resolutions are not multiples of each other. The very device independence of PDLs ensures that scaling will result in parts of letters not of integral size.

The problem is illustrated in Fig. 6.15. Choosing the nearest pixel

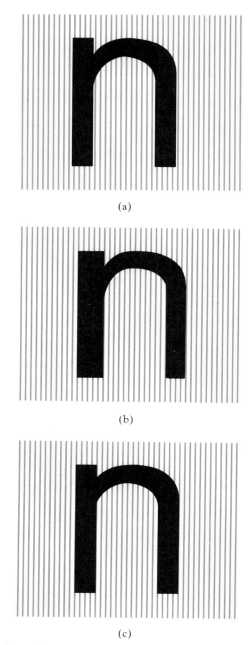

(a)

(b)

(c)

FIGURE 6.15 Rounding errors can result in uneven stroke widths when out-lines are scaled. In (a), the scaled letters are shown on the resolution grid. If merely rounded, the result is (b). Using information about the stem widths and other properties of the font results in image (c), which is more sensitive to the design and far more uniform.

A modern modem.
A bum can burn yarns.

FIGURE 6.16   Distributing rounding error across lines results in occasional tight letter spaces, as shown here. Certain letter combinations are affected more severely than others, as illustrated by the 'rn' sequence shown here.

boundary after scaling outlines causes differences of ± 1 pixel in stem width, counter size, and interletter space. For example, a typical letter may have a nominal six-pixel-wide stem at 600 dpi. If some stems are rounded to five pixels, and others to seven, the unevenness will be quite apparent in the result. This amounts to a 29% difference in stroke width, making an otherwise good typeface look very bad.

To solve this problem, the PDL implementation must carefully adjust the stroke and space values to keep these dimensions consistent at any given size and resolution, and across the width of the line. This means that at any size requested, the PDL decides the correct integral number of pixels to use for strokes and spaces within each letter in order to create harmony across the font. Thus proper scaling involves nonlinear adjustment of feature dimensions in the resulting letterforms [Hersch 1987].

Finally, in laying out whole lines, some unevenness of spacing can still result from accumulated error across a whole line. It is possible to place symbols only at integral positions (on a laser printer, at least). Thus it is impossible to distribute the rounding error for positioning letters across a whole line. Frequently a one-pixel error must be made between adjacent letters or words. If this error is placed between letters, in certain cases it will be quite noticeable (see Fig. 6.16). The best place for these errors is thus between words, whenever possible.

Chapter Summary

With the What You See Is What You Get or wysiwyg approach, the user sees a screen image that is a facsimile of the printed version of the document. Attaining an exact match between screen and paper is impossible, and is limited by a number of problems.

Differences in resolution result in trade-offs between matching appearance and achieving the best quality with each resolution. Differences in fonts are inevitable if quality is maintained for each device. Also, spacing is affected by differences in resolution. Letters cannot be spaced as tightly and evenly at low resolution as at higher resolution. Without care, differences in line and page breaks can appear between versions.

Because users may view a screen at greater distance than they read paper, text that is the right size for a given purpose on the screen may look much too large when printed on paper. Similarly, margins, often not shown on screens, are expected on paper. This also gives rise to differing expectations.

Because of these problems, what the user sees on the screen cannot match the result on paper. Nor should this be an absolute goal, because rigid adherence to WYSIWYG results in less than optimal quality in one or both presentations. An alternative standard is to avoid user surprises (WYGINS), which can be achieved by making differences in appearance be part of the user's understanding of how the system works, and by employing mechanisms such as the ability to show a proof of printer output.

Relatively few typefaces and variations are required for general office publishing and printing. A generic approach, amenable to intentional specification, provides a single family of typefaces. Included are subfamilies of serifed, sans serif, and monospaced fonts and variations, as well as symbol fonts. A decorative face is a necessary addition because offices often print fancy material such as invitations.

Communicating documents between systems can surprise users because different systems may handle the same document quite differently. Formatters such as T$_E$X, which provide their own communication format, avoid some of the incompatibility problems.

Another class of interchange format is page description languages or PDLs. They are used primarily to communicate documents for printing. Three PDLs in common use are DDL, Interpress, and PostScript. They differ in emphasis, but all are raster-oriented programming languages for transmitting and expressing the contents of documents, both graphics and text.

_7

Automatic Layout

What a crop of rubbish is daily printed by the possible regrouping of only 25 letters.

— Wilhelm Junk

W HEN someone sits down to create and typeset a document, he or she must determine how the document will look, page by page, and must also decide how to express the desired look to the typesetting system. Part of the problem of laying out pages is handled automatically by the system, and part is the user's responsibility.

Page makeup, also called *pagination,* is laying out the parts of a large document into pages. Pagination is complicated by the number of constraints and goals that must be satisfied. Human interface for typesetting and printing also comes under the heading of automatic layout; it is the human interface that the user sees and manipulates to achieve (or not achieve) the desired effect. Human-interface designers must find compromises between the complexity of typesetting and the user's need to understand the system and be in control.

Consider the simplest layout problem, that of paginating a book containing only text, but no figures, charts, or other nontextual items. What's hard about that? Actually, it is not very hard, and can be approached by applying the same methods used to break paragraphs, but on a page-by-page basis. Nonetheless, many considerations affect the quality of the result.

First, the pages must match in depth when the document is printed two sided; the vertical extent on the page must match on left and right pages for each opening (pair of facing pages). If the entire document were one long paragraph with lines of equal depth, this would be easy.

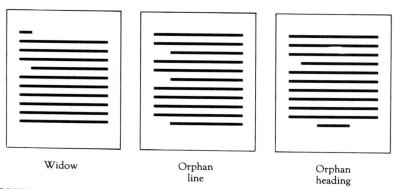

FIGURE 7.1   Widows and orphans resulting from improper pagination.

Simply take the total number of lines of text and allocate them equally among the pages. The last page, of course, might be an odd length, but that is acceptable. However, most documents have many paragraphs and sections, frequently with lines of varying depth. This results in additional constraints, even on an all-text book such as a novel. In particular, *widows* and *orphans* must be avoided. A widow is an isolated line set at the top of a new page, the last line of the paragraph on the previous page. An orphan is a single line left alone at the bottom of a page. Orphans can be the first line of a new paragraph, or a title or header line associated with the next paragraph. Widows and orphans do not look good, a valid consideration in typesetting, and they can confuse the eye in reading because they do not necessarily give the reader enough information to parse the page correctly. Figure 7.1 shows these situations.

It is also bad form to hyphenate a word across a page break. Looking ahead to the facing page or turning a page interrupts the flow of reading. A hyphenation may not seem very disruptive under these circumstances, but the interruption may make it harder to glean the sense of the hyphenated word and the sentence in which it occurs. The result is that the reader may have to return to the first part of the sentence, on the previous page, which otherwise would not have been necessary. Although returning to a previous word or line is fairly common in reading, a hyphenated word at the end of a page makes returning to the previous page more likely.

Therefore text cannot be divided into pages blindly. Some pages must be adjusted to prevent unacceptable situations. Since facing pages must match, it is necessary to look ahead a bit, at least to the next page. Then a line or two can be moved ahead of a problem area to avoid a widow or orphan.

In fact, pagination can interact usefully with paragraph breaking. The badness function used to break paragraphs in TEX, for example, includes a penalty proportional to the number of lines in the paragraph. This creates a bias in favor of shorter, tighter paragraphs. Similarly, a large penalty for hyphenating a word across a page break can be used to minimize such occurrences. Penalties for widows and orphans can be brought to bear when breaking the paragraphs that would otherwise contain them. Thus paragraph breaking and pagination can be combined, with the goal of improving the layout of the entire document.

In a certain sense, line breaking is harder than page breaking. The format of a document normally prescribes a specific line length. The formatter has no choice in the matter, and has only one degree of freedom, the amount of text placed on each line. In contrast, page breaking usually has another degree of freedom because the depth of the page can be adjusted somewhat from page to page to avoid widows and similar problems. The requirement that facing pages in a book must match in depth is thus a weaker constraint than is a fixed line length, leaving more room to maneuver when pages are typeset.

One obvious solution to the equal-depth-of-facing-pages problem is to adjust the space between paragraphs or lines. However, altering leading between lines, by even a small amount, is more noticeable and may adversely affect the look, feel, and legibility of the text. This should generally be avoided, even though great typographers do it when necessary, as long as the work remains consistent with their quality goals. Consider this report from the typographer Bruce Rogers [1979:160]:

> Unfortunately the preceding Book [of Homer's *Odyssey*] ended with only a few lines on the left-hand page, leaving the opposite a full blank. So with the addition of thin cards we reduced the lines per page from thirty-one to thirty throughout Book XXI, thereby gaining enough lines to fill the short page and carry over six lines to the blank page preceding Book XXII. I have never heard of anyone's noticing this discrepancy in Book XXI. It was only one of the tricks of the trade, resorted to by many early printers.

Nonetheless, programs must make such changes very conservatively. Whatever adjustments the formatter makes must be consistent across the whole document, or at least between facing pages. For example, differences in interline spacing from page to page would be very noticeable. It is also good typesetting practice to match the text baselines on facing pages, since the juxtaposition of facing pages invites comparison.

A difficulty arises with another constraint that sometimes applies to book work. Because print can show through the paper from the other side, it is often a requirement of the book design that lines *back up*— that they match in vertical position on the opposite sides of each sheet. This means that if interline or interparagraph spaces are adjusted, the adjustments must be made for whole chapters, or perhaps for the whole book, when backing up of lines is specified.

Paginating Complex Documents

Now consider a more realistic, complex document. It may include the following:

- Footnotes;
- Marginal notes or illustrations;
- Multiple columns;
- Figures;
- Illustrations;
- Tables;
- Equations, formulas, or other formal notation;
- Cross-references;
- Bibliographic references.

Each element poses its own problems and constraints on the pagination of the whole document. Footnotes quickly create a dilemma for a simple-minded formatting program. It is required that the footnote begin on the page on which the footnote mark appears.

Imagine a page on which the footnote mark would appear within the last couple of lines. If the text containing the mark were added to the page, no room would be left for the footnote, but if the lines were moved to the next page, the page would be left short. This problem provides another argument for more-global optimization. Note that some book designs allow footnotes to be continued on the next page, though there is a bias against continuing them *overleaf* when the next page is the left-hand page of a new opening (the page would have to be turned for the rest of the footnote to be read).

Marginal notes and illustrations behave much like footnotes. More common in the days of hand typesetting, they are nonetheless hard to set with metal type. The use of the Linotype machine for most book work early in this century created an additional bias against marginal notes because usually they could not be set with the machine. Although marginal notes are easier to place on pages than footnotes because they do not cause lines of text to be displaced, they are subject to the same problems of carryover onto subsequent pages. Normally a marginal note starts at the vertical position of the line to which it refers, and continues down the column. Although there is a bias against continuing marginalia on subsequent pages, a particular document design could allow it. Fortunately these notes are usually short, identifying the subject of a paragraph, or making a short comment that is more appropriate in close proximity than at the bottom of the page or the end of the section.

Some document designs specify multiple columns. Short lines permit greater density of information and greater economy, consistent with good legibility. This works because smaller type and less leading are appropriate in the shorter lines (see Chapter 5). Multicolumn work is common in newspapers, magazines, and newsletters, and is often found in large-format books. In pagination, columns can be treated much like pages, except that all the columns visible at one time—such as a newspaper page or magazine opening—usually must match in depth.

Figures, illustrations, and tables—*floating objects* that must be positioned with the running text at appropriate places—create pagination problems. These objects can be said to float over the text because the formatter is free to place them in various relations to the text and each other, though order must be preserved. The difficulties arise from the need to look at figures in relation to passages in the text. Frequently the reader encounters a reference to a figure and then immediately tries to find it. Life is much easier if the referenced object is close at hand, on the same page or the facing one.

In traditional typesetting, figures, tables, cuts (photographs or line drawings), and other matter not part of the main body of text are assembled in separate galleys (type trays). When it is time for page makeup, the printer merges the separate sequences of items into a sequence of pages. Obviously this requires a substantial amount of skill, which may be hard to duplicate with a program.

The following constraints apply to the placement of figures, illustrations, and tables:

- Each should appear on the same opening as its first reference.
- None should create an on-page widow or orphan, that is, should not break up a paragraph to leave a single line on either side of a figure or illustration.
- Sequence must be maintained. The first referenced item should appear first within the paginated document.
- A footnote or marginal note that refers to a figure should appear on the same page as the referenced object.
- Related figures, those the reader must compare, should be placed on the same or facing pages.

Many formatters do attempt to place figures to create the minimum disruption of text and to equalize page length. One approach is to allow the user to specify preferences and constraints on the placement of figures, tables, and other objects. For example, the user specifies that an object must appear in one of the following positions:

- Exactly where it appears in the sequence of text, as an in-line figure or display;
- At the top of a page;
- At the bottom of a page;
- On a page reserved for figures;
- Anywhere on a page.

This provides a useful amount of information that the formatter can use to optimize pagination. However, additional information can also be useful. For example: Must certain figures be compared? Must certain items not appear on the same page or opening (e.g., quiz answers)?

Meeting all the constraints of pagination, a computationally difficult problem, is an area of current research [Plass 1981].

Another pagination problem is splitting complicated objects across pages. This difficulty is common in typesetting mathematical material when a formula or equation is longer than one line. Similar difficulties befall the formatter in trying to split a table between pages. Sequences of lines of mathematical notation, called *displayed formulas,* present similar problems. The same is true of any kind of formal notation, such as that of music, dance, and other disciplines. The situations that arise with complex notations, formulas, and tables all require that the meaning of the displayed material be understood. Chaundy, Barrett, and Batey [1954:37] describe the situation this way:

> When a formula is too long for the page-width and has to be broken into successive lines...it should be broken, if possible, at the end of a natural 'phrase'; if, for example, it is a much-bracketed formula, it should be broken at the end of one of the major brackets and not at an inner symbol. This natural phrasing (as in music or speech) makes for intelligibility between writer and reader and should not be left to the compositor. An author, when he finds himself writing a longish formula, should indicate a con-venient point of fracture in case of need.

That the meaning of notation is relevant to breaking it across lines or pages is demonstrated by the following example. When a formula of the form

$$\{\ldots\} + \{\ldots\}$$

is split across lines or pages, it is usual to repeat the operator:

$$\{\ldots\} +$$
$$+ \{\ldots\}.$$

Similarly, the formula

$$(\ldots)(\ldots),$$

which includes an implied multiplication, when split across pages would be written out as

$$(\ldots) \times$$
$$\times (\ldots).$$

These conventions require additional symbols to be used in the course of breaking formulas. Typesetting such material is not merely a matter of positioning a supplied list of symbols—there must be contex-tual adjustments.

A related problem is typesetting cross-references, bibliographic ref-erences, and the like. These items vary in length, depending on the placement or content of the referenced items. For example, if a referenced page falls on page 99, a word added to page 1 could move the referenced item to page 100. The number 100 takes up more space than the number 99, forcing the line and page breaks for the text containing the reference to be reconsidered. Some formatters deal with this problem with a simplifying restriction—for example, that all such references must be predeclared or of constant length. In general, multiple passes over the document specification are required to process references. When optimizing page breaks, it may be necessary to recompute references for each set of breaks considered, since a particular choice of breaks could change the value of a reference to a subsequent item, and thus its width. Obviously this activity can be computationally expensive.

References are more than a matter of syntactic rules. Where to break a notation still requires human judgment. An interesting research area would be development of an expert system that understands enough of the meaning of a notational system to perform this kind of page break.

Until such artificial intelligence programs are developed and incorporated into formatters, what should be done? The germ of the answer is in the quotation from Chaundy, Barrett, and Batey. It is appropriate that the user of a typesetting system, if he or she is the author, provide the breaking information. This communication is more comfortable when interactive—an analogy to communication between an author and a human typesetter. The author and the system have a conversation to solve page-breaking problems.

Automatic Pagination

What resources, or degrees of freedom, can a program (or person) work with to achieve the best pagination of a document? One obvious variable is the position of figures in relation to the text. The depth of individual pages is another—the document style must establish minimum and maximum depths. Within these bounds, it is necessary only that facing pages match.

Another resource is the amount of white space around figures. Again within the bounds established by the document style, adjustments can free a little white space or use a little, as needed. As noted previously, adjusting interline or interparagraph spacing is usually not acceptable, but is sometimes done.

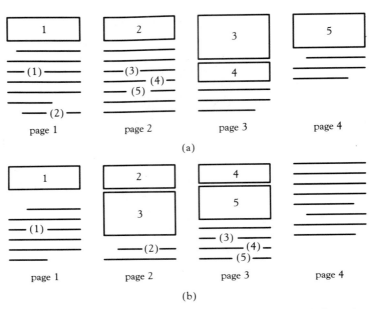

FIGURE 7.2 Two ways to paginate a small book [Plass 1981]. Page 1 is a right-hand page; pages 2 and 3 constitute an opening and are visible together; and page 4 is a left-hand page. In (a) there are two overleaf figure references. In (b) there are none. (Courtesy of Michael Plass.)

Some resources are best kept under human control. Generally, the size of type, the tightness with which it is set, the width of lines, the order of figures, and the content of the text are all matters about which a human typesetter will consult the author or book designer. Similarly, typesetting programs should be circumspect about making changes in these areas in order to solve pagination problems.

Plass [1981:2–3] gives a nice example of the alternatives in paginating a small book. Even as small a book as the one in his four-page example presents difficult choices for illustration placement. Figure 7.2 shows two ways to lay out the book. The numbers in parentheses are references to illustrations. In the first approach (Fig. 7.2a), illustrations 2 and 5 are overleaf from their references. References to illustrations 3 and 4 are within the same opening, which is fine. The second pagination (Fig. 7.2b) is noticeably better, with all references appearing within view of their target illustrations.

How can a program achieve good results, satisfying the many con-straints that apply to the various parts of a complex document? Plass's approach uses badness functions, in the same way that TEX uses a badness function to break lines. These numeric penalties for various arrangements of the pages, considered across a whole document or section such as a chapter, capture the relative undesirability of faults.

The multiple-galley approach used by human printers provides a convenient conceptual structure for paginating. Items in the figure and table galleys are sorted in the order of their first reference in the text. Items are taken as needed from the galleys, creating provisional paginated documents to which the badness functions are applied. Alternatives that result in large penalties are discarded, with no need to evaluate similar possibilities. By pruning the search space in this way, relatively few cases need be considered.

Complex situations, such as figure references within captions, can be hard to handle with the galley scheme. Such situations represent constraints on the relative placement of figures or tables. Such con-straints can certainly be accommodated by badness functions for ref-erences, but it may be simpler to discover the required relationship between related figures, and to associate penalties with failure to meet them.

Plass describes ways to find the unequivocally best pagination, which makes the problem much harder. He uses dynamic programming to search the space of possible paginations to find the best one, without explicitly considering most of the bad ones. But the best pagination is not necessarily required. By analogy to computers playing chess, a solution is acceptable if it meets the needs of the system user—that is, it plays a good game. A document formatter can legitimately miss the very best solution if it finds an acceptable solution in a reasonable time. To the extent that the badness numbers reflect what matters to the human user of the document, optimizing their sum will produce an acceptable document.

There are two difficulties with this general approach to pagination. First, the amount of computation needed to search the set of possible paginations grows exponentially with document size. For large docu-ments, the amount of computation can be far more than practicable with current hardware. In fact, as Plass has shown, many choices of badness functions produce intractable search problems, of the type known in computation theory as NP-complete. Thus compromises in searching for optimum solutions are necessary.

As with other human activities involving judgment, people are able to make good choices in a modest amount of time, often without explicitly searching alternatives. For example, an architect can produce several building designs that meet most of the constraints on the problem. A chess player can make good moves without explicitly considering the millions of possibilities that combinatorial programs seem doomed to check. We do not yet know how to make computers perform these essentially perceptual and cognitive acts.

The second difficulty is that numerical badness functions do not completely capture the concerns of a human author, book designer, or printer. When people paginate, they find creative solutions. For example, in a particular case it may be acceptable to make an overleaf figure reference because of the author's intent. It may be acceptable to reduce or enlarge a particular figure because of its role in the document. These creative solutions amount to changes in the document design that fulfill a larger purpose. Current technology is very far from being able to operate in this realm.

Taxonomy of Layout Programs

Automatic layout programs can be categorized in three ways: They are either interactive or batch; they format text automatically, in real time, as changes are made, or only on demand; and they require the user to describe the desired output either intentionally or extensionally. Each of these dimensions warrants discussion.

While most of the desktop, personal-computer world operates in an interactive mode, many programs that run on mainframes are batch-like. These programs accept an input file, process it in some way, and produce an output or an output file. Until recently, the vast majority of formatting programs fit this mold. Some form of editor, usually a so-called screen editor, is used to prepare the input file, which is really a computer program for generating the desired document. In addition to the text of the document, numerous commands are present that specify spacing, indentation, headings, and other formatting information. The style of document specification that includes instructions about formatting within the source file is called a *markup language*. Markup languages can be thought of as an analogy to an author's manuscript, marked up in colored pencil by a human editor with instructions to a human typesetter.

In contrast, interactive formatters allow formatting information to be specified directly by commands, menus, or direct manipulation (for example, pointing and dragging with a mouse). Interactive formatters are not programming interfaces.

Actual formatting of text may take place as changes are made, or only on request. Formatting as changes are made must be done in real time, that is, fast enough to keep up with the user. This does not mean instantly, but rather fast enough for the user to see what he or she is doing and avoid confusion. Obviously a mixture of these options is possible; some parts of the formatting, such as line breaking, may be updated in real time, and other parts, such as page breaking and figure placement, only on demand.

The final dimension, extensional versus intentional specification, expresses the degree to which a document's typographic style is separated from the specification of its details. An extensional specification of a quotation, say, could indicate that the left and right margins are to be moved in, and the spacing and typeface changed to set off the quote. An intentional specification declares that the text is a quotation of a certain type such as verse, leaving the detailed look to be determined by the document definition or other declared style. The corresponding distinction in programming languages is between *procedural* and *declarative* languages, respectively. These latter terms are used widely to describe formatters.

Figure 7.3 shows intentional and extensional specifications that result in the same output. This dimension is continuous—systems can be compared in terms of the degree to which their specifications are intentional or extensional. Figure 7.4 shows a rough categorization of several formatting systems based upon this taxonomy. Traditional programs such as RUNOFF, NROFF, TROFF, and GML [Furura, Scofield, and Shaw 1982] can be described as batch, demand, extensional formatters. These formatters each provide the basis for a more intentional system by including macros, an idea imported from programming languages. Macros are routines that a user or programmer can define and invoke within a document specification. They are a shorthand for a collection of extensional changes, and can be used to create an inten-

```
itself; for 35 per cent, increase it one-eighth itself, etc.
Hence, to mark an article at any per cent profit, we have the
following
.skip 1 .small caps .center
General Rule
.no small caps .left margin +.25 .right margin -.25 .italic
.rag right
First find 20 percent profit, by removing the decimal point one
place to the left on the price the articles cost a dozen; then, as
20 per cent profit is 120 per cent, add to or subtract from this
amount the fractional part that the required percent added to 100
is more or less than 120.
.left margin -.25 .right margin +.25 .roman .justified .skip 1
Merchants, in marking goods, generally take a per cent that is an
aliquot part of
```

. . .

(a)

. . .

```
itself; for 35 per cent, increase it one-eighth itself, etc.
Hence, to mark an article at any per cent profit, we have the
following
.begin{general rule}
First find 20 percent profit, by removing the decimal point one
place to the left on the price the articles cost a dozen; then, as
20 per cent profit is 120 per cent, add to or subtract from this
amount the fractional part that the required percent added to 100
is more or less than 120.
.end{general rule}
Merchants, in marking goods, generally take a per cent that is an
aliquot part of
```

. . .

(b)

. . .

itself; for 35 per cent, increase it one-eighth itself etc. Hence, to mark an article at any per cent profit we have the following

GENERAL RULE

First find 20 percent profit, by removing the decimal point one place to the left on the price the articles cost a dozen; then, as 20 per cent profit is 120 per cent, add to or subtract from this amount the fractional part that the required percent added to 100 is more or less than 120.

Merchants, in marking goods, generally take a per cent that is an aliquot part of

. . .

(c)

FIGURE 7.3 Extensional (a) and intentional (b) specifications resulting in the same formatted output (c).

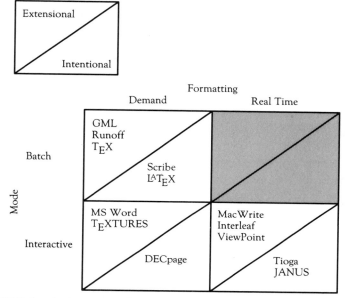

FIGURE 7.4 A taxonomy of automatic text-layout programs.

tional environment that implements a document style. Preprocessors such as EQN, which translates formulas for input to NROFF and TROFF, have a similar intentional effect.

Screen-oriented preparation systems that attempt to continuously display the formatted document as it will appear on paper are classified as interactive and real time. Most existing commercial programs in this category are extensional in character, but intentional programs are possible. Other formatters, because of their batch origins or their complexity, operate in an interactive demand mode. Most current interactive systems are extensional, but interactive, real-time, intentional systems are also possible—research systems such as Tioga [Paxton 1983] at Xerox and JANUS at IBM [Chamberlin *et al.* 1981] are of this type. Finally, batch and real-time formatting do not make much sense in combination, so this quadrant of Fig. 7.4 is vacant.

The use of intentional information to specify documents was materially developed and extended in Scribe, a formatter developed at Carnegie-Mellon University [Reid 1980]. Scribe successfully separates the definition of a document type from its content. For example, a

Scribe programmer can define a corporate-report document style. Users of this document type need only reference it, and then describe their document in terms of the kinds of objects contained in the definition. Later systems such as LATEX have adopted similar structures.[1]

This scheme has many virtues. It allows document design to be separated from document creation. While this is not always a goal, it is useful when there is a standard to be followed, as in the creation of a book or magazine by a group of people or in the establishment of a corporate look for letters and reports. When different people are responsible for the content and design of a document—for example, a book written by one person and designed by another—the separation is very practical. Separation is also valuable when communicating across systems with different output devices; the style descriptions can be adjusted to accommodate the differences at the two ends.

There are only a few intentional interactive formatters, and it is interesting to speculate on the future of this kind of tool. One way to achieve intentional interactive formatting is to present both an intentional language and the resulting formatted document in two separate windows. This is the approach taken by JANUS [Chamberlin *et al.* 1981], Etude [Hammer *et al.* 1981], and TEXTURES [Kellerman and Smith 1987]. In each of these systems, the user interacts with an intentional form of the document and sees the typeset result at the same time. The basic concept is that of two different conceptual views of the document: as specified and as realized when typeset.

None of these systems allows editing changes in the typeset output to be reflected in the intentional form of the document. In other words, the transformation is unidirectional. While it is possible to have multiple editable representations of a document, with changes in one representation reflected in one or more of the others, this remains an area for research.

In another possible approach to intentional interactive typesetting, the formatted, typeset document would be shown on the screen, and access to intentional information would be provided by some indirect mechanism. The text could be altered directly, and intentional information could be altered when called up and made visible. This is the basic approach taken by the Bravo editor [Lampson 1978] and the

---

[1] LATEX is in fact a macro package that runs atop TEX. From the user's viewpoint, it is an intentional system.

Xerox product based on it called VP: Document Editor [Xerox 1985]. In these editors, objects such as words, sentences, and paragraphs have *property sheets*—interactive windows, normally hidden, that contain formatting information for each object. For example, the fact that a paragraph is to be double spaced is recorded on the paragraph's property sheet. Interleaf [Morris 1986], a similar product, has style sheets that serve the same purpose.

User Interfaces for Typesetting Systems

In order to operate, typesetting systems must of course have user interfaces. Most desktop-publishing systems in particular are intended primarily for nonspecialists, and their success depends on their quality in terms of human factors. Some aspects of interface design arise directly from typographical issues.[2]

The traditional relationship of an author to a typeset work like a book is as provider of the content—the text, illustrations, pictures, and other components that are assembled to form the finished work. However, the author does not supply those pieces in finished form. The text is a typed (originally handwritten) manuscript to be edited; figures are sketches for an artist to work from; and so on. Desktop-publishing systems are changing this relationship. Depending on the goals of a particular author and the capabilities of the system used, the author may also take on the roles of editor, book designer, and graphic artist. Since few authors are also skilled designers, editors, and artists, it falls to the system to help in these areas.

Desktop-publishing systems are easiest to use when they present a coherent external behavior, called an *external myth*, from which the user can build a conceptual model of how the system works. Many different external myths are possible. Whether the system designer chooses a good external myth depends on a knowledge of users and how they think about their work, and on skill in expressing system behavior comprehensibly and consistently. It also depends on the intended relationship between author and system—how much of the production process the author is responsible for.

Interactive, real-time systems usually opt for a *document model* (also

---

[2] For a discussion of user-interface design methodology, see [Rubinstein and Hersh 1984:12–58].

called a desktop model) in which the user is presented with a screen representation of the document he or she is creating as it will appear when printed. In other words, WYSIWYG is a human-interface design in the sense that it specifies a particular external myth. In conjunction with a direct-manipulation style of interaction, a document model can be very compelling and readily understood.

The ability to perform sophisticated typographical operations within a system conflicts with the conceptual simplicity offered by the WYSIWYG model. The more information is hidden from view in the document—the style of headers, where page numbers go, how to place figures, and so forth—the greater the conceptual complexity imposed on the user. Less and less of the information that controls the document is directly accessible. What you see becomes less and less what you have, even if it is what you get.

As they become more sophisticated and capable, typesetting systems run the risk of becoming far too complicated conceptually. From the user's viewpoint, is is not the number of features included in a particular system that determines its complexity, but rather the number of things the user must know and understand to be able to use these features. If a simple understanding is possible, one that allows predicting and inventing correct ways to accomplish desired goals, the system will be learnable, convenient, and easy to use.

Intentional systems represent a useful trade-off between power and user-specified detail. Users are limited by the available set of document designs unless they are willing to specify more designs themselves. Within the range of supplied designs, a lot can be expressed with very little effort on the user's part. Scribe and other systems make the further compromise of allowing modest modifications to the intentional specifications. For example, if the user of the system of Fig. 7.3 wanted the "General Rule" insert to be justified, rather than the standard ragged right, the modification could be inserted in the *begin* statement, perhaps as

```
.begin{general rule, justified}
```

Two basic questions must be answered before the user interface of a desktop-publishing system can be designed: What will the system be able to do, and how will the user express these capabilities? The answer to the first question depends on the goals of the system; to the second, on the skill, taste, and energy of the interface designer.

Intentional systems make strong statements about the degrees of freedom given users. Making such statements is good design because they specify what the system is and is not, what it will do and will not do. The user need not decide what the system is or how it should behave. Whatever style of interface the system designer creates, if the system is to be coherent and simple, choices of appropriate degrees of freedom for users must be made. Depending on the purpose of the system and the needs and abilities of its users, more or less freedom is appropriate in various categories—matters of document style like page layout, and matters of editing such as operation syntax. The point is that these are the typographically relevant dimensions along which system designers must choose when designing typesetting systems.

It is *not* good design to provide every thinkably useful feature in a typesetting system, even if it is intended for professional graphic artists, book designers, or printers. Unnecessary facilities introduce unnecessary complexity, and extra complexity also results in additional development time and cost. More important to potential users, complexity makes systems harder to learn and use.

An important overall issue in designing a formatting system is *scoping*. Whether the system operates intentionally or extensionally, there is the choice of whether contexts—the collection of settings in force at a particular place in the document—can be nested or remembered in some way. If not, not only must the user make each change in parameters, but also must restore them to their previous values when returning to the previous context. The ability to declare ranges within the document (corresponding to blocks within a programming language), in which declared parameter values temporarily replace those in the surrounding contexts, is most valuable. Scoping of this type avoids many user errors.

In a batch-oriented formatting system, scoping can be textual, similar to the programming language ALGOL. *Begin* and *end* instructions can establish the scopes, or the scopes can be delimited by intentional units such as sections. In interactive systems, the same scoping effect can be achieved by associating parameters with objects such as paragraphs, figures, and sections. This approach is familiar to users of object-oriented programming languages, in which data and instructions are combined within programming entities—*objects*—that have behavior. In other words, natural units within a document, such as paragraphs and sections, can record the invisible, intentional properties that they embody.

Document Style

Good typographic quality in typeset material demands that the document have a consistent overall style—a design for its form that is used throughout. For simple, short, or informal documents, a publishing system need supply little in support of style. Systems for general use that are intended to create more sophisticated documents, however, have the responsibility to support style. Intentional formatters can play this role.

Document-style specifications come from several sources. Most publishers have one or more house styles. Many corporations have established styles for their reports and other publications. A particular document may have a custom design, created by a designer or the author. Alternatively, some systems, DECpage, Scribe, and LaTeX among them, provide a few basic document styles with the formatter itself.

There are several ways in which formatters can help institute document style in regard to page layout, as discussed in Chapter 5. Providing a grid as a basis for a document design helps. In the context of this grid, the user creates a specific layout design. The system should treat this design as a unit, allowing it to be named, reused, and modified. Another useful facility is a mechanism for supplying standard material on each page, such as page numbers and running heads. Similarly, when made the accounting responsibility of the formatter, the style of document elements such as paragraphs, lists, inserts, and section headings is controlled and kept uniform.

It is considerably harder to achieve uniform style when preparing tables, figures, and illustrations. In current publishing practice, most illustrative material is prepared by hand and pasted up to create a master copy of the document for printing. Responsibility for consistency of illustrations, and for conformity to the overall document design, rests with editors and illustrators. Automatic formatting of graphics from descriptions provided by users offers the possibility of a unified working environment that makes the preparation of tables, figures, and diagrams easier [Kernighan 1981; Mackinlay 1986]. Publishing systems that prepare and include graphic materials in compound documents must provide for stylistic requirements [Beach 1985].

One issue is the matching of text style in the body of a work to text that appears in tables, figures, and illustrations. If these elements are prepared with different tools, variations in font, size, and formatting must be avoided. This argues either for suites of coordinated preparation programs that reference the same style information, or for integrated systems in which one document style can be applied to all parts of the document.

Graphical problems also arise. In illustrations and figures, many components must be coordinated across the document, and thus are part of the document style. Included are:

- Line widths;
- Line style (solid, dotted, and so on);
- Size and shape of boxes and other material in diagrams;
- Tick marks and legends on graph axes;
- Shading and the use of color;
- Emphasis (how attention is called to an item).

When some artwork is to be pasted into an otherwise electronically produced document, matching style is difficult. The system and the illustrator must work to the same specifications. Further, in traditional pasteup, illustrations are usually produced oversize and reduced to increase reproduction quality. Different amounts of reduction play havoc with line widths and type sizes, resulting in a poor match to document style. Illustrations produced with machine aid must also avoid this problem, either by generating all artwork at the same scale or by scaling lines and text appropriately. This latter approach requires that the system know what degree of reduction will be used in reproducing graphical output.

The ideal situation, of course, is to produce all illustrations in an integrated way, as part of one compound document. However, the need will always exist to incorporate external materials into a compound document.

Editing

Interactive systems must provide some facility for editing. More and more editing is integrated with formatting in publishing systems, within the confines of a single user interface. There is a substantial literature on interactive editors.[3]

---

[3] For a review, see [Meyrowitz and van Dam 1982].

At a minimum, interactive editors must deal with the following issues:

* Modes;
* Operation syntax;
* Selection;
* Feedback and attributes;
* Interaction style;
* Operations;
* Windows.

Modes   Modes exist in a user interface when the same action by the user has different meanings, depending on the state or history of the interaction. Two examples of modes are distinctions between input and command states (as in the VI editor of the UNIX system), and between overstriking entered text or inserting it. Some believe that *modeless* interfaces in editors are superior because users need not remember the current state of the interface, nor must they learn how to make transitions between states. It is enormously difficult, however, to completely avoid states in interfaces.

Operation Syntax   Operations are performed on some portion of the document. The syntax specifies how the operation and document portions are specified. In *postfix* syntax, the user first specifies an object to be operated on. Then the operation (the '-fix' in postfix) is applied to the object. The reverse is true in *prefix:* The user selects an operation, and then selects the operand or operands to which it will be applied.

In general, postfix syntax is associated with modeless interfaces, or at least with those having few modes. Conversely, prefix editors have many modes—at least one for each operation. Many modes are necessary because the advance specification of an operation in a prefix editor leaves the interface in a state of requiring one or more operands to be picked; to change the operation, some special action must be taken to escape from the waiting-for-operand mode. However, prefix editors work better when two or more operands must be selected, a somewhat awkward problem in postfix syntax.

Selection   The portion of the document to be operated on must be identified to the system. This action is called *selection*. In selection by pointing, an input device such as a mouse is used to indicate the location or extent of the portion desired. Alternatively, the part is described by its location or name. Finally, in implicit specification, the part is described by one of its properties, such as when a search is performed for a particular word.

Feedback and Attributes   Parts of a document must be distinguished on the screen independent of font, size, or other usual properties of objects. For example, when some text is selected, the editor must indicate which parts are selected, and which are not. Some systems do this by inverting the image—thus black-on-white text, when selected, appears white on black. Similarly, "invisible" items that do not actually print must have a distinctive appearance.

Interaction Style   There are three overall styles of interface: command, menu, and direct manipulation [Rubinstein and Hersh 1984:108–130]. These styles mix the way primary colors do; different combinations are possible.

In the command style of interface, users use some language (usually a textual one) to describe what to do. This is the traditional, familiar kind of user interface, known to all users of time-sharing systems. Commands have the virtue of allowing users to express a wide variety of actions with precision. The disadvantage of commands is that users must learn the command language and remember what it is possible to say, as well as how to say it.

Menu systems offer an explicit list of options. Much of the burden on the user's memory is relieved because a menu is self-prompting. The disadvantage of menu interfaces is that a system may require many menus and levels, with the result that users may lose track of the state of the interface. ("How did I get here?" "How do I get to such-and-such a menu?")

Finally, direct-manipulation systems substitute pointing and visual representations of objects in a system for part of the function that would otherwise be done less directly. An analogy to a physical situation is made, such as documents on a desk that the user can work with, thereby diminishing the need for many named operations.

These three styles are frequently blended within interfaces. In particular, most direct-manipulation interfaces also have menus and commands for specifying some operations and data.

Operations   The set of functions must be determined. Some functions are almost always required: insert, erase, move, copy, replace, change attribute (such as font and style), and undo a previous operation or operations.

Windows   More than one view of the document may be available. For example, the user may be able to look at two parts of a document simultaneously, which may be convenient when moving a section from one place to another. Or two distinct representations of the document may appear on the screen, as when both markup and typeset versions are presented. Similarly, style and other out-of-band information has a natural place in a window adjacent to the typeset version of a document.

Compound Documents   The editing of compound documents presents its own set of issues. If modeless operation is the goal, modes may creep into the design when objects of different types are dealt with. Consider a textual document with an embedded line drawing. To the extent that the same editing functions—select, erase, copy, and so on—apply to the line drawing, no special accommodation is needed. But different graphic entities must be handled with different operations. How do you create a rectangle with the common set of functions?

One approach is to insist on a common set of generic commands for only operations of broad utility, and carry out specialized operations via menus that adjust dynamically, depending on the characteristics of the object being edited. The virtue of this approach is the small number of functions that need be learned to do many operations; menus remind users of the more specialized ones.

If modes are used, each particular graphical type—text, line drawings, image, and so on—has its own set of functions. The user must realize what kind of object is being worked on at any one time.

The problem is compounded when an object of one kind is embedded in another. In the example shown in Fig. 7.5, illustrations are included in a larger text document. Each illustration is an editable compound object containing within itself a mixture of text, line art,

FIGURE 7.5 Graphical objects of different types, embedded within one another.

and graphics. Changing modes at each level, as the user edits various parts, is potentially confusing. Great care must be taken in designing the user interface to make the state of the interaction visible and available to the user in this situation.

A Catalog of Typesetting Features

Many features can be included in a typesetting or desktop-publishing system, but such a list can never be complete, since new ideas and greater degrees of control are always possible. As the field of digital typography matures, researchers and developers understand more and more about what printers and typographers do manually. When these functions are analyzed and understood, they will appear as new features and capabilities in typesetting systems.

Typeface Functions

Users need to distinguish among different portions of text. Is a choice of variation—roman, italic, bold, bold italic—sufficient for the users of the system? Or will they need to distinguish among more subtle styles and moods? Do users know typefaces by name, or can they better choose them by appearance or functional description? Are different sizes needed? If so, can they be specified by their function? Specifications of intention, such as footnote, quotation, or heading, will provide sufficient control for some applications, but be insufficient for others.

Specifications of typeface, variation, and size must have some identifiable scope. Does the user make these specifications for whole units of text, or on a section, paragraph, word, or letter basis? For example, can a single letter be specified to be in a different typeface, variation, or size from its neighbors?

Table 7.1 shows the features and operations that relate to typefaces.

Justification and Line Breaking

Justification is often associated closely with the design of a document. Thus intentional formatters will supply most justification information from the document-style specification supplied by the designer or user. Extensional systems provide justification control on an item-by-item basis.

Line breaking, on the other hand, is performed automatically in most systems, and is thus intentional. Only in exceptional cases will users explicitly describe alterations to line breaking—for example, when the breaking algorithm fails to produce an acceptable line or paragraph. Giving information about how to hyphenate words unknown to the system is a more comfortable (and more intentional) form of user input.

The system designer must answer a number of questions to arrive at a strategy for justification and line breaking. Does the document style specify how parts are justified, or is this under the user's control? Is

Feature	Description
Typeface	Typeface is chosen by name, description, function, or example. Descriptions can be analytic, for example: • Display or text; • Serif or sans serif; • Script or normal. • Monospaced or proportionally spaced; • Old style, transitional, or modern; Alternatively, they can be stylistic: • Formal or informal; • Old or modern; • Ornamental or plain text; • Dense (economical) or sparse (opulent).
Size	Size is chosen by measurement (points, inches, etc.), description (display, text, footnote, bibliography), or example.
Variation	Variations within the basic typeface are chosen. The following are possible: • Roman; • Italic (oblique); • Bold (various degrees possible); • Bold italic; • Condensed (various degrees); • Expanded (various degrees); • Caps and small caps. Variations outside the scope of traditional typographic practice may also be specified. Frequently these versions are created algorithmically, rather than by using special fonts. • Underlined; • Overlined; • Line through center; • Outline; • Drop shadow; • Reversed (white on black); • Slant right (oblique; pseudo-italic); • Slant left (used in advertising and Japanese).
Vertical placement	Indicate variations from the normal positioning of inline characters along the line of text: • Superscript; • Baseline; • Subscript.
Horizontal placement	Adjust horizontal placement of symbol or group of symbols. Relative positioning is used to adjust kerning or to set unusual symbols or logos, such as LaTeX. Absolute positioning is used for manual control of objects within a line, without the artificial necessity of padding with spaces or tabs.
Tracking	Adjustments may be made to the relative tightness of interletter and word spacing, in proportion to the normal spacing. This is useful for display work, and is sometimes used in place of condensed or expanded variations.
Overprinting	Allows symbols to overprinted, creating accented letters or other useful modifications to the standard character set.
Color	Select the chromatic color or gray level of the text or its background.
Special notation	Enables special placement rules for proper setting of mathematical formulas, music, or other formal notations.

TABLE 7.1 Typeface functions.

justification, when specified, indicated on a section, paragraph, or line basis? Can justification information in the document style be overridden? At what level of detail? Can justification be performed against a nonlinear shape, as when text must flow around an illustration? How is the continuation of text from one column to the next expressed? Can the user indicate preferences, or otherwise influence where lines are broken? Is a dialog initiated with the user when unacceptably loose or tight lines would be set? Can users set their own standards for loose and tight, or are these standards predefined?

Table 7.2 details the various considerations.

Pagination

Like line breaking, pagination is intrinsic to many typesetting systems, and thus intentional at least in part. The question remains, however, of the user's degree of control over pagination.

Pagination is especially hard to specify in systems in which the user cannot see the result in real time, or at least see it quickly on demand. The result of too little feedback is inaccurate expectations and repeated trials to get the desired result.

Pagination is complicated by relationships between the text and floating objects. When the system is automatically calculating the best location for floating objects, real-time display can be confusing. At the extreme, changing a single letter, say an 'i' to an 'm', could dramatically affect the location of a figure or table. This could be very surprising.

One way to minimize the surprise is to perform the highest level of optimization, including the placing of figures, on a demand basis. This approach meshes well with the substantial computational demands of performing the optimization, which is hard to do in real time.

Alternatively, separate windows can present figures, tables, footnotes, and so on in parallel with the text. This corresponds to the traditional method of preparing separate galleys for floating material. The system displays the relevant part of each galley as a function of the part of the document undergoing modification by the user. Previewing or final printing causes the separate streams to be merged.

Direct instructions that conflict with other rules, such as explicitly forced breaks, cannot be resolved algorithmically. Situations like this call for an interaction between system and user. See Table 7.3.

Feature	Description
Paragraph	Select the basic justification scheme for a block of justified text. Possibilities include: • Left justified, ragged right; • Right justified, ragged left; • Justified (left and right); • Centered; • Quad center (space in middle, around a marker). For information tabulated in each column of a table, it is also possible to specify these kinds of justification on a column basis.
Force line break	A line break is created at the specified point. When line breaking depends on ratings or demerits, a more general operation can encourage a break at a point or within a range.
Suppress line break	A line break is prevented within a specified scope. When line breaking depends on ratings or demerits, this operation can discourage a break at a point or within a range.
Last line in paragraph	The last line in a paragraph is a special case when justifying. When the line is nearly full, it should be filled out and justified. The possible conditions when this should happen are: • Never; • When the tightness criteria for the paragraph are met; • When the remaining space is less than a specified amount.

TABLE 7.2 Justification and line breaking.

Tabular Material

Typesetting tabular material is complex and difficult. In traditional document production, authors had the luxury of leaving the detailed design of tables to the graphic artist or printer. But again, publishing systems are now called upon to fill a role once held by a human being.

Tables are difficult to typeset because their shape and details depend on their content, and because there are many constraints on their layout [Beach 1986]. Consider the table in Fig. 7.6. Reproduced from

Feature	Description
Force page break	A page break is created at the specified point. When page breaking depends on ratings or demerits, this operation can encourage a break at a point or within a range.
Prevent page break	A page break is prevented in the specified range. When page breaking depends on ratings or demerits, this operation can discourage a break at a point or within a specified range.
Identify floater	A floating object is identified as a graphical object, unit of text, or other aggregate. It may be given a constraint that helps it to be placed: • Place here, relative to text. • Place at next fit. • Place at top of page. • Place at bottom of page. • Place on figures-only (tables-only) page. • Place at end of section (chapter, etc.).
Group objects	A collection of objects (tables, figures, paragraphs, etc.) are constrained to stay together. • On the same page; • On the same opening (facing pages).
Separate objects	Occasionally it is useful to force objects to appear on different pages, as when two similar figures might be confusing if viewed together: • Not on same page; • Not on same opening.
Control widows and orphans	Adjust breaks to prevent widows and orphans. In a globally optimizing system, when page breaking depends on ratings or demerits, a degree of importance may be assigned to the prevention of widows and orphans. This function may be global to the document, or localized to ranges of objects within the document.
Match depth	Apply a constraint on the depth: • Facing pages must match. • Pages in a chapter (etc.) must match. • Columns on each page must match. • Columns in a chapter (etc.) must match. • Lines must back up on pairs of overleaf pages.

TABLE 7.3　Pagination.

TABLE des inclinaisons de l'horizon visuel avec l'horizon vrai.											
Elév. au-dess. de la mer.		Inclinaison de l'horizon.			Elév. au-dess. de la mer.	Inclinaison de l'horizon.			Elév. au-dess. de la mer.	Inclinaison de l'horizon.	
pi.	po.	m.	s.	d	pieds	m.	s.	d.	pieds	m.	s.	d.
0.	6	0.	44		28	5.	26	11	94	9.	58	12
1.	0	1.	1	17	30	5.	37	11	98	10.	10	12
1.	6	1.	15	14	32	5.	48	10	102	10.	22	11
2.	0	1.	27	12	34	5.	58	11	106	10.	33	12
2.	6	1.	38	11	36	6.	9	10	110	10.	45	12
3.	0	1.	47	9	38	6.	19	10	114	10.	57	11
4.	0	2.	3	16	40	6.	29	10	118	11.	8	12
5.	0	2.	18	15	42	6.	39	9	122	11.	20	11
6.	0	2.	31	13	44	6.	48	9	126	11.	31	12
7.	0	2.	43	12	46	6.	57	9	130	11.	43	11
8.	0	2.	54	11	48	7.	6	9	134	11.	54	10
9.	0	3.	4	10	50	7.	15	9	138	12.	4	10
10.	0	3.	14	10	52	7.	24	9	142	12.	14	10
11.	0	3.	24	9	54	7.	33	9	146	12.	24	10
12.	0	3.	33	9	56	7.	42	8	150	12.	34	10
13.	0	3.	42	8	58	7.	50	7	154	12.	44	9
14.	0	3.	50	8	60	7.	57	8	158	12.	53	10
15.	0	3.	58	8	62	8.	5	7	162	13.	3	9
16.	0	4.	6	8	64	8.	12	8	166	13.	12	10
17.	0	4.	14	7	66	8.	20	7	170	13.	22	9
18.	0	4.	21	7	68	8.	27	8	174	13.	31	10
19.	0	4.	28	7	70	8.	35	7	178	13.	41	9
20.	0	4.	35	7	72	8.	42	7	182	13.	50	9
21.	0	4.	42	7	74	8.	49	7	186	13.	59	9
22.	0	4.	49	6	76	8.	56	11	190	14.	8	11
23.	0	4.	55	7	79	9.	7	10	195	14.	19	11
24.	0	5.	2	6	82	9.	17	10	200	14.	30	11
25.	0	5.	8	6	85	9.	27	11	205	14.	41	11
26.	0	5.	14	6	88	9.	38	10	210	14.	52	11
27.	0	5.	20	6	91	9.	48	10	215	15.	3	11
28.	0	5.	26		94	9.	58		220	15.	14	

FIGURE 7.6 A complex table. The choices of column width and row height depend on content. This table has the further complication that the column labeled "d" is intentionally set between the lines of the column to its left, since these numbers represent differences between adjacent numbers in the "s" column. Reproduced from *Tables Portatives de Logarithmes* by François Callet, Paris: Firmin Didot, 1795.

an old book, it shows many of the possible problems. Widths of columns depend on the data presented in them, as well as the number of words in the headings. At the same time, economy of space demands that the columns be narrow. A balanced structure depends on making similar columns equal in width across the table. Note also the vertical structure, suggested effectively by the double vertical rules between equivalent thirds of the table. Similar comments apply to the horizontal dimension. Thus tables are two-dimensional objects in which the constraints on each dimension interact.

Tables often include both vertical and horizontal rules to separate their various parts. Expensive to typeset by traditional means, vertical lines were once avoided by publishers, but in electronic publishing they create no extra expense. Rules must join properly where they meet, a problem complicated by the presence of varying widths, shadings, and shapes of rule in a table (see Fig. 7.7).

Text in any particular column or box in a table may be aligned on the left, aligned on the right, centered, or justified. Because very narrow columns are frequently necessary, justification is usually unsatisfactory; ragged-right is the norm for running text within tables. Long text entries are usually *folded* into several lines to avoid making the column too wide. Exactly where to fold a particular entry may be a matter sensitive enough to require the author's attention.

Similarly, text in tables must be aligned vertically. It may be set at the top of a box, in the center, or at the bottom. Where adjacent columns include different numbers of lines, aligning the baselines is usually necessary to avoid an untidy appearance.

Another source of difficulty is the complex structure of many tables. Subheadings may span two or more columns or rows, as may entries in the body of the table (Fig. 7.8). Table making also has an æsthetic

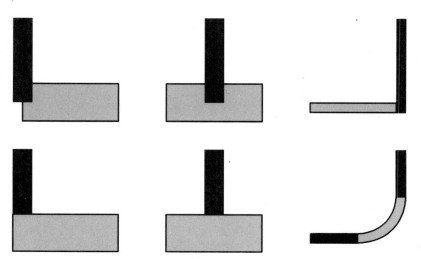

FIGURE 7.7   Rules within tables must join neatly. The situation is complicated by shaded lines and regions [Beach 1985]. (Courtesy of Richard Beach.)

A: Xxxxx Xxx Xxxx				
B: Xxxx	C: Xxxx			D: Xxxx
	E: Xxx	F: Xxx	G: Xxx	
H: Xxxx	I: Xxx	J: Xxx	K: Xxx	L: Xxxx

FIGURE 7.8 A table in which entries span more than one row and more than one column.

component: Space should be allocated so as to please the eye, items in columns and rows should align visually, and the style of text and graphic elements within the body should match each other and the larger document. Many æsthetic considerations are hard to encode as style information, and tinkering with the results of machine-set tables is the norm in many publishing environments. Therefore iterative construction and modification of tables is a very desirable feature in a publishing system.

Meeting all the constraints on tables requires considerable computational sophistication in the formatting program. Beach [1985] uses a constraint solver to generate a workable table layout, thus resolving the requirements of style and content.

See Table 7.4 for a listing of table features.

Margins and Page Layout

Margins and page layout are integral to the design and look of any document. As noted in Chapter 5, the presentation of margins on screen and paper is often different. When this is the case, the user should be made aware of the difference. The designer must also determine how much control the user will have over presentation. Will margins be represented accurately on the screen? Will there be a page-viewing mode in which overall spatial relationships on the page will be visible on the screen? Table 7.5 shows the possibilities.

In extensional formatters such as Runoff, margins could be changed within running text. Intentional formatters that incorporate a document design must behave differently, since local changes in margins could disrupt the overall layout. When a layout is defined for the document, text is "poured" into text regions. Provision must be made for the text to flow from one part of the document to another as more text is added.

Feature	Description
Tab position	Only the simplest tabular material can be set using the type-writer tab-stop model. Tabs may have differing alignments in this model (see below).
Table structure	Table structure may be expressed separately from table content. The structure identifies headings that span more than one column or row.
Table data	Data are supplied relative to a given table structure. When entries occupy more than one nominal position, that is, span rows and/or columns, this fact may be treated as part of the table data.
Alignment	Horizontal alignment offers several possibilities: • Left aligned; • Right aligned; • Center aligned; • Decimal aligned (comma in Europe); • Aligned on a specified character. Note that decimal alignment includes the case in which the decimal is omitted (integer). Alignment on a specified character permits more specialized alignment internal to an entry: $10 \times 10 =\quad\ \ 100$ $100 \times 10 =\quad 1000$ $1000 \times 10 = 10000$ Similarly, vertical alignment permits: • Top aligned; • Centered; • Bottom aligned.
Leaders	A horizontal series of dots or dashes, a *leader*, helps lead the eye between corresponding columns, for example, between a chapter title and page number in an index.

TABLE 7.4 Table features.

Feature	Description
Set margin	Margins are altered beginning at a point in the document, or within a specified range in the document (extensional): • Move left/right margin to absolute position. • Move left or right margin relative to current position. • Specify each margin as a fraction of the page dimensions.
Define grid	A constraint for describing the page is defined as a grid geometry. Other definitions are forced to conform to its boundaries.
Layout page	Margins, columns, etc. are described as rectangles with properties (intentional): • Contained text (marginal notes, page numbers); • Adjustable (matching page length in openings); • Gutters; • Page layout in terms of the proportions of margins, illustrations, text blocks, column widths, and so on.
Specify text flow	The topology of the layout, how text continues from one part of the design to another, must be specified as part of the layout design (intentional).

TABLE 7.5 Margins and page layout.

Multiple-column typesetting is complicated by constraints on the relationship between columns. Usually columns on the same and facing pages must be set with the same depth. Complex page layouts with columns must also specify how text overflows from one part of the page to another. It may be difficult for the system to react to an arbitrary editing change in real time when these constraints are taken into account.

Hyphenation

When it works well, hyphenation does not usually come to the user's attention. Hyphenation is an intentional function. Does the user control it? Is the control only high level (on or off), or is it detailed? Can users provide global hyphenations for words peculiar to their documents? Can hyphenation points be specified invisibly within text? Can hyphenation be suppressed where desired? Table 7.6 details the choices.

Feature	Description
Hyphenation-dictionary entry	The places at which a particular word may be hyphenated are declared globally for a document or set of documents.
Set hyphenation dictionary	Use a specified dictionary to hyphenate this document or range.
Hyphenation permitted	Declares a single place or range where hyphenation is permitted. In rating systems, a weighting may be provided.
Inhibit hyphenation	Declares a location or range in which hyphenation is not permitted (or discouraged in a rating system).
Hyphenation optimization	Limitations on hyphenation are established for a range, or for a whole document. Possible constraints include: • Do not hyphenate. • Limit hyphenation to n consecutive lines. • Do not hyphenate capitalized words.

TABLE 7.6   Hyphenation.

Unlike most other features of a typesetting system, hyphenation is language dependent. Each language for which the system will be used requires the appropriate dictionary. Also, in many countries it is common to create documents that contain more than one language. Systems used in these situations must make it possible to designate which hyphenation dictionary is to be used for each passage.

Leading

How is interline spacing determined? Is it automatic? Part of the document style? Under detailed user control? How are difficult passages handled, such as those with superscripts, subscripts, and varying sizes of type on the same line? Table 7.7 shows these various controls.

Leading is usually an intentional function in a defined document style or design. If the system adjusts leading in the course of pagination, either interline or interparagraph, the user must understand this. Otherwise very uneven results will be obtained when the user constrains some parts of the document to have specific spacing, and the system modifies other parts. In certain applications, such as advertising layout,

Feature	Description
Declared leading	Several types of general interline spacing can be applied to a text object or aggregate of objects. It is always desirable to adjust spacing to type size and line length, even within these general specifications: • Close line spacing (as in books); • Loose line spacing (as in letters); • Open line spacing (as in manuscripts); • Space x between lines. May be negative. (This overrides automatic leading.)
Interparagraph leading	The document design may specify interparagraph leading. Leading may be of several forms: • Space x before paragraphs. • Space x after paragraphs. • Minimum x and maximum y space between paragraphs (allows adjustment for depth matching on facing pages)
Absolute vertical positioning	The absolute position relative to the top or bottom of the page, or relative to another object, is specified.
Backing-up control	Books and other documents printed on both sides of the paper may require that vertical line positions match on opposite sides of each sheet of paper, preventing distraction if the text on the other side of the paper were to show through. This setting specifies that text is to back up, or specifies a penalty for failure to back up in a rating system.

TABLE 7.7 Leading.

leading is a central focus, and must be under the direct control of the user.

Optimization

The degree of optimization performed in a document may be specified globally, applied locally to objects or ranges in the document, or treated as a mode to be turned on and off as desired. Usually the user should not be burdened with synthetic parameters, such as demerit values, because these parameters do not relate directly to any physical quantity. Nor do such numbers have much intuitive basis; they are hard to understand and remember, and represent a substantial amount of learn-

Feature	Description
Paragraph break optimization	Enable or disable the optimization of paragraphs to produce the best set of line breaks, in terms of: • Minimizing hyphenation; • Controlling line tightness; • Minimizing rivers. These optimizations can be controlled together or selected individually.
Kerning control	Is the best possible interletter spacing to be achieved, or can interletter spacing be compromised to achieve other goals?
Widow and orphan control	Enable or disable optimization to prevent widows and orphans.
Depth control	Enable or disable the matching of depth of text on facing pages.
Backing-up control	Enable or disable the matching of vertical position of lines on opposite sides of a sheet of paper.

TABLE 7.8   Optimization.

ing if they are to be used effectively. They should remain part of an arbitrary scale best kept internal to the formatting algorithms.

Table 7.8 brings together items listed elsewhere that relate to good optimization. Most desktop-publishing users will want very simple choices relating to optimization. The only reason the office user has to suppress optimization is the time it takes the computer to optimize. Whether formatting is done in real time or on demand, optimization control is an issue only when the user perceives that he or she is waiting for the system to do something that is optional. In cases in which optimization dramatically increases processing time, users may choose a draft mode with less optimization before they create a final version.

Demand Formatting

Table 7.9 shows the few choices that relate to the timing of formatting. What formatting functions, if any, are not performed except upon request? Under what circumstances can the user see a less-than-accurate representation of a document? How can the user tell whether the

Feature	Description
Real-time versus demand	Keep the screen representation up to date or not.
Optimize versus draft	Format in real time with or without optimizations.
Page break versus galley	Present galleys or pages (or previous page breaks).

TABLE 7.9 Demand formatting.

presented version is or is not representative of the printed result? The answers to these questions will have a profound effect on the user's perception of the system. It will seem fast or slow, abstract or concrete, powerful or inefficient based on how these issues are handled in the interface and the overall design.

Undoing and Reversion

In both interactive and batch systems, user mistakes should not result in the loss of work. Batch systems have long been structured so that rerunning a job or program does not cause data to be lost. Similarly, interruption of a job must leave files in a known state, preferably as though the job had never been run.

In interactive systems, providing for user errors not only avoids the loss of work, but also leads the user to experiment with new aspects of the system, which helps increase expertise. Functions that allow actions to be reversed within a direct-manipulation editor are invaluable. When otherwise-destructive actions can be undone, it is safer to experiment with features. Also, various alternatives for the layout and content of a document may be considered in "what if" scenarios that can be reversed if desired. Many different models for reversing the effect of actions are possible. The important issue for user-interface design is making sure that users recognize the states to which they will be able to return with the undo functions. See Table 7.10 for a list of useful interactive functions.

Computed Values and Embedded Views

A wonderful service possible with a formatting program is automatic cross-references and computed values. There are many kinds, listed in Table 7.11.

Feature	Description
Whoops	Reverse the effect of the last action.
Undo	Successively reverse the effect of preceding operations. The tree of states can quickly become confusing, so some concrete model is required, for example, a storyboard or time line with a marker showing the current state. It could be possible to: • Go back a step; • Go forward a step; • Go forward to the most recent state; • Make the current state the new starting point. A potential confusion results from moving backward in time, as it were, making changes relative to the historical state and then attempting to revert to later history that may no longer be reachable. Whether or not all previous states are reachable, the confusion must be avoided.
Examine history	Show previous major versions either of the entire document or of some specified part, for example, a paragraph, section, or chapter. Selecting a historical version makes it current. This form may correspond to file versions.
Revert	Revert to the previous major version of the entire document. In traditional computer systems, this corresponds to the last saved version. More flexibly, reversion may be to a state purposefully identified by the user. This facilitates "what if" scenarios and other experimentation.

TABLE 7.10 Undoing and reversion.

The problem of making specification of computed values easy is significant. For a desktop-publishing system, nothing that looks like mathematical notation or a programming language will gain ready acceptance. Thus the user-interface challenge is to create these facilities without imposing an undue conceptual burden on the nontechnical user.

An issue in the implementation of cross-references is the possible computational problems. Cross-references are similar in behavior to forward references in assemblers and compilers. If input is processed sequentially, more than one pass may be required to compute all the reference values. In a typesetting system this may be unacceptable,

Feature	Description
Number pages	Page numbers are generated and placed as specified. Numbering may be reset to a new value at a point within the body of a document, as often done between the preface and body of a book. Also, a pattern in which to embed the number can be specified, such as '—*n*—'. Various numbering notations are possible: • Arabic numerals (123); • Roman numerals, uppercase (CXXII); • Roman numerals, lowercase (cxxii); • English words (one hundred twenty-three); • Relative English description (next page, overleaf, etc.).
Cross-reference	Create a reference pointer that can be referred to at another point in the document: • For a cross-reference, to a page, for example; • For a bibliographic citation; • For a chapter, section, or item or line number; • For an index entry; • For a glossary entry.
Value reference	It is frequently useful to include within text the value of some quantity known to the typesetting program, such as: • Page number; • Chapter number; • Section number; • Chapter or section title; • Page of a cross-reference; • Chapter and/or section of a cross-reference; • Citation for a bibliographic reference; • Page and/or number of a footnote; • Relative location of a reference, in textual form (top of this page, bottom of the next page, above, below, left, center, right); • The title of the current chapter, section, etc.
Reference section	Sections in documents may be created to list various reference points that are marked throughout the text: • Table of contents; • Glossary; • Bibliography; • Index; • User-defined items such as theorems or guidelines.

TABLE 7.11 Computed values and embedded views.

Feature	Description
Itemization	A list of bulleted or unbulleted items is created with the identified items. The specification may include: • The bullet symbol (•, ˙, ☛, etc.). • With nested items, a sequence of symbols is needed. For example, succeeding levels might use •, ˙, -, and · as the line markers.
Enumeration	A list of numbered items is created with the identified items. The specification may include: • The notation for the number (123, cxxiii, etc.). • With nested items, a sequence of notations is needed. For example, succeeding levels might use ABC, 123, abc.
Description	Items are typeset against corresponding descriptions, as frequently seen in the descriptions of features in computer manuals. The item provides its own marker. This explanation of the description list type is itself a description.

TABLE 7.12   Itemization and enumeration.

especially in a WYSIWYG, real-time system, which requires a different strategy.

Itemization and Enumeration

Many documents contain lists, and it is natural to provide an intentional construct that makes it easy to format them. Many stylistic variations are possible with lists. For example, items may be marked in various ways, indented in different ways, numbered with Arabic or Roman numerals, and justified in various ways. With extensional specification, many commands are needed at the beginning and end of the list to achieve the desired effect. For this reason, intentional specification, relative to a style definition, is to be preferred. See Table 7.12.

Out-of-Band Material

Material is often expressed at some meaningful point in the sequence of the document, but appears at another physical location. Footnotes are one example. Such objects explicitly depart from the WYSIWYG philosophy, but in a way that makes sense in terms of the layout of the document. Nonetheless, the challenge for interface design here is to make the information accessible in an unsurprising way, perhaps both where it is specified and where it occurs in a real-time, direct-manipulation system. See Table 7.13.

External References

Large or complex documents are frequently created in segments. For example, books are usually written in chapters, and it may be impracticable to work on the entire book as a single file or document. Therefore it is useful to be able to link documents and also to reference one document inside another. In terms of implementation, segmenting large documents has the advantage of dividing the computational load into manageable units. As with modular compilation of programming languages, global context and dynamic linkage are required to achieve the right behavior when a single piece is altered. See Table 7.14.

Output Devices and Publishing Functions

Is output device independent, or must the user adjust for the particular output device to which the document will be directed? The simplest interface results from not having to worry about the output device, of course, but this situation is not always attainable. When it is not, what characteristics of the output device must the user specify? It is important that the terms the user must employ in this description be familiar. Most users will not know the technical device designations for printers, nor the technology employed in them. Worse still is the possibility of exposing users to choices in output protocol—PostScript, Interpress, and so on. These choices are best handled implicitly in the user-specified destination. See Table 7.15.

Some characteristics of output devices are of unavoidable interest to users. For example, documents that include color will require some degree of modification when printed on monochrome printers. If the user can avoid having to make choices in this area, so much the better. The use to which the output will be put may determine how color is to be handled, however, resulting in choices for the user.

If the output device collates and binds documents, the user will want to control these functions, which may be simply selecting stapling, two-sided printing, choice of paper, and the like. The possibilities could be much more elaborate, however, allowing entire books to be

Feature	Description
Footnote	A footnote is declared. It includes: • A textual body or content; • A reference mark, possibly one created in sequence such as 1, 2, 3, a, b, c, i, ii, iii, or †, ††, †††. Footnotes must also have a specified position: • At the bottom of the page of occurrence; • At the end of a section or chapter (endnotes); • In a special notes section. Long footnotes may be allowed to overflow onto the next page, or may not be.
Other notes	A second category of note may be indicated for placement in a different location in the document. For example, if footnotes are placed at the bottom of pages, chapter notes might be placed at the ends of chapters.
Marginal notes	Notes associated with a location or section of the text are typeset in the margin near the associated body text.
Alternate text	Complex documents, such as computer documentation, may call for different texts to be substituted under different printing conditions. (This is like conditional assembly in programming languages.) In a WYSIWYG system, the alternative texts must be placed outside the scope of the presented document, for example, in another display window on the screen.
Remarks	Notations not to be typeset, but for the benefit of the composer of the document, may be included within the document. Here is another intentional violation of WYSIWYG, albeit a useful one. Remarks can be made to appear in a separate window, in supermargins outside the document margins, or in other locations where they will not confuse the user about the actual content of the document.

TABLE 7.13   Out-of-band material.

Feature	Description
Continue	Declares the next file (chapter, segment) that is part of the current document.
Static embedding	An external document (or picture, table, graphic, etc.) is copied into the document. When copied its form remains unchanged, even if the external document changes at a later time.
Dynamic embedding	An external document is referenced in the document. It appears, and shows any changes that may be made to the referenced document. Time and date behave like dynamic embeddings.

TABLE 7.14 External references.

gathered into signatures and bound—and requiring considerable control by the user.

Chapter Summary

The automatic layout of documents is complicated by the many typographical constraints that apply to the finished result. In addition to the requirements of a document's style, it is often necessary that facing pages have the same depth, that text line up across openings, and that lines back up on opposite sides of the paper. There are further constraints on multicolumn documents—for example, that baselines must match between columns, and that adjacent columns must match in depth. Figures, tables, and other illustrations must be placed so they are visible where referenced.

There are many degrees of freedom that allow different arrangements of text and illustrations. Although facing pages must match in depth, the depth of pages for different openings need not be identical; a line or two of difference is usually acceptable. Similarly, the white space around figures allows for some adjustment. Other variables can be changed by the user: size of text, interline and interparagraph spacing, size of figures and illustrations, and wording of the text.

Finding the uniquely best solution to paginating a document is computationally very expensive. The number of cases to consider

Feature	Description
Output resolution	Prepare text for an output device of a specified resolution. Resolution may be specified functionally: • Draft resolution; • Proof resolution; • Typeset resolution; Or resolution may be specified by device name or type.
Color simulation	Does the output device support color printing? How is color information to be handled on black-and-white printers? • Print colors as halftones representing intensity. • Encode colors with line patterns (cross-hatching, etc.) • Print colors by printing separation originals for multicolor offset press printing. • Ignore colors other than black, white, and gray. Print the latter as specified patterns or shades.
Color printing	If the output device does support color: • Print the best match to colors. • Simulate colors with color halftones. • Encode black and white shades as colors (false color). • Adjust colors for photo reproduction or separation.
Publishing features	Will output be collated and bound? • Specify paper (size, color, weight); • Image orientation (landscape; portrait); • Print on both sides (duplex); • Print two-up, four-up, etc.; • Print for signature binding; • Bind output (staple, perfect binding).

TABLE 7.15 Output devices.

grows exponentially with the size of the document, and in most cases searching the full range of possibilities is computationally impracticable. However, heuristic methods that yield good though not necessarily optimal results are acceptable for both desktop- and professional-publishing systems. Because the best solution may not be found, users must interact with the system to make adjustments or add constraints.

Layout programs may be interactive or batch, they may format in real time or on demand, and they may accept intentional or extensional descriptions of documents. Many desktop systems now integrate editing functions into the formatting operations, resulting in a direct-manipulation document model as the basis of the user interface. The challenge of user-interface design for these systems is to keep them conceptually simple while providing a complete and useful set of functions relative to the user's needs.

_8
Conclusions

I hate quotations. Tell me what you know.
— *Ralph Waldo Emerson*

T HE goal of this final chapter is to summarize what we know
about the infant technology of digital typography, of whose future
course we can be none too sure. It is no accident that more knowledge
comes to this new area from the older disciplines of typography and
psychology than from computer science. But computer technology
contributes essential life to the endeavor, not to mention the machines
that make it possible.

What we know is the sum of what we know, together with what we
know we don't know. This book summarizes what is known of digital
typography; this chapter expresses that knowledge as a number of broad
principles and guidelines. What is not known is partially described in
the remainder of the chapter.

Principles of Digital Typography

What is the essence of digital typography? What publishing system
properties will best serve the needs of users and of readers of documents
produced electronically? Digital typography must fit into the larger
scheme of things—perception, graphic design, economics, and technical feasibility. From this point of view, the following seven principles
summarize the state of the art.

1. Typography should be invisible. It is the goal of typography
   and printing, however performed, to communicate, not to call
   attention to itself as the vehicle. Electronic publishing should
   be no different.

2. Typography is part of "literacy." An appreciation of the average user of desktop-publishing systems suggests the wisdom of minimizing the typographic and computer-specific knowledge necessary to use the machinery. Nonetheless, the freedom of owning publishing technology presents the user with issues of layout, quality of presentation, and effectiveness of print. The meaning of literacy is changing to include not only reading and writing but also presenting of information.

3. Typography is part of the quality of human interface. Systems that display printed material now depend on typographic quality as a component of their overall human interface. The user's satisfaction and productivity will depend more and more on the quality of presentation of textual information in user interfaces.

4. Technology and typographic quality are linked. Printing technology has long been reflected in printed letterforms, and this remains true. Not only is quality affected by such technical properties as output resolution, but the shapes themselves reflect what is easiest and most economical using available technology.

5. The human vision system is reflected in the shape of letters. Letterforms have evolved so as to make good use of the human visual apparatus. The characteristics of the visual system can help us choose how letterforms should be presented by computers.

6. The person is part of the system. People have a huge investment in the shapes of letters, and also in conventions for laying out pages. Radical changes in typography will not be accepted both because of the nature of visual perception and because of well-established habits. To buck this trend would not be productive; rather it behooves us to accept it and use knowledge about human behavior to advantage in choosing how to present text. All systems must be designed with the user clearly in mind; systems that present text are no different.

7. Digital typography is interdisciplinary. Like many new fields, digital typography benefits from a number of technologies and disciplines, including computer hardware technology, computer science, human factors technology, psychology, and

typography. Practitioners in each of these areas have ideas and information to offer. The challenge is to be mutually intelligible, avoiding the Tower of Babel.

Issues in Digital Typography

Over time, the resolution of output devices will improve dramatically. One role for researchers in digital typography is to discover what is sufficient resolution, taking into account what people can perceive, what facilitates reading, and what compromises can be made in constructing equipment.

At the limit, better digital output technology will convert many issues in digital typography to purely typographic ones. With increasing resolution, type design and layout will eventually come to depend principally on how good particular letterforms are for particular purposes, and where they should be placed. If improvement in resolution is rapid, then pure and applied research in perception and reading performance will pay off, but efforts to adapt to low resolution will be of little long-term value.

On the other hand, an important question is the level of system that will become the commodity low-end standard for desktop publishing. Many low-quality dot-matrix printers are still in use for printing business letters and other personal documents. But there is no reason to believe that the least-expensive desktop-publishing systems of the future will continue to operate under severe constraints in resolution. For these inexpensive systems, the challenge of producing high-quality letterforms and layouts with a minimum of hardware resources will remain. Good type designs in low-resolution versions for both screens and low-end printers will continue to be in demand.

One goal for system designers is to establish new minimum standards for low-cost electronic printing and publishing systems with the best-possible typographic quality. Low-cost systems need not present low-quality images. There is no reason that high-quality documents should not be created and proofed on low-cost systems, for typesetting elsewhere. Attention to issues of visual perception, typographical sensibilities, device characteristics, wygins, and user-interface design will make cost-effective systems a reality.

Some directions for research are unlikely to be fruitful. For example, developing fonts without descenders (in order to conserve space on

> After this he lifted uP his head, and seeing the moon rising, walked towards the Palace. As he Passed through the fields, and saw the animals around him, "Ye, said he, are haPPy, and need not envy me that walk thus among you, burthened with myself; nor do I, ye gentle ones, envy your felicity; for it is not the felicity of man. I have many distresses from which ye are free; I fear Pain when I do not feel it: I sometimes shrink at evils recollected, and sometimes start at evils anticiPated: surely the equity of Providence has balanced Peculiar sufferings with Peculiar joys

FIGURE 8.1 Rusher's "patent types," a typeface without descenders [Goudy 1940:142]. (Frederic W. Goudy, *Typologia*, ©1940. Reproduced courtesy of the University of California Press.)

screens and paper) is of no value. Radical changes in the shapes of letterforms are poorly received by readers, whatever the economic advantages that might motivate such changes. When typefaces without descenders were first tried, in 1804, they were a worthwhile experiment, but one that should not be repeated today (see Fig. 8.1).

Some low-resolution environments will be with us for a long time. In particular, television standards and the large number of installed TV sets ensure that low-resolution text will be presented in this medium, as is, for a long time. Any methods that improve the typographic quality of text presented on TV screens, therefore, are certainly worthwhile.[1]

Industry will probably find a way around the broadcast standard. Work is underway at the MIT Media Lab to generate acceptable high-resolution images in real time from standard transmissions [Media Lab 1986]. When high-resolution displays are incorporated in standard TVs, digital transmission of text on a subcarrier will allow the local use of higher-resolution fonts to generate better text on the screen.

R&D Projects

Here is a list of research, development, and technology-transfer projects that would advance the state of the art. There is more we do not

---

[1] For example, van Nes [1986] is working to improve the readability of Teletext.

know about digital typography than we do know. Possible projects to increase our knowledge can be categorized along a dimension ranging from pure research, at one end of the spectrum (denoted "P" in the list), through applied research ("A"), to system development, at the other ("D"). Roughly speaking, pure research extends basic understanding and applied research uses this understanding to resolve issues more directly related to technology, while development involves the construction of systems. In addition, there is technology transfer ("T"), activity that converts knowledge from one discipline to another, synthesizes new ideas using knowledge from other fields, or communicates useful information to those who need it.

Of course, not every activity fits neatly under one of these labels. Rather, projects operate over a range within the spectrum, but are identified in terms of the part of the spectrum to which they apply most closely.

Convert Knowledge

It is useful to convert typographic and psychological knowledge into a form useful for engineering. This is partly a matter of translating and communicating, partly of synthesizing ideas, and partly of identifying experiments that would produce useful engineering results, all attempted in this book. (T)

Size Expectations

How can the user's expectations about typeface size and feel, as well as line breaks and page layout, be made to match between screen and paper presentations? Full-page displays will not eliminate this problem because of differences in viewing distance. Should margins be represented accurately on screens? (A,D)

Design of Output Devices

What characteristics of output devices best facilitate high-quality text output? How should pixels be best arranged in LCD displays to optimize typographic performance at a given resolution? How can high-quality halftones on laser printers be achieved most economically? For example, are dithering techniques sufficient, or would variable dot size as a hardware function be better? (A,D)

Font-Design Tools for Typographers

Some typographers who have tried to use font-production tools such as METAFONT complain that they cannot describe the essential properties of a design in programmatic terms. A design paradigm and interface that is comfortable for traditional typographers would help them produce new high-quality typeface designs. An object-oriented, direct-manipulation approach appears promising. Knowledge of the shapes of letters and their interrelationships should be built into these systems. (A,D)

Degrees of Freedom

What degrees of typographic freedom do users need? For example, how simple can the interface to a desktop-publishing system be and still meet most of the needs of most office users? The right compromise between guidance and flexibility is essential for productivity and for good-quality output. Structure, such as grids and standard documents, may be as important as specific defaults or recommendations. (A,D)

Psychology of Continuous Reading

What characteristics of typefaces and the arrangement of text and graphics are most important to continuous reading [Trollip and Sales 1986]? Tinker's work would be the starting point for this research. Can relevant typeface characteristics be analyzed well enough to offer the user good choices of line width and leading? (P)

Formatting

The final word certainly has not been written about how to format text automatically. Work is required on languages and interfaces for expressing layout and text. In particular, there is a gap between real-time WYSIWYG formatters and batch formatters in terms of ease of use, on the one hand, and capability, on the other.[2] (D)

Few current formatters attempt to globally optimize line and page breaks. Better and faster algorithms are needed. (A,D)

Hyphenation remains a problem in spite of much excellent work on the problems of encoding dictionaries and performing checking quickly. A thorough investigation of the effect of hyphenation on confusion and reading-speed degradation would be worthwhile. (P)

---

[2] See [van Vliet 1986] for several relevant papers.

Artificial Intelligence and Page Layout

Could an expert system do a good job of page design? How about chapter- or book-level pagination as an alternative to the Plass-Knuth algorithmic approach? (A)

Typography

Many purely typographic issues deserve the attention of psychologists and other scientists. While there is every reason to believe that typographers are usually right about what is legible, a theory based on visual perception and verified by experiment would help us predict legibility more accurately and guide system design—not to mention that the issues in perception and reading are of intrinsic interest. Here are just a few topics:

> Does nonlinear scaling of fonts (changing the design of a given typeface from size to size) improve legibility? How can nonlinear scaling be characterized algorithmically, allowing variations at different sizes to be produced automatically? (P,A)
>
> What is a good theory of letter spacing? Is it possible to characterize variations in reading performance due to spacing in the spatial-frequency domain? (P)
>
> What is an objective basis for choosing typefaces and layouts? (P)

New Document Structures

Computer systems offer a much more dynamic kind of reading environment than possible with paper books. Experimental ideas such as Hypertext [Nelson 1979; Brown 1986; Burrill 1986], in which text is not organized linearly, are fascinating. Do they help people learn, acquire information, or communicate more effectively? (P) What is the effect of including other "media" within documents—movies, sound, interactive programs? (A)

Newspapers and magazines present far more information at a glance than do high-resolution displays. Moreover, by thumbing through them, books give the reader a kind of quick access and overview that has yet to be simulated effectively with computers. Can dynamic presentations—movies in documents, tailoring of documents to individual needs, real-time updating, rapid paging within documents—close the gap in utility [Media Lab 1986]? (A,D)

Organizational Role of Typography

There is much for sociologists and those interested in the organizational effect of technology to discover about electronic publishing. Like word processing, desktop publishing will undoubtedly change many people's jobs. It is part of a trend away from centralized typing pools and production facilities and toward vertical integration of jobs, the broadening of skills and responsibility. How will desktop publishing affect the quality of work life? Will it affect interpersonal relationships and communication in the workplace, as did word processing? Will organizational issues and personal preferences limit its use, as has been the case with dictation equipment (many managers will not dictate to a machine) and electronic telephone exchanges (most users do not use most of the features)? (P)

Fatigue in Reading

Although many studies of legibility as gauged by reading speed and comprehension have been performed, less is known about the effects of typographic quality on fatigue and concentration. Is fatigue strongly associated with reading speed (for an individual), or do certain properties cause fatigue without impairing reading performance? Is page layout a fatigue factor? (P)

Grayscale Fonts

What is the effect of grayscale fonts (anti-aliasing) on reading rates and fatigue when this technique is employed on CRT displays? Which anti-aliasing methods produce the most-legible print? Display hardware can be built to do anti-aliasing in real time, based on high-resolution versions of fonts. Is this cost effective? (A,D)

Flicker

What is the effect of refresh rates on reading performance and fatigue? One trade-off in display technology is resolution versus refresh rate. Also, using interlaced displays, resolution can be doubled without doubling the data rate out of memory. The result, however, is a display that has alternate fields refreshed at half the noninterlaced rate, which means that a large component of this half-rate frequency is in the flicker. Well below the flicker-fusion rate for most people, this rate may have significant effects on reading rate, comprehension, concentration, and fatigue. (P,A)

Communication Protocols

New or refined vehicles for communicating compound documents are needed. Presentation-level protocols and page-description languages allow the correct appearance of documents to be expressed, but they cannot be edited. Also, they systematically discard relationships among components that were known by the creating program. Modifiable formats, in contrast, trade editability against simplicity and speed. A middle ground that solves both problems would improve system integration and ease of use. (A,D)

Seeing the Invisible

A real problem with WYSIWYG editors is that information that will not appear in the printed document must always be displayed. Many screen editors have facilities for showing formatting characters, "hard carriage returns," and other formatting information. Turning the presentation of this metainformation on and off creates modes in the user interface. When the information is presented, the departure from "What You Get" can be dramatic. Better user-interface approaches to this problem are much needed. (A,D?)

Document-Design Specifications

Currently, when information about document style is provided separately from the document itself, the form is very much like a program. It includes variable declarations, macros, and executable programs. A form closer to the way that typographers and book designers work would give these art professionals better access to and control over the electronic medium, without forcing them to learn computer jargon and methods. (A,D)

Generic Fonts and Specification

Device independence of fonts has been a goal of recent work in digital typography. While the ability to render fonts similarly on different devices is improving, and will continue to improve, the way in which fonts are specified needs work. Can generic fonts be thoroughly characterized by the requirements of the document design? Can a common format for expressing font design be developed and brought into general usage? (D)

WYGINS

Work is required to develop effective interfaces that do not surprise users when they see the printed results. In addition to size expectations, the use of "graphics text," which does not share all the properties of text, and the relationship between text and graphics need evolutionary work. (D)

Guidelines

In the future, many nontypographers will be specifying document layouts, fonts, and other typographic information. These people need guidelines for making specifications that are reliable both typographically and technically. Guidelines should be expressed both as the default behavior of programs, and as design rules that make sense to nontechnical as well as engineering minds. (T)

Spatial Frequency Model

Can examining spatial frequencies, in conjunction with models of human perception, help us understand differences in reading speed among various typographic conditions—monospaced, serifed, upper-case? (P)

Parsing Pages

Studies of the perception of page structure could shed light on the quality of layout. A related area is how documents are recognized by their appearance, which provides one basis for information retrieval. This, too, might be a criterion in designing documents for on-line use. (P)

Concluding Thoughts

The ability to create typeset-quality documents easily may well change people's attitudes about type and printing. For example, a merchandising executive relates how he can no longer gauge the metaqualities of memos. When memos were typed on conventional typewriters, he could hold the document up to the light to see how much correction fluid had been expended. The more corrections, the less the sender must have cared, or else the memo would have been retyped. With computers, only the uncorrected errors show. For this executive, word processing has meant the loss of some information that used to come with his interoffice mail.

Since laser printers and photocopiers use the same marking technology, the distinction between copies and originals has become weak. However, many organizational procedures depend on this distinction.

A similar situation arises out of expectations about the quality of printing itself. Through experience, most people associate typesetting with a good-quality document. After all, much care, attention, and revision are required to put a document into typeset form in a book, journal, or magazine. But now, memos, drafts of articles, and business letters enter homes and offices in near-typeset form. Unconsciously, people attribute quality to the content, based on the form.

The reverse also happens. Nonspecialists with no flair whatsoever for typographic design are designing and producing documents that have worse form than content. Our high expectations for graphic quality from commercial printing will be brought to bear on everything printed. The same thing has happened with film and television. We are so used to a high level of production quality in movies that even Grade B movies must rise to this level. Amateur productions can scarcely be shown on television today unless they meet minimum professional standards of production quality.

What will be the social consequences of inexpensive, accessible, high-quality printing? Will more people be able to communicate more easily and quickly? Potentially, their communications will be of better quality. Will they communicate more information more effectively?

With centralized typesetting, much of the control over the final product must sit with the editor, publisher, art department, and printer. But soon the locus of control of documents may well shift to the author. Authors can now deliver their manuscripts in computer-readable form. Electronic publishing gives them more control, if that is what they wish.

Electronic printing may also increase publishing on demand. Instead of printing many copies of a low-volume publication, it can be printed in very small batches as required. For example, music publishing requires keeping a large inventory of expensive sheet music. Retailers of sheet music must also inventory large numbers of items. Demand publishing allows only music that is requested to be printed, on the spot. The selection could be very large, because the inventory would be electronic.

In 1970, Warren Chappell [1970:228] worried about what technology must be doing to printing: "The difficulties of operating the equipment can be staggering even for those who can afford ownership." The new digital technology is reversing this trend, placing the means of publishing into many more hands. By combining knowledge of typography, psychology, human factors technology, and computer technology, we can prove Chappell's worries to be unfounded. If the quality of print is foremost in our minds as we design and build new systems, everyone will benefit.

Appendix: Teaching Digital Typography

IT is always hard to keep courses in technology-related areas up-to-date. A brand-new area such as digital typography presents a special challenge, first in providing current material, and second in providing appropriate student projects and activities.

The following exercises, which differ substantially in scale and difficulty, can be used in a variety of ways. Many students will find it useful to choose projects centered outside their own disciplines. This gives them a clearer interdisciplinary sense, and may help them learn more than projects restricted to their specialties.

The projects can be assigned to individuals or groups. For graduate students and some undergraduates, research projects included in Chapter 8 may also be approachable in whole or part. The activities listed here, however, are not aimed at advancing the state of the art, but rather at advancing students' knowledge of it.

Projects

1. Font Design

Consider the analog designs shown in Fig. A-1. For a CRT with 72-dpi resolution, design versions of the letters A, J, Q, S, a, b, d, and g. Design 10- and 12-point text sizes, and a 24-point display size. Use a collateral approach, trying to balance truth to the original design, on the one hand, and making the various sizes similar, on the other. Pay attention to matching x-height, weight, and contrast. Write a report describing the difficulties you encountered, and the compromises you struck.

ABCDEFGHIJKL MNOPQRSTUV WXYZ&abcdefghi jklmnopqrstuvwxyz 1234567890$

FIGURE A.1   An analog type design on which to base the designs in exercise 1.

2. Legibility Study

Conduct a legibility study to determine the relative quality of two print typefaces of your choosing. The typefaces may be traditional, laser output, or one of each. The test will be based on a proofreading task.

Prepare two one-page samples of running text. Make the sheets as nearly identical as possible, except for the difference in typefaces. The samples should contain exactly the same words, and should match as nearly as possible in justification, size, and leading. Each sample should contain 10 obvious typographical errors. Avoid subtle errors because you will want each subject to find all the errors.

The task is to read the page through, circling any errors found. Tell the subjects the number of errors and allow them to work until all are located. Discard the test results for any subject who does not find all the errors. Measure the time each subject takes to complete the task.

Use enough subjects so that at least 10 complete the task. Each subject will read both samples, but half must read one first, and half the other first. This experimental design minimizes the effect of different performance from person to person and the effect of learning how to do the task.

Compute and compare the average completion times for both samples. The difference can be described as the difference in legibility of the two typefaces. You should consider a difference of less than 5% to be insignificant.

Write a report describing your results. Be sure to describe any difficulties encountered in running the experiment. The experimental design is a simplified one. How might it be improved to get more reliable results?

3. Typeface Classification and Identification

Classify 20 different "found" typefaces according to the taxonomy in Chapter 2. Include at least 5 faces from electronic publishing or printing systems. Next, using a copy of *Rookledge's International Typefinder* [Perfect and Rookledge 1983], identify each sample by name. Describe those that cannot be identified uniquely in terms of the closest "name" faces.

4. Riverless Paragraphs

TEX goes to some length to optimize line breaking within paragraphs. Knuth and Plass [1981:1117–1178] assert that rivers are rarely a problem in TEX, so long as reasonably tight spacing is maintained. Exceptions include pathological cases such as narrow paragraphs and paragraphs containing repetitive items such as a list of attendees at a party, which might be printed in a newspaper.

Develop a formula that calculates a badness value for paragraphs in terms of the rivers they contain. Calculate the river badness of a number of paragraphs set by two different formatters. If TEX is available to you, use it as one of the formatters. Does the function identify rivers as well as you can visually? Be sure to test a variety of paragraph samples.

5. Font Extension

Design six new glyphs to match an existing font. Choose letters or symbols that are familiar to you but that are not in the font. For example, add the following symbols to a font that does not have them:

$$\exists \; \Psi \; \Pi \; \forall \; \Lambda \; \mu \; \cup \; \aleph \; \Sigma$$

Be sure to match style, weight, x-height, and similar characteristics, as appropriate.

6. Laser Printer Characteristics

Using a bitmap font editor, modify four letters from an existing serifed font to include half-bitting. Print the letters on a laser printer. See whether you can improve the quality of these letters in terms of the sharpness of corners and the subtlety of curves, for example in the serifs. Do some experiments to understand how the printer actually prints various shapes, as specified by its input. For example, print vertical and horizontal lines of the same pixel width and measure the actual width of the printed marks. Do straight edges print straight? Do square corners print square?

7. Electronic Mail

Develop a design for integrating typographic information into electronic mail. Bear in mind that existing electronic-mail systems may be constrained to transmitting only ASCII text information. Express your design in the form of a proposal for a standard. How should font and formatting information be expressed to allow nonconforming mail programs to read the messages? Take a position on how much typographic information should be captured in electronic mail.

8. Publishing System Evaluation

Evaluate an existing electronic-publishing system in terms of its typographic quality, flexibility, and ease of use. Report on the quality of the user interface, the extent to which output meets user expectations, and the quality of the output itself. What layout tools are provided? Does the system support WYSIWYG? What kinds of misunderstandings and surprises do users encounter?

9. METAFONT

Use METAFONT to construct a letter similar to the Optima 'f' shown in Fig. A.2. Write a report detailing the difficulties that arose, both

FIGURE A.2   An Optima semibold letter 'f'.

technical and æsthetic, and explain how the problems were addressed (or not addressed) in your program.

10. T_EX

Create a set of T_EX macros to recreate the format of a particular journal or book, for example, *Communications of the ACM*. Format some text using the macros and evaluate the result by comparing it with the original journal or book.

11. Grids as a User Interface

Design a user interface for a desktop-publishing system that specifies page layout with grids. Allow page layouts defined in terms of the grid to be modified themselves, or to be modified implicitly by changing the basic grid design. Make all interactions direct manipulations on the screen, rather than textual or command oriented. Describe the design in a detailed specification document. What actions can users perform? What entities or objects are users aware of, and which can they manipulate? How are they represented to the user? What are the modes? When does the user see and manipulate information that is not printed in a finished document?[1]

---

[1] Two references for user-interface design are included in the bibliography: [Rubinstein and Hersh 1984] and [Shneiderman 1987].

Annotated Bibliography

Achugbue, James O. [1981] "On the Line Breaking Problem in Text Formatting." *SIGPLAN Notices*, Vol. 16, No. 6, 117–122.

Adobe Systems, Inc. [1985a] *PostScript Language Reference Manual.* Reading, Mass.: Addison-Wesley. *This reference book completely describes the PostScript formatting language.*

Adobe Systems, Inc. [1985b] *PostScript Language Tutorial and Cookbook.* Reading, Mass.: Addison-Wesley. *The companion instructional book to the reference manual. Well written, with many examples.*

Apley, Phillip G. [1987] "Automatic Generation of Digital Typographic Images From Outline Masters, or HCD: A Framework for Representing Character." *Proc. of AI '87, The Third Annual AI & Advanced Computer Technology Conference,* April, Long Beach, Calif., 219–229.

Ayers, R. M., J. T. Horning, B. W. Lampson, and J. G. Mitchell [1984] *Interscript: A Proposal for a Standard for the Interchange of Editable Documents.* Palo Alto, Calif.: Xerox Palo Alto Research Center.

Barnett, Michael P. [1965] *Computer Typesetting: Experiments and Prospects.* Cambridge: MIT Press. *An early book on computer-aided typesetting; mostly about programming and formatting issues.*

Beach, Richard J. [1985] *Setting Tables and Illustrations with Style.* Report No. CSL-85-3. Palo Alto, Calif.: Xerox Palo Alto Research Center, May. *A very readable thesis on the problems of typesetting tables, diagrams, and other illustrations. Provides methods of two-dimensional constraint satisfaction for tables. Includes an extensive survey of prior work.*

Beach, Richard J. [1986] "Tabular Typography." In [van Vliet 1986]. *A short but nonetheless thorough survey of the problems of typesetting tables.*

Becker, Joseph D. [1987] "Arabic Word Processing." *Communications of the ACM*, Vol. 30, No. 7, July. *An interesting description of the many problems of processing non-Latin writing systems, including Arabic and Hebrew script.*

Beldie, Ion P., Siegmund Pastoor, and Elmar Schwarz [1983] "Fixed versus Variable Letter Width for Televised Text. *Human Factors*, Vol. 25, No. 3, 273–277. *A comparison of fixed and variable width bitmap fonts for use in television.*

Bell, Carolyn F. [1985] "High-Resolution Printing without a Frame Buffer."

Report No. 85-290. Stanford, Calif.: Stanford University Computer Systems Laboratory. *A Stanford thesis directed at a future in which typesetters operate at extremely high resolution. Proposes an alternative to staging a page to be printed as full bitmap.*

Bhushan, Abhay and Michael Plass [1986] "The Interpress Page and Document Description Language." *IEEE Computer*, Vol. 19, No. 6, 72–77, June.

Bigelow, Charles [Private Communication]

Bigelow, Charles [1981] "Aesthetics vs. Technology: Does Digital Typesetting Mean Degraded Type Design?" in *The Seybold Report on Publishing Systems*, Vol. 10, No. 24, 24 Aug. 1981; continued in Vol. 11, No. 11, 8 Feb. 1982, and Vol. 11, No.12, 22 Feb. 1982. *An authoritative and thorough discussion of the issues of type design in the digital domain. Included is a good discussion of the history of letterforms and writing. Similar to [Bigelow and Day 1983].*

Bigelow, Charles and Donald Day [1983] "Digital Typography." *Scientific American*, Vol. 249, No. 2, Aug. 1983. *This is the best short introduction to the issues of digital typography in an article that can be read in one sitting. A good history of letterforms and writing is included.*

Bigelow, Charles [1985] "Font Design for Personal Workstations," *Byte*, Vol. 10, No. 1, Jan. 1985.

Bigelow, Charles, and Kris Holmes [1986] "The Design of Lucida®: an Integrated Family of Types for Electronic Literacy." In [van Vliet 1986].

Bigelow, Charles, and Lynn Ruggles, eds. [1985] "The Computer and the Hand in Type Design: Proceedings of the Fifth ATypI Working Seminar, Part I." *Visible Language*, Vol. 19, No. 1, Winter. *A special issue of the journal devoted entirely to æsthetic and technical issues in the design of digital type.*

Biggs, John R. [1954] *The Use of Type: The Practice of Typography*. London: Blandford.

Brown, P. J. [1986] "A Simple Mechanism for Authorship of Dynamic Documents." In [van Vliet 1986].

Buckler, Andrew T. [1977] "A Review of the Literature on the Legibility of Alphanumerics on Electronic Displays." Aberdeen Proving Ground, Md.: U.S. Army Human Engineering Laboratory, May.

Burrill, Victoria A. [1986] "VORTEX: VictORias TEXT Reading and Authoring System." In [van Vliet 1986].

Casey, R. G., T. D. Friedman, and K. Y. Wong [1980] "Use of Pattern Processing Techniques to Scale Digital Print Fonts." *Proceedings of the Fifth International Conference on Pattern Recognition, Miami Beach, Fla*: IEEE, Dec. 1–4, 1980. 872–878.

Chamberlin, D. C., *et al*, [1981] "JANUS: An interactive system for document composition." *SIGPLAN Notices*, V. 16, No. 6, June, 82–91.

Chappell, Warren [1970] *A Short History of the Printed Word*. New York: Knopf.

Chaundy, T. W., P. R. Barrett, and Charles Batey [1954] The Printing of Mathematics. London: Oxford University Press. *A good book about how mathematics used to be typeset. Useful both historically and as a catalog of problems that must be solved to typeset mathematics.*

Conrac Corporation [1985] *Raster Graphics Handbook*, 2nd ed. New York: Van Nostrand Reinhold. *A useful reference book containing much technical data on CRTs and other displays, color systems, and graphics programming.*

Cornsweet, Tom N. [1970] *Visual Perception*. New York: Academic Press. *A very substantial and detailed discussion of the behavior of the human vision system considered as an information-processing machine. Useful descriptive engineering data.*

Coueignoux, Philippe J. M. [1975], "Generation of Roman Printed Fonts." Ph.D. dissertation, Cambridge: MIT, June.

Coueignoux, Philippe J. M. [1981] "Character Generation by Computer." In *Computer Graphics and Image Processing*, Vol. 16, 240–269. New York: Academic Press. *A thorough discussion of methods for encoding and generating symbols in a digital, bitmap environment.*

Cowan, D. D. and G. de V. Smit [1986] "Combining Interactive Document Editing with Batch Document Formatting." In [van Vliet 1986].

Cowan, William B., and Colin Ware [1985] *Color Perception Tutorial Notes: SIGGRAPH '85.* (Cowan's address: Division of Physics, National Research Council of Canada, Ottawa, Ontario, Canada K1A 0R6.) *A set of notes based on a SIGGRAPH course, providing an introduction to color perception, including much material that is independent of color.*

Dair, Carl [1967] *Design with Type*. Toronto: University of Toronto Press, paperback reprint 1985. *A good survey of traditional typography with many useful rules of thumb.*

Digital Equipment Corporation [1984] *DECpage User's Guide*. Maynard, Mass.: Digital Equipment Corporation, March 1984.

Downing, Cathryn J., and Steven Pinker [1985] "The Spatial Structure of Visual Attention." In *Attention and Performance XI. Search*, eds. M.I. Posner and O. Marin. Hillsdale, N.J.: Erlbaum.

ECMA [1985] *Standard ECMA-101: Office Document Architecture*. Geneva: European Computer Manufacturers Association, Sept.

Fabrizio, Ralph, Ira Kaplan, and Gilbert Teal [1967] "Readability as a Function of the Straightness of Right-Hand Margins." *Journal of Typographic Research*, Vol. 1, No. 1, Jan. 1967. *An early study that found no difference in reading rate between justified and ragged-right setting of type.*

Flesch, R. F. [1949] *The Art of Readable Writing.* New York: Harper.

Flowers, Jim [1984] "Digital Type Manufacture: An Interactive Approach." *IEEE Computer.* Vol. 17, No. 5, May. *A brief, well-written survey of digital typography and its problems. Describes an interactive design system developed for capture and interactive editing of outline typefaces.*

Foley, James D., and Andries van Dam [1982] *Fundamentals of Interactive Computer Graphics.* Reading, Mass.: Addison-Wesley. *An excellent introduction to the subject of computer graphics.*

Fuchs, David R., and Donald E. Knuth [1982] "Optimal Font Caching." Report No. STAN-CS-82-901. Stanford, Calif.: Stanford University Department of Computer Science, March. *Proposes an algorithm that minimizes the amount of data transfer to communicate font information to a printer. Interesting because as the resolution of printers rises, the minimization of data transfer becomes an increasingly important issue.*

Furuta, Richard, Jeffrey Scofield, and Alan Shaw [1982] "Document Formatting Systems: Survey, Concepts, and Issues," *ACM Computing Surveys,* Vol. 14, No. 3, Sept. *A useful and detailed survey of formatting systems.*

Gaines, Helen Fouché [1939], "Source of Digraph and Trigraph Statistics for Various Languages." In *Cryptanalysis.* New York: Dover, reprint 1956.

Geisler, Wilson S. [1984] "Physical Limits of Acuity and Hyperacuity," *Journal of the Optical Society of America A,* Vol. 1, No. 7, July, 775–782. *A summary of observations of hyperacuity, and the results of a theory and related experiments aimed at understanding them.*

Ghosh, Pijush K. [1983] *An Approach to Type Design and Text Composition in Indian Scripts.* Report No. STAN-CS-83-965. Stanford, Calif.: Stanford University Department of Computer Science, Apr. *There is painfully little in print about the typography of non-Latin writing systems, and even less on producing them by computer. This thorough study explains Indian writing systems and gives* METAFONT *programs for creating the symbols.*

Ghosh, Pijush K. [1984] "Study of Fourier Features for Discrimination of Digitized Letterforms." *International Conference on Computers, Systems, and Signal Processing.* Bangalore, India, 10–12 Dec.

Ghosh, Pijush K., and Charles A. Bigelow [1983] *A Formal Approach to Lettershape Description for Type Design.* Report No. STAN-CS-83-966, Stanford, Calif.: Stanford University Department of Computer Science, May. *A study of the use of* TEX *to produce letterforms by carefully reusing graphical components from letter to letter in the alphabet.*

Ginsburg, Arthur P. [1978] "Visual Information Processing Based on Spatial Filters Constrained by Biological Data." Aerospace Medical Research Laboratory. Wright-Patterson AFB, Ohio.

Ginsburg, Arthur P. [1980] "Specifying Relevant Spatial Information for Image Evaluation and Display Design: An Explanation of How We See

Certain Objects." *Proceedings of the SID,* Vol. 21/3. *Readable article that describes the spatial-frequency channel-filtering theory of the perception of visual objects.*

Goldfarb, C. F. [1981] "A Generalized Approach to Document Markup." *SIGPLAN Notices,* Vol. 16, No. 6, June. *A discussion of the GML markup language.*

Goudy, Frederic W. [1940] *Typologia: Studies in Type Design & Type Making.* Berkeley: University of California Press, reprint 1977. *An idiosyncratic account of type design and letter founding by one of the most prolific twentieth-century type designers. Worth reading for the history and the spirit of the man, though his comments on legibility are not useful for engineering purposes.*

Gould, John D. [1987] "Reading Is Slower from CRT Displays than Paper: Attempts to Isolate a Single-Variable Explanation." *Human Factors,* Vol. 29, No. 3, 269–299. *John Gould and his colleagues are trying to understand why reading speed is lower on CRTs than paper.*

Gould, John D. [1987] "Why Reading Is Slower from CRT Displays than from Paper." *CHI+GI Conference Proceedings: Human Factors in Computing Systems and Graphics Interface,* Apr., 7–11.

Gould, John D., and Nancy Grischkowsky [1984] "Doing the Same Work with Hard Copy and with Cathode-Ray Tube (CRT) Computer Terminals." *Human Factors,* Vol. 26, No. 3, 323–337. *A careful study aimed at understanding differences between reading from screens and paper. No differences in performance, fatigue, or visual acuity were observed in this experiment, although a substantial speed difference in favor of paper was observed.*

Gould, John D., and Nancy Grischkowsky [1986] "Does Visual Angle of a Line of Characters Affect Reading Speed?" in *Human Factors,* Vol. 28, No. 2, 165–173. *This study demonstrates that the angle subtended by reading matter is not a source of difference at the distances from which screens and books are read.*

Gray, Bill [1983] *Tips on Type.* New York: Van Nostrand Reinhold. *A pleasant, informal introduction to the use of type in design.*

Gress, Edmund G. [1917] *The Art & Practice of Typography: A Manual of American Printing.* New York: Oswald.

Grolier [1986] *Academic American Encyclopedia.* Danbury, Conn.

Haber, Ralph N., and Lyn R. Haber [1981] "Visual Components of the Reading Process." *Visible Language,* Vol. 15, No. 2. *A good review article on how information is picked up from the page in reading.*

Hammer, M., et al. [1981] "Étude: An Integrated Document Processing System." Office Automation Group Memo OAM-028. Cambridge: MIT Laboratory for Computer Science, Feb.

Heppner, Frank H., J. G. T. Anderson, A. E. Farstrup, and N. H. Weiderman [1985] "Reading Performance on a Standardized Test Is Better from Print than from Computer Display." *Journal of Reading,* Jan. 321–325.

Hersch, Roger D. [1987] "Character Generation Under Grid Constraints." *Computer Graphics,* Vol. 21, No. 4, July, SIGGRAPH '87, Anaheim, Calif., July 27–31, 243–252. *A detailed description of a method for adjusting outline characters for rasterization so as to preserve their typographic properties.*

Hershey, Allen V. [1972] "A Computer System for Scientific Typography." *Computer Graphics and Image Processing* Vol. 1, 373–385. *An early paper on technical computer typesetting.*

Hess, Stanley [1981] *The Modification of Letterforms.* New York: Art Direction.

Hou, H. S. [1983] *Digital Document Processing.* New York: Wiley. *A good technical introduction to the problems of scanning, storing, enhancing, and printing documents digitally as facsimiles of printed pages. Some material is relevant to synthesizing and formatting documents.*

Hurlburt, Allen [1978] *The Grid: A Modular System for the Design and Production of Newspapers, Magazines, and Books.* New York: Van Nostrand Reinhold. *A complete introduction to using grids in newspaper, magazine, and book design.*

Imagen Corporation [1986] *DDL™ Reference Manual.* Santa Clara, Calif.: Imagen Corporation, Nov.

Joloboff, Vania [1986] "Trends and Standards in Document Representation." In [van Vliet 1986]. *A useful survey of revisable interchange formats, and issues relating to them. Badly edited, but worth the trouble.*

Kajiya, J., and M. Ullner [1981] "Filtering High Quality Text for Display on Raster Scan Devices." *ACM SIGGRAPH Computer Graphics,* Vol. 15, No. 3, Aug. *An analysis of anti-aliasing procedures for use with CRTs.*

Kak, A. V. [1981] "Relationships between Readability of Printed and CRT-displayed Text." *Proceedings of the 1981 Human Factors Society 25th Annual Meeting,* Rochester, N.Y., 137–140.

Karow, Peter *et al.* [1979] "Ikarus-System: computer-controlled font production for CRT and Lasercomp." Hamburg, Germany: Karow Rubow Weber GmbH, September.

Keen, A. J. [1979] "Advanced Technology in Printing: The Laser Printer." *ICL Technical Journal,* May.

Kellerman, David, and Barry Smith, [1987] T_EXTURES: User's Guide. Reading, Mass.: Addison-Wesley.

Kernighan, Brian W. [1981] "PIC—A Language for Typesetting Graphics" *SIGPLAN Notices,* Vol. 16, No. 6, 92–98.

Kindersley, D. [1987] Letter in *The Seybold Report on Publishing Systems,* Vol. 16, No. 15, 13 Apr., 2, 34. *A good though short example of Kindersley's work on optical spacing algorithms.*

Kindersley, D., and Neil Wiseman [1979] "Computer-Aided Letter Design," *Printing World*, 31 Oct., 12–13, 17.

Klauber, James [1984] "The Use of Typography in Office Communication." In *The Practical Aspects of Engineering Communication*, IEEE PCC 84 Conference Record.

Knuth, Donald E. [1984] *The T$_E$Xbook*. Reading, Mass.: Addison-Wesley. *This is the manual for the document formatting language T$_E$X. Among other things, it explains Knuth's ideas about justification (glue), hyphenation, and line-breaking.*

Knuth, Donald E. [1985] "Lessons Learned from METAFONT." *Visible Language*, Vol. 19, No. 1, Winter.

Knuth, Donald E. [1986] *The METAFONT Book*. Reading, Mass.: Addison-Wesley. *A readable introduction to and manual for the METAFONT typeface description language.*

Knuth, Donald E., and M. F. Plass [1981] "Breaking Paragraphs into Lines." *Software—Practice and Experience*, Vol. 11, No. 11, 1119–1234. *A thorough exposition of the paragraph-level optimization methods that went into the T$_E$X formatting system—boxes, glue, and penalties.*

Lamport, Leslie [1986] *L*A*T$_E$X: A Document Preparation System*. Reading, Mass.: Addison-Wesley. *This is the user's manual for a batch formatter that combines the virtues of Scribe—intentional specification and separate document descriptions—with the virtues of T$_E$X—careful setting of text, hyphenation, and high-quality setting of mathematics.*

Lampson, B. W., [1978] "Bravo Manual." In *Alto User's Handbook*, eds. B. W. Lampson and E. A. Taft. Palo Alto, Calif.: Computer Science Laboratory, Xerox Palo Alto Research Center.

Lawson, Alexander [1971] *Printing Types: An Introduction*. Boston: Beacon. *A useful introduction that includes a taxonomy of typefaces.*

Lee, Marshall [1979] *Bookmaking: The Illustrated Guide to Design/Production/ Editing*, 2d ed. New York: Bowker. *A course in the design and production of books by traditional means, a useful reference.*

Leler, William J. [1980] "Human Vision, Anti-aliasing, and the Cheap 4000 Line Display." *Computer Graphics*, Vol. 14, No. 3 (SIGGRAPH '80 conference proceedings), July, 308–313.

Lewis, John [1978] *Typography: Design and Practice*. New York: Taplinger. *Introductory typography book containing a section on phototypesetting and discussions of various early computer-controlled typesetting devices.*

Liang, Franklin Mark [1983] *Word Hy-phen-a-tion by Com-put-er*. Ph.D. dissertation, Stanford University. Report No. STAN-CS-83-977. Stanford, Calif.: Stanford University Department of Computer Science, Aug. *A well-written dissertation that carefully describes issues in dictionary construction for hyphenation. This work is the basis for the hyphenation algorithms in* T$_E$X.

Mackinlay, Jock D. [1986] *Automatic Design of Graphical Presentations.* Ph.D. dissertation, Stanford, Calif.: Department of Computer Science, Stanford University, Dec.

Mañas, José A. [1987] "Word Division in Spanish." *Communications of the ACM,* Vol. 30, No. 7, July.

McLean, Ruari [1980] *The Thames and Hudson Manual of Typography.* London: Thames and Hudson. *A broad, very readable introduction to conventional typography. This is the best recent general book if you read only one.*

Media Lab [1986] *MIT Media Laboratory.* Videotape Produced and directed by Guy Guillet; introduction and narration by Walter Cronkite. Cambridge: MIT Media Laboratory. *The typographically related projects described include a customized newspaper and a program for designing business cards.*

Mei, Tung Yun [1980] "LCCD, A Language for Chinese Character Design." Report No. 80–824. Stanford, Calif.: Stanford Computer Science Department, Oct.

Mendelson, Jerry [1985] "A Comparison of Interpress and PostScript." Palo Alto, Calif.: Xerox Corporation, Apr.

Merriam-Webster [1983] *Webster's Ninth New Collegiate Dictionary.* Springfield, Mass.: Merriam-Webster.

Mewhort, D. J. K. [1966] "Sequential Redundancy and Letter Spacing as Determinants of Tachistoscopic Recognition." *Canadian Journal of Psychology,* Vol. 20, No. 4, 435–444.

Meyer, Gary W., and Donald P. Greenberg [1980] "Perceptual Color Spaces for Computer Graphics." *Computer Graphics,* Vol. 14, No. 3 (SIGGRAPH '80 conference proceedings), July, 254–261.

Meyrowitz, Norman, and Andries van Dam [1982], "Document Formatting Systems: Survey, Concepts, and Issues." ACM *Computing Surveys,* Vol. 14, No. 3, Sept.

Moitra, Abha [1979] "Design and Analysis of a Hyphenation Procedure." *Software—Practice and Experience,* Vol. 9, 325–337. New York: Wiley.

Morris, Robert A. [1986] "The Interleaf User Interface" *Protext III, Proceedings of the Third International Conference on Text Processing Systems, J. J. H. Miller, ed.* Dublin, Ireland: Boole.

Morrison, Robert E., and Albrecht-Werner Inhoff [1981] "Visual Factors and Eye Movements in Reading." *Visible Language,* Vol. 15, No. 2, Spring. *A good survey article linking reading speed to typographic variables. Largely an analysis of Tinker's much-earlier work.*

Mudur, S. P. and R. Sujata [1982] "Three Systems for Typesetting: A Survey." *Computer Science and Informatics*, Vol. 12, No. 1. A comparison of three batch page-layout systems: DIP, Scribe, and T_EX.

Naiman, Avi C. [1985] "High-Quality Text for Raster Displays." Ph.D. dissertation, University of Toronto, Jan. *A definitive study, including much useful background material on perception and color.*

Naiman, Avi C., and Alain Fournier [1987] "Rectangular Convolution for Fast Filtering of Characters." *Computer Graphics*, Vol. 21, No. 4, July, SIGGRAPH '87, Anaheim, Calif. July 27–31, 1987, 233–242. *A detailed article describing a computationally-efficient method for generating grayscale fonts.*

Neisser, Ulric [1967] *Cognitive Psychology.* New York: Appleton-Century-Crofts. *Excellent, classic, and very readable introduction to the subject. Unfortunately, little of direct relevance to typographical issues emerges due to the low level of detailed knowledge of the mechanisms of reading.*

Nelson, T. H. [1974] *Dream Machines—New Freedoms through Computer Screens.* South Bend, Ind.: Ted Nelson.

Newman, William M., and Robert F. Sproull [1979] *Principles of Interactive Computer Graphics*, 2d ed. New York: McGraw-Hill. *An excellent introduction to and reference for interactive computer graphics; includes several chapters on raster graphics techniques.*

Pardoe, F. E. [1975] *John Baskerville of Birmingham: Letter-Founder & Printer.* London: Frederick Muller. *A readable account of the life of a great printer who was responsible for a substantial advancement of the art, as well as for typefaces still very much in use.*

Patterson, Donald G., and Miles A. Tinker [1940] *How To Make Type Readable: A Manual for Typographers, Printers and Advertisers.* New York: Harper & Brothers.

Paxton, Bill [1983] "The Tioga Editor." Xerox Corporation Internal Memo.

Payne, Donald E. [1967] "Readability of Typewritten Material: Proportional versus Standard Spacing." *Journal of Typographic Research*, Vol. 1, No. 2, Apr.

Perfect, Christopher, and Gordon Rookledge [1983] *Rookledge's International Typefinder.* London: Sarema. *Intended to help professional graphic designers and typographers identify typefaces. As such, it is not only useful for identifying type, but also is an excellent eye trainer and tutorial on the elements of typeface design, presenting an analytic scheme of classification. An expensive paperback, but fun if one is hooked on the diversity of typefaces.*

Plass, Michael F. [1981] *Optimal Pagination Techniques for Automatic Typesetting Systems.* Ph.D. dissertation. Report No. STAN-CS-81-870. Palo

Alto, Calif.: Stanford University Department of Computer Science, June. *A thoughtful approach, using dynamic programming, to the problem of optimizing the pagination of a document considered as a whole. Based on the T$_E$X box, glue, and penalty model.*

Pratt, Vaughan [1985] "Techniques for Conic Splines." In *SIGGRAPH* '85, Vol. 19, No. 3. *An excellent tutorial on conic splines, to which cubic splines are compared for their utility for describing letter shapes. The work described was done specifically for storing and generating letterforms.*

Pratt, William K. [1978] *Digital Image Processing.* New York: Wiley. *A good basic reference that includes information on image sampling, enhancement, analysis, and coding.*

Proudfoot, W. B. [1972] *The Origin of Stencil Duplicating.* London: Hutchinson. *This is a fascinating, historical account of early methods of office duplication.*

Rayner, Keith, ed. [1981] *Visual Cues in Word Recognition and Reading.* Special issue of *Visible Language,* Vol. 15, No. 2, Spring. *A survey of typographical and psychological factors in the reading process.*

Reid, Brian K. [1980] "Scribe: A Document Specification Language and Its Compiler." Ph.D. dissertation, Carnegie-Mellon University, Oct. *The original report on Scribe, an innovative intentional document formatter.*

Reid, Brian K. [1986] "Procedural Page Description Languages." In [van Vliet 1986].

Robinson, Arthur H. [1952] *The Look of Maps.* Madison: University of Wisconsin Press. *Much of this book concerns the legibility of text as used on maps—isolated, in various colors and sizes, and in different variations. Interesting for its different requirements for visibility and legibility of print, compared with running text.*

Roetling, Paul G. [1977] "Binary Approximation of Continuous Tone Images." *Photographic Science and Engineering,* Vol. 21, No. 2, Mar./Apr. *A description of various dithering methods for producing halftone images.*

Rogers, Bruce [1979] *Paragraphs on Printing.* New York: Dover, "An unabridged republication of the work first published by William E. Rudge's Sons, New York, in 1943." *Thoughts and examples from one of the masters of book design.*

Rogowitz, Bernice E. [1983] "The Human Visual System: A Guide for the Display Technologist." *Proceedings of the SID,* Vol. 24/3. *An excellent survey of spatial information processing by the visual system.*

Rogowitz, Bernice E. [1984] "The Human Visual System: The New Key to Making Better Images." *SIGGRAPH* '84 seminar.

Rubinstein, Richard [1974], "Computers and a Liberal Education: Using LOGO and Computer Art." Ph.D. dissertation, University of California, Irvine.

Rubinstein, Richard, and Harry Hersh [1984] *The Human Factor: Designing Computer Systems for People.* Bedford, Mass.: Digital Press. *Contains a chapter on conceptual models in user-interface design. Useful for its methodology and guidelines.*

Rubinstein, Richard, et al. [1985] "Digital Typography and the Human Interface: Proceedings of the Typography Interest Group at CHI '85." *SIGCHI Bulletin*, Vol. 17, No. 1, July. *Edited transcripts of short papers given by typographers, software designers, and human factors specialists provide a summary of issues in digital typography.*

Ruggles, Lynn [1983], *Letterform Design Systems.* Report No. STAN-CS-83-971. Palo Alto, Calif.: Stanford University Department of Computer Science, Apr. *A useful survey of design systems, including information about ITSLF, CSD, ELF, PM Digital Spiral, Ikarus, and METAFONT.*

Sauvain, Richard and Elizabeth Wayman [1987] "Typefounder—A Collection of Digital Font Creation Tools," *PROTEXT IV; The Fourth International Conference on Text Processing Systems*, 10–22 Oct.

Schmandt, Christopher [1980] "Soft Typography." In *Information Processing 80,* ed. S. H. Lavington. IFIP. *A clear explanation in engineering rather than perceptual terms of the virtues of gray levels in fonts, in this case those displayed on conventional TV screens.*

Schmandt, Christopher [1985] *Grayscale Fonts Designed from Video Signal Analysis.* Report No. 11-51-85. Cambridge: MIT Industrial Liaison Program.

Sekuler, Robert, Hugh R. Wilson, and Cynthia Owsley [1984] "Structural Modeling of Spatial Vision." *Vision Research*, Vol. 24, No. 7, 689–700.

Shani, Uri [1980] "Filling Regions in Binary Raster Images: A Graph-Theoretic Approach." *Computer Graphics*, Vol. 14, No. 3 (SIGGRAPH '80 conference proceedings), July, 321–325. *When working with bitmaps, filling regions with a color or pattern presents problems of identifying closed regions, and of performing the operations efficiently. This paper presents a useful approach to these problems.*

Shneiderman, Ben [1987] *Designing the User Interface: Strategies for Effective Human-Computer Interaction.* Reading, Mass.: Addison-Wesley.

Siegel, David R. [1985] *The Euler Project at Stanford.* Palo Alto, Calif.: Stanford University Department of Computer Science. *A wonderful account of a project to develop a new digital typeface. Much of the struggle is described.*

Simon and Schuster [1967] *The Way Things Work: An Illustrated Encyclopedia of Technology.* New York: Simon & Schuster.

Simon, Oliver [1945] *Introduction to Typography.* Cambridge: Harvard University Press. *A good traditional typography book, sadly out of print.*

Southall, Richard [1985] *Designing New Typefaces with METAFONT.* Report

No. STAN-CS-85-1074. Palo Alto, Calif.: Stanford University Department of Computer Science, Sept. *A study of the difficulties of font design, using METAFONT. Includes an elaborate set of terminology for describing electronic and paper documents as virtual, actual, copies, and so on.*

Taylor, Insup, and M. Martin Taylor [1983] *The Psychology of Reading.* New York: Academic Press. *A broad and interesting introduction to reading and how people do it.*

Tinker, Miles A. [1963a] "Influence of Simultaneous Variation in Size of Type, Width of Line, and Leading for Newspaper Type." *Journal of Applied Psychology.* Vol. 47, No. 6, 380–382.

Tinker, Miles A. [1963b] *Legibility of Print.* Ames: Iowa State University Press. *A most-readable summary of the work of more than 30 years by Tinker, his coworkers, and others. Tinker's studies on legibility are sophisticated typographically, careful psychologically, and represent an immense effort involving tens of thousands of experimental subject sessions.*

Tinker, Miles A. [1965] *Bases for Effective Reading.* Minneapolis: University of Minnesota Press. *A slightly later book than* Legibility of Print *summarizing much of the same work. Very readable.*

Tobin, Georgia K. M. [1985] *The Elements of METAFONT Style.* Preliminary Version, 4 August. *Course notes for a course of the same name, offered at Stanford by the T_EX Users Group.*

Trollip, Stanley R., and Gregory Sales [1986] "Readability of Computer-Generated Fill-Justified Text," *Human Factors,* Vol. 28, No. 2, 159–163. *A study that shows that ragged-right text is read faster than right-and-left justified text containing the same words on each line. Unfortunately, the study was done with monospaced type.*

Tschichold, Jan [1967] *Asymmetric Typography.* New York: Reinhold. *Translation by Ruari McLean of Tschichold's classic book (Basle:* Typographische Gestaltung, *1935). This is the bible for the revolt against the old ways of laying out pages in totally symmetric form. It is the basis for most of today's layout; our modern eyes expect the kind of images that were revolutionary when Tschichold described them.*

Tschichold, Jan [1975] "Penguin Composition Rules." In *Jan Tschichold: Typographer,* ed. Ruari McLean, 94–95. Boston: Godine.

Turba, Thomas N. [1981] "Checking for Spelling and Typographical Errors in Computer-Based Text." *SIGPLAN Notices,* Vol. 16, No. 6, June, 50–60. *Includes a survey of data representation for very large dictionaries.*

Ulichney, Robert [1987] *Digital Halftoning.* Cambridge: MIT Press. *Based on a doctoral thesis, this book provides detailed examples of a wide range of choices for spatial dithering. It analyzes these patterns in terms of their Fourier transforms, and proposes a new method based on "blue noise."*

Updike, Daniel Berkeley [1980] *Printing Types: Their History, Forms, and Use.*

Vols. 1 and 2, 2d ed. Cambridge: Harvard University Press (Dover reprint). *Voluminous history of old typefaces and their development, with many examples reproduced.*

van Nes, Floris L. [1986] "A New Teletext Character Set with Enhanced Legibility." *IEEE Transactions on Electron Devices*, Vol. ED-33, No. 8, Aug. *An effort to improve the quality of text presented on TV screens.*

van Vliet, J. C., ed. [1986] *Text Processing and Document Manipulation: Proceedings of the International Conference, University of Nottingham, 14–16 Apr.* New York: Cambridge University Press. *An interesting set of papers on various subjects, including type design, layout, structured editing, formatters, page-description languages, and document retrieval. Individual papers from this volume are listed separately in this bibliography.*

Van Wyk, Christopher John [1980] "A Language for Typesetting Graphics." Ph.D. dissertation. Report No. STAN-CS-80-803. Palo Alto, Calif.: Stanford University Department of Computer Science, June. *A textual, declarative language for describing two-dimensional pictures.*

Waern, Yvonne, and Carl Rollenhagen [1983] "Reading Text from Visual Display Units (VDUs)." *International Journal of Man-Machine Studies*, Vol. 18, 441–465. *An analysis of the task of reading from CRTs from a psychological viewpoint.*

Warnock, John E. [1980] "The Display of Characters Using Gray Level Sample Arrays." *Computer Graphics*, Vol. 14, No. 3 (SIGGRAPH '80 conference proceedings), July. *The original grayscale font paper, well written, concise, and useful.*

Warnock, John E. and Douglas K. Wyatt [1982] "A Device Independent Graphics Imaging Model for Use with Raster Devices." *Computer Graphics*, Vol. 16, No. 3, Proceedings of SIGGRAPH '82, July, 313–319.

Westheimer, G. [1979] "The spatial sense of the eye," *Invest. Ophthalmol.*, Vol. 18, 893–912. *A description of early observations of hyperacuity.*

Wiggins, Richard H. [1967] "Effects of Three Typographical Variables on Speed of Reading." *Journal of Typographic Research*, Vol. 1, No. 1, 5–18, Jan. *This journal is now called* Visible Language.

Williamson, Hugh [1956] *Methods of Book Design: The Practice of an Industrial Craft.* New York: Oxford University Press. *A very complete reference book.*

Wilson, Adrian [1974] *The Design of Books.* Salt Lake City: Peregrine Smith. *A lively book by a master contemporary book designer, providing a basic introduction to book design.*

Wilson, Hugh R., and Douglas J. Gelb [1984] "Modified Line-Element Theory for Spatial-Frequency and Width Discrimination." *Journal of the Optical Society of America*, Vol. 1, No. 1, Jan.

Witten, Ian H. [1985] "Elements of Computer Typography." *International*

Journal of Man-Machine Studies, Vol. 23, 623–687. *Extensive, well-written survey, including many useful algorithms for line breaking and hyphenation.*

Wolcott, Norman M., and Joseph Hilsenrath [1976] *A Contribution to Computer Typesetting Techniques: Tables of Coordinates for Hershey's Repertory of Occidental Type Fonts and Graphic Symbols.* Washington, D.C.: National Bureau of Standards, Apr.

Xerox [1985] "The Xerox 6085 Professional Computer System." El Segundo, Calif.: Xerox Corporation, Apr.

Zapf, Hermann [1968] "Changes in Letterforms Due to Technical Developments" *Journal of Typographic Research,* Vol. 2, No. 4, Oct.

Zapf, Hermann [1970] *About Alphabets: Some Marginal Notes on Type Design.* Cambridge: MIT Press. *More of a loose autobiography of Zapf than a general study of type design, but very interesting as the perspective of an important contemporary type designer.*

Zapf, Hermann [1985] "Future Tendencies in Type Design: The Scientific Approach to Letterforms." *Visible Language,* Vol. 19, No. 1, Winter.

Glossary

accent. A diacritical mark near or through a letter indicating a variation in pronunciation. Examples: ç, à, ò, é, Å.

addressing resolution. The degree of fineness of position that the computer can specify for an output device.

aliasing. The misrepresentation of high frequencies from the original signal as low frequencies in the sampled result, due to undersampling. Aliasing distorts letterforms and letter spacing.

alphabet. The set of abstract symbols employed in a particular writing system.

Alto computer. An early raster-graphic workstation developed at Xerox Palo Alto Research Center. It was the vehicle for work such as the Bravo editor that helped in the development of WYSIWYG editors, compound documents, and direct-manipulation user interfaces.

analog letterform. A glyph, drawn or printed, sometimes used as a model for creating a similar digitized shape. Analog letterform designs may be expressed as smooth curves that are then digitized.

anisotropic scaling. Enlarging or shrinking letters nonlinearly, so that, for example, they become disproportionately less bold and narrower for their height as they are enlarged. Such transformations can create some of the traditional variations in shape of typefaces at different sizes.

anisotropy. A property of some output devices that gives different results on the x- and y-axes. In CRTs, for example, black features crossed by the scan are narrowed preferentially compared with those running parallel to the scan.

anti-aliasing. Removing alias frequencies from the sampled signal. In letterforms, jaggedness can be minimized during reconstruction by using varying gray levels at the edges of strokes.

arc. Segment of a circle or ellipse, sometimes used to describe part of the boundary of a letterform.

ascender. That part of a lower case letter that rises above the x-height, as in the letters 'b', 'd', 'f', 'h', 'k', 't', and 'l'.

ASCII. The American Standard Code for Information Interchange, a standard character set defined by ANSI, the American National Standards Institute.

aspect ratio. The ratio of width to height.

assimilation. The symmetry property possessed in varying degrees by a typeface that creates mirror relationships and other similarities of form between letters.

asymmetry. Aspects of letterforms that depart from mirror image relationships between letter pairs, especially 'b–d' and 'p–q', and within individual letters, such as 'T' in some typefaces.

back up. To match the vertical position of lines on the opposite sides of a sheet printed on both sides.

background. The field on which a letter or graphic appears; the blank paper or screen on which the image is formed.

bandwidth. The information capacity of a channel or medium. The spatial bandwidth of a printer or display is the number of on-off cycles per unit of length that it can resolve.

baseline. The imaginary line upon which printed letters without descenders appear to rest.

Baskerville, John. Eighteenth-century printer and typefounder noted for his precise, high-quality printing. A modern version of Baskerville's type that bears his name is still popular.

Bézier splines. A class of third-degree interpolating splines useful for representing letterform shapes.

Bigelow, Charles. A contemporary digital typographer and type designer.

binding of variables. The association of values with abstract variables, for example, when the formal parameters to a subroutine are assigned values in a particular call. In document preparation, making decisions (about resolution, for example) that determine the prop-

erties of the result and the relationship between draft and final versions.

bitmap. An array of intensity values, normally rectangular, used to create an image, as on a screen or on paper. The bits are "mapped" onto the screen or paper.

bitmapped display. An output device that portrays a bitmap image. A raster display is a bitmap display in which the bitmap data are scanned line by line.

blackness. The apparent darkness of type as it appears on the page. Blackness depends on the broadness of the parts of the letter (boldness), as well as on the x-height and set.

bleed. An image that extends to the edge of the paper (after trimming).

Bodoni. A modern typeface with unbracketed serifs, vertical stress, and very high contrast.

bold. A blacker, heavier variation of a typeface, relative to the roman variation.

bowl. The loop in a letter that encloses a counter (white space), as in the letters 'a' and 'g'.

Bravo. Early, innovative WYSIWYG, bitmap editor that ran on the Alto computer.

break. Deciding how much text shall appear on each line or page of a document.

brightness. The perceived intensity level of light in a visual scene.

brilliance. Property of a typeface related to its typographic contrast. Also referred to as sparkle.

bullet. A mark used to set off items in a list, frequently a filled circle (•), whence its name.

CAD. Computer-aided design.

calligraphic display. An image-display device that produces images by directly creating lines, arcs, and so on, as opposed to a bitmap display. Also called a stroke display.

cap-height. The height above the baseline of capital letters.

captions. Text associated with pictures, figures, or tables within a larger document.

Carter, Matthew. Contemporary typographer and digital typeface designer.

Caslon, William. An eighteenth-century printer, type designer, and type founder. The modern typeface that bears his name is based on one of his designs.

cathode ray tube (CRT). Display device that creates an image by selectively activating a light-emitting phosphor with a beam of electrons.

cell text. A monospaced typeface, usually associated with older display devices.

centered. Text set so as to distribute residual space on the line equally to the right and left.

character. An abstract symbol, represented within a computer by a numeric code. Also, a symbol in a font, or a glyph.

character set. An ordered set of abstract symbols, used to represent and exchange information, in which a particular symbol is represented by its index.

chromatic aberration. An aberration in the eye (or any optical system) that causes light of different colors to be focused in different planes.

CIE. Commission Internationale de l'Éclairage, a standards organization that developed a standard for the precise description of colors.

collateral font design. The author's term. A font-design method in which the quality of low- and high-resolution versions is compromised to achieve uniform quality.

colophon. A description of how a book was produced, normally placed at the end. Also, a printers mark or emblem.

color. (physics) The spectral distribution of light, that is, the collection of wavelengths it contains.

color. (typography) The overall blackness of a page of text, that is, its average density. By extension, the blackness of a typeface when set in a block.

color. (vision) The perception that results from viewing light of a particular spectral distribution.

compound document. A document that contains, in addition to text, graphics, images, or other nontextual components.

Computer Modern. A coordinated family of typefaces designed by Donald Knuth and expressed by him in the METAFONT language.

conceptual model. The idea or the understanding that the user of a computer system develops in the course of learning to use the system. Conceptual models are constructed on the basis of prior knowledge and system behavior.

condensed. A type-design variation with less than normal set; thus a tightly spaced font.

cone. A light-sensitive cell in the retina of the eye that responds differentially to color. There are three classes of cones in the human eye, with differing absorption spectra.

conic spline. A spline curve of order two.

constraint. A condition that must be satisfied. For example, if two lines in a picture are constrained to be parallel, this property must be maintained when the image containing the lines is transformed.

continuous tone. A picture with continuously varying levels of intensity, as contrasted with bivalued images.

contrast. (typography) The ratio of thickness of vertical to horizontal strokes in letterforms.

contrast ratio. (engineering) The ratio of signal to noise. For images presented on screens or on paper, the brightness contrast is the ratio of the intensity of the foreground to background parts of the image.

counter. (typography) The inside of a loop or bowl in a letterform.

critical-fusion frequency. The rate at which a flickering light appears to be constant.

CRT. Cathode ray tube.

cubic splines. A spline curve of order three.

cursive. Typefaces that resemble handwriting, frequently having joins or the suggestion of joins between letters. Scriptlike.

DDL. A page-description language developed by Imagen Corporation.

decode. In reading, to identify letters and words.

DECpage. A document-formatting system developed by Digital Equipment Corporation.

demand publishing. Creation of printed documents in small runs or even in single copies, as needed.

demerits. A point system used to rate the quality of a particular arrangement of type, for example, when line breaking in TeX. Lines receive demerits for faults such as being too loose or tight; paragraphs, for defects such as consecutive hyphenations.

dentation. The manipulation of the edges of graphic images so as to minimize the effects of aliasing and reconstruction errors. Also called half-bitting.

depth. The vertical extent on the page of a block of print.

descender. That portion of a letter that falls below the baseline, as in 'j', 'g', 'q', 'p' and 'y'.

desktop publishing. Direct printing of typeset material using small, relatively inexpensive computers and printers under the direct control of the creator of the material.

diacritical mark. An accent or other ancillary mark added to a letter to distinguish it or change its pronunciation.

Didot point. Unit of type measurement in Europe (except Britain); 1 Didot point = 0.3759 mm.

digital halftoning. The simulation of continuous-tone pictures by the algorithmic arrangement of bivalued picture elements. Also called spatial dithering.

digital typography. The technology of using computers for the presentation of text, in which the letters themselves are created and positioned under digital control.

digitization error. The loss of information in the sampling of a signal. The broader class of errors of which aliasing is an example.

digitize. To sample an analog signal and represent the results in a numeric form.

digraph-spacing adjustment. The author's term for kerning in digital type. Adjusting the spacing of letters pairwise to achieve optically equal interletter spacing.

dingbat. A special symbol not a part of any particular typeface, including arrows, mathematical signs such as square root, and bullets, for example: ♠ ✔ ✂ ☛ ∉ ® √ ♠ ○.

direct manipulation. Style of user interface in which the user modifies or moves parts of the document using a pointing device such as a mouse.

display. (engineering) Machine or device for presenting text and graphics dynamically, under computer control.

display. (typography) Large sizes of type, for use as headlines, titles, and so forth.

displayed formulas. Sequences of lines of mathematical notation included within running text.

dithering. Spatial dithering, the method of creating digital halftones.

document model. An external myth that presents textual and graphical information as (simulated) paper documents.

document. Any "printed" image stored in a computer or realized on a piece of paper.

dots per inch (dpi). Measure of the resolution or addressability of input and output devices.

draft printing. Printing a test copy of a document before printing it in final form.

dyslexia. A perceptual aberration, one form of which causes confusion of mirror-image letter pairs, especially 'p–q' and 'b–d'.

ECMA. European Computer Manufacturers Association.

edge enhancement. (image processing) An image-processing technique that identifies the boundaries of objects and increases their contrast.

edge enhancement. (perception) The sharpening of edges in an image by the visual system.

electrographic printer. A printer that uses a direct electrostatic-printing process in which charge is placed directly on the paper and then developed to form an image by the application of toner.

electronic publishing. Digital typography.

elite. A typewriter (monospaced) typeface with a pitch of 12 characters per inch.

em. A horizontal space equal to the type size. Thus, in 12-point type, an em equals 12 points.

en. Half an em.

endnote. A piece of text associated with the body of a document, like a foot-note but placed at the end of a section or chapter.

erosion. The thinning of the vertical strokes in letter forms that results from characteristics of the output device.

expanded or extended. A type design variation with more than normal set. Thus, a loosely spaced or wider than normal font.

extensional specification. In a document formatter, the detailed specification of formatting information such as spacing, margins, and font, as opposed to intentional specification, in which the purpose of a passage is described, for example, verse.

external myth. The external behavior of a computer system, as observable via the user interface. Users develop an understanding of how the system works in large part by observing this behavior. The external myth may represent internal technical details accurately, or it may present an entirely synthetic reality for the user's benefit.

facsimile. Electronic representation of images, often entire documents, for transmission over a distance, frequently by a telephone or computer network using digital encoding.

family. A related set of typefaces.

fatigue. The subjective feeling of tiredness. Also, the physical inability to continue with an activity because of loss of strength or control in muscles due to strenuous use.

fields. The portions of a displayed frame that are scanned alternately in an interlaced refreshing scheme. In broadcast television, the lines in the two fields alternate, and each field contains half of the scan lines.

figure. (perception) The object seen, as separated in the act of seeing from everything else in the image.

figure. (typography) A picture or diagram that may be included within the body of a typeset document.

figures, lining. Modern numbers, all of which rest on the baseline.

figures, nonlining. Old-style numbers, some of which (3,4,5,7,9) descend below the baseline. For example, 0 1 2 3 4 5 6 7 8 9.

fill. The graphical operation of reproducing a pattern or color throughout a bounded area.

fixation. The stopping of the eye to sample the visual scene. Even during fixations, there are continual small motions of the eye.

fixed pitch. Monospaced type.

fleuron. A printer's flower or ornament, for example: ❁ ❤ ❊ ᭥.

flicker fusion frequency. The temporal rate of intensity variation of a light or image at which a particular person sees the light as steady. Flicker-fusion frequency varies from person to person, with the degree of modulation of the intensity variation, and with the angle from the center of the visual field.

floating object. An illustration, table, or diagram that the document formatter is free to place in various places relative to the running text.

flower. A printer's decorative symbol. Also called a fleuron.

flush left. Setting lines of text so that any extra space is on the right, and the text is against the left margin. Also called ragged right.

flush right. Setting lines of text so that any extra space is on the left, and the text is against the right margin.

folio. A page number, for example as part of a running head or foot.

font. A fixed example or instance of a typeface, usually of a single size and variation, and often tailored to a particular output device.

footnote. A floating note associated with a location and reference mark in a text and displayed at the bottom of the page on which the mark occurs.

foreground. The image or figure, as opposed to the background.

foundry. Originally, a factory in which metal type is made; now any maker of type.

Fourier transform. The mathematical transformation that allows a function in time or space to be examined in terms of its frequency components.

fovea. In the eye, the small, central region of the retina that exhibits the greatest sensitivity to detail and color.

galley. In traditional typesetting, a proof of the running text, tables, or figures, before these parts are combined to form pages.

Garamond, Claude. Sixteenth-century type designer. The Monotype Corporation typeface that mistakenly bears his name was based on a typeface later discovered to be the work of Jean Jannon; the corresponding italic is based on a face by Robert Granjon.

gestalt. The perceptual process of separating figure and ground to create an overall visual understanding of an image.

glyph. A single graphic symbol, as actually realized on paper or a display screen.

Goudy, Frederic W. Prolific twentieth-century type designer. Among other faces, he designed Goudy Oldstyle, in which this book is typeset.

grayscale fonts. Fonts that use variations in intensity at the edges of the letters to suppress the effects of aliasing and thus improve the apparent sharpness and fineness of letterforms.

grid. (engineering) A control structure in a CRT, used to modulate the intensity of the electron beam, and thus the brightness of spots on the phosphor screen.

grid. (typography) A graphical layout

for the design of pages of a book or other document. Variations on pages must match divisions in the grid.

ground. (perception) That part of an image that is seen as the background, rather than the perceived object, called the figure.

Gutenberg. (unit of measure) A unit of linear measure equal to 1/7200 inch, or about 1/100 of a point.

Gutenberg, Johann. The generally acknowledged inventor of printing with movable type.

gutter. The inside edge in a book where facing pages meet. When printing a book, extra margin width is usually needed on gutter edges to allow for the binding. Also, the white space between columns.

h and j. Also H/J. Typesetting abbreviation for hyphenation and justification.

hairline. The thinnest part of a letter other than the serif. Joins are frequently hairlines. Also, a fine line or rule, the thinnest that can be reproduced in printing.

half-bitting. The manipulation of the edges of graphic images so as to minimize the effects of aliasing and reconstruction errors. Also called dentation.

half tone. A method of simulating continuous-tone images with a device that has a small number of output tones, colors, or intensities. The patterns used are called dithers.

heading. Text that introduces sections of text, set off from the text by differences in size, typeface, or position.

Helvetica. A popular sans serif typeface.

Hershey fonts. A public-domain set of typefaces specified as strokes, originally for pen-and-ink plotters, still used in rasterized bitmap form.

Hertz. A unit of frequency, cycles per second. Abbreviated Hz.

Holmes, Kris. A contemporary calligrapher and type designer, the designer of the Isadora typeface.

hue. The perception of light that corresponds to changes in wavelength.

hyperacuity. A perceptual phenomenon in which spatial frequencies much higher than usual are detected.

Hypertext. A system proposed by Ted Nelson and others in which a rich structure of interconnections is created and used within on-line electronic documents.

hyphenation. The splitting of a word across lines, as an aid to uniform line breaking.

illusions. Perceptions created in the visual system and brain that differ from the "objective" environment as measured by physical instruments.

image. Bitmap pictures, often representing real scenes as viewed by a camera, as opposed to text or line graphics.

image contrast. The ratio of the maximum luminance (intensity) in an image to the minimum luminance.

imposition. In printing, the arranging of pages on a larger sheet in the correct order and orientation so that when the sheet is folded the pages will appear in order.

indentation. Insetting a line of text in from the margin, as at the beginning of a paragraph or within an outline, or to set off a quotation.

inking. The electronic filling of regions on a display.

inline font specification. A pen path that, in conjunction with a pen shape for marking along the path, specifies a letterform.

intensity. The luminance of light.

intensity contrast. See image contrast.

intentional specification. In a document formatter, the functional specification of formatting information without providing details of spacing, margins, font, or the like, as opposed to extensional specification, in which detailed formatting changes are described.

interchange protocol. A communications convention or standard that describes how information is represented and transmitted from point to point or between (dissimilar) systems.

interlaced display. A technique used with CRT displays to reduce the data rate at which the display must be refreshed. Two fields, containing alternate lines, are refreshed alternately.

Interleaf. A compound-document editor for workstations, created by Interleaf Corporation.

interletter space. The horizontal space between individual letterforms within a single word. Interletter space may be adjusted as a function of the letters (see kerning), but its proper value is an integral part of the typeface design.

interpolating curves. Parametric curves that are constrained to pass through the control points that specify them.

Interpress. A page-description language developed by Xerox Corporation.

Interscript. A machine-parsable, modifiable transmission format developed at Xerox Palo Alto Research Center.

interword space. The horizontal space between words on a line. Interword space can be adjusted to achieve justification.

inverse video. Also, reverse video. Literally, the reversal of black for white and white for black in a bitmap screen image. Incongruously used by computer people to indicate light letters on a dark background, which is the inverse of the historically more common dark letters on a light background. Also, reversal of foreground and background colors.

ISO. International Organization for Standardization.

italic. A type design that is both slanted and scriptlike (cursive).

ITC. International Typeface Corporation, a major vendor of typefaces.

jaggies. Roughness in the edges of letterforms, most notably on curved and diagonal parts. Jaggies may result from aliasing, or from improper reconstruction of the image from the data. See aliasing.

join. The thin stroke that connects two main strokes in a letter form.

joint. The point in common between two adjoining segments of a spline curve.

justification. Generically, placing lines of text in a particular relationship to one or both margins. As distinct from flush left or flush right, justified text has both the left and right margins even.

kern. (electronic typesetting) To adjust the interletter spacing of two or more letters so as to equalize optical spacing.

kern. (traditional typesetting) A part of a letter that extends onto the space occupied by an adjacent letter's type body.

knot. The point where connected curves join.

Knuth, Donald. Contemporary computer scientist responsible for the TEX formatter and the METAFONT font-production language.

landscape orientation. A layout wider than it is high, whether on screen or paper.

laser printer. A device similar to an office copier in which the image is created on a photosensitive surface, usually a drum, via a computer-controlled beam of light from a laser.

lateral inhibition. The basic means by which edges are detected in the retina. Adjacent excitatory and inhibitory regions signal differences in illumination between them.

LCD. Liquid crystal display.

leading. Interline spacing added to improve the legibility of blocks of type. So called because strips of lead were used in letterpress printing for this purpose.

left justify. Setting text against the left margin, that is, with unused space all placed at the right. Also called ragged right.

legibility. The ease with which text is read in ordinary, continuous reading, usually gauged by reading speed and error rate. Readability.

letterform. A single glyph or letter, such as might be found on a page or screen. Also, the design of such a letter.

letterpress. Traditional method of relief printing in which individual pieces of type, called sorts, are assembled from cases into lines and blocks of text and printed by inking and direct contact with paper.

letterspacing. Adjustment of the interletter space within words so as to achieve equal optical space, or sometimes line justification.

ligature. In traditional typesetting, letters sharing a single type body. This was generally done because the letter combination required the letters to touch, overlap strongly, or differ in shape because of the combination. In digital typesetting, combinations of letters that are treated as a single unit for these reasons. Examples: Æ, fl, fi.

linearity. (engineering) The degree to which an output device preserves the fixed proportional relationship between addressing and physical dimensions in the output.

lines per inch (lpi). The spatial resolution of a device, photographic emulsion, and so forth, expressed as the greatest number of parallel lines per inch that can be resolved. Related only indirectly to dots per inch, which specifies addressing resolution, but not the greatest number of lines that can be sensed or created, which will be at least two times smaller.

Linotype. A typesetting machine, invented in 1886 by Ottmar Mergenthaler, that casts slugs containing whole lines of type for relief printing.

liquid crystal display (LCD). A screen-display technology that uses optically active organic materials to selectively reflect light under electronic control.

logotype. A typographic trademark or symbol, frequently using distorted letterforms.

loose line. A line of print that contains too much blank space (normally between words) compared with adjacent lines and general norms. The nominal interword space used in conventional printing is between a quarter and a third of the point size.

low-pass filter. A filter that allows low frequencies through, but eliminates high frequency components.

lowercase. Small letters used in printing that evolved from the Caroline minuscules of approximately 800 A.D. So called because they are found in the lower part of the printer's type case.

Lucida. A typeface designed by Bigelow & Holmes specifically for digital output. Its low-resolution screen version is known as Pellucida.

macros. Open subroutines, often used to create new commands within a markup language.

MacWrite. A direct-manipulation, WYSIWYG editor and formatter for the Macintosh computer.

majuscule. A capital (or other large) letter.

margin. The blank space to the left, right, above, and below the text on a page. Margins may contain up to 50% of the area of a well-designed book page.

marginalia. Notes, titles, summaries, or other information in the margins of a document.

markup language. A formatting language, usually run in batch mode, that includes textual instructions to the formatter, intermingled with the text to be formatted.

mechanical. A camera-ready original, ready for reproduction by offset printing.

METAFONT. Font production language developed by Donald Knuth.

metal type. Typesetting technology prior to phototypesetting, a kind of relief printing. See letterpress, linotype and monotype.

minuscule. A lowercase letter.

modeless editor. An editor without states (such as text versus command mode) in the user interface.

modern typeface. Any of a group of serif typeface typified by high typographic contrast and flat, thin serifs.

monochrome display. Display that presents images in black and white (or some other pair of foreground and background colors). Some monochrome displays are capable of grayscale, that is, gradations of intensity.

monospaced printing. Printing in which each letter or symbol occupies the same horizontal space.

Monotype. Typesetting machine invented in 1893 by Tolbert Lanston that casts individual letters and assembles them into a block of type, following instructions punched on a paper tape.

mood of type. The subjective feeling imparted by a typeface, layout, or page of type.

movable type. What Gutenberg invented—individual letters cast on independent metal bodies, for assembly into blocks for printing.

noise. (engineering) That part of a signal, image, and so forth that is independent of the information content of the message.

nroff. The UNIX batch-oriented document formatter, closely associated with troff, which is used for phototypesetting. It has some programming features such as environments.

Nyquist frequency. The sampling rate at which sufficient information is captured so as to be able to reproduce a signal of a given bandwidth. The Nyquist frequency is exactly twice the highest frequency to be resolved.

object. In programming-language methodology, an object is a unit of a program that contains both code and data. It exhibits a behavior as a unit, and can be thought of as the simulation of a physical object or system.

oblique. A slanted type design, following the letter shapes of the roman variation, as opposed to italic, which is also cursive.

ODA. Office Document Architecture, an interchange format for expressing revisable, structured documents, not intended to be human readable.

office typography. The design and printing of documents for everyday business, scientific, professional, and engineering use. Before desktop publishing, a generally haphazard affair.

offset printing. Printing method in which an image is developed on one surface and transferred (offset) onto another, and eventually onto the paper.

oldstyle typeface. A group of typefaces typified by oblique, bracketed serifs.

optical spacing. Positioning of letters so that they are perceived as having equal spaces between them. Exact geometric spacing does not have this property.

orphan. A header or the first line of a paragraph that appear as the last line on a page.

outline font description. Specification of the shapes of letters by defining their boundaries (to be filled with the ink color).

overleaf. The other side of a sheet printed on both sides, specifically the page in a book after a right-hand page.

page-description language (PDL). An executable description that expresses the appearance of a typeset page or series of pages. DDL, Interpress, and PostScript are examples.

page independence. The property of a page description language that allows the pages within a document to be processed and printed in any order.

pagination. Laying out the parts of a document into pages.

parse. To decode and understand, relative to a grammar. Written and spoken language is parsed in reading or listening. Visual images can also be spoken of in these terms.

pattern recognition. The process of extracting information and structure from a signal or image, by reference to known signals or images.

pel. A *picture element* or *pixel*.

perception. Seeing and understanding objects by human beings.

Perpetua. Serif typeface created by Eric Gill that matches a sans serif face, Gill Sans.

persistence (of a phosphor). The time it takes for the light output of a phosphor to decay to 10% of its original brightness when excited.

persistence (of vision). The property of the visual system that allows a short flash of light or exposure to an image to be perceived over a longer period of time.

phosphor. Light-emitting material, such as that on the inner surface of a CRT screen, that creates an image when selectively stimulated.

photo-offset printing. A printing process in which ink adhering to a photographically processed plate is transferred to paper via one or more intermediate surfaces (rollers).

photocomposition. Typesetting method in which images of letterforms are set by photographically imaging master versions onto film or photographic paper.

phototypesetting. Photocomposition.

pi font. A font of special symbols not in the standard character set.

pica. A unit of typographic measure, equal to 12 points, or about 1/6 inch. Also, a typewriter (monospaced) typeface with a pitch of 10 characters to the inch and a vertical spacing of six lines per inch (hence the name).

pixel. A picture element, which is also called a pel. The spot of graphical information displayed at a single location on a screen or other output device, or on paper.

plasma display. Screen-display technology that uses ionized gas (plasma) to create an image. In some plasma devices, the light emitted by the plasma is used to stimulate a phosphor, which then emits visible light.

point. A unit of measure used by printers, equal to $1/72.27$ inch. See also Didot point.

point size. The height of a font, expressed in points.

polarity asymmetry. The property in an output device that results in changes in shape when image polarity is reversed.

polygons. A straight-line representation sometimes used to express typefaces in outline form.

portrait orientation. A vertical-format page or screen, one higher than it is wide.

postfix. The sequence of specifying instructions and data in which the operation follows the data. For example, adding one and two would be done as 1 2 +. Postfix is also referred to as reverse Polish notation. In the case of a user interface, postfix order requires that an object or objects be selected first. Then the operation to be applied is specified.

PostScript. A page-description language developed by Adobe Systems, Inc.

power spectrum. The graph of the energy in the component frequencies of a signal.

prefix. The sequence of specifying instructions and data in which the operation precedes the data. For example, adding one and two would be done as + 1 2. Prefix is also referred to as Polish notation. In the case of a user interface, pre-

fix order requires that the operation be identified, and then the operand or operands.

proof. A working copy of typeset material printed for the purpose of checking content and format and of making corrections.

property sheet. A form that describes the formatting characteristics of an object within a WYSIWYG editor/formatter. The sheet is normally hidden, but may be made visible for inspection or modification.

proportional spacing. Printing in which each letter or symbol occupies an amount of horizontal space that depends upon its design.

psychology. That branch of science that studies the cognitive, perceptual, and behavioral characteristics of human beings.

quad. (printing) A space equal to the type size. Also, to fill a large blank space in a line with spacing material.

ragged right. Left-justified text that is flush with the left margin and ragged at the right margin. Unused space in each line is at its right.

random-access display. A display device that draws the image in any specified order. Calligraphic displays are random access. Raster devices are not.

raster device. A device that produces an image by scanning it as a series of lines.

rasterize. To convert an image to raster form, as from a vector-display list.

readability. Legibility. The speed at

which continuous text can be read.

reading for comprehension. Continuous reading, as of a block of text in a book.

real-time formatting. Presentation of an electronic document in (nearly) printed form while it is being edited.

reconstruction error. Artifact introduced into a sampled image when it is reconstructed (imaged) by an output device.

recto page. Right-hand page in an opening. Has an odd page number.

reference mark. A symbol such as a dagger (†) used to refer the reader to a footnote or other information outside of the immediate context of the mark.

reflection. Light impinging upon a scene that returns back from the scene. Reflections from display screens reduce image quality by reducing contrast. Light reflected from paper (but not the ink) increases image contrast.

refresh. To redisplay information on a display device. CRT displays, for example, refresh the image many times per second to achieve the appearance of constancy.

relief printing. A printing process in which a raised surface accepts ink, which is then transferred to paper by direct contact.

replicating pixels. A method of enlarging an image by mapping each original pixel onto more than one pixel in the enlarged image. Simple transformations like this result in poor-quality enlarged images.

resolution. The fineness of position and detail produced by an output device or sampled by an input device.

retina. The photosensitive part of the eye, upon which the lens images the scene being viewed.

river. A perceived white rift in a block of type that results from the alignment of interword spaces from line to line. Proper layout and typesetting minimize or eliminate rivers.

rods. Light-sensitive cells in the retina that respond to intensity but not color.

roman. The classical style of type that is upright, as opposed to oblique, is of normal weight as opposed to light or bold, and has graduated thick and thin strokes as opposed to being cursive.

rule. A thin line, either vertical or horizontal, often used to separate parts of a table or columns of text.

run-length encoding. A data-compression technique that represents sequences of values by counts of sequential items of the same value, instead of representing the values individually.

running head. Text such as the title, chapter, or section headings that is repeated on the tops of pages of a book.

Runoff. A number of document-formatting programs of related ancestry that operate in batch mode and use a highly extensional set of formatting commands. Macros within Runoff allow more intentional formatting.

saccade. Motion of the eye between fixations.

sans serif. A typeface without serifs.

saturation. The purity of color, the degree to which light is pastel versus spectral.

scoping of variables. (programming languages) The inheritance of values by program variables as a function of context, such as textual inclusion of code, nesting of function definitions, and dynamic calling of functions within other functions.

screen coordinates. Specification of a location on a screen in terms of the discrete pixels, as two integers (x,y), as opposed to world or application coordinates, which relate to a simulated coordinate system that may be expressed in real numbers and may be completely independent of screen position.

Scribe. A batch-mode document formatter developed by Brian Reid, much more intentional in its specifications that such formatters as Runoff.

script. A form of typeface based on writing, having generally continuous strokes that connect letters.

sector kerning. One method of automatic kerning that calculates the interletter spacing based on stored information about the lateral extent of each letter, assessed in a number of horizontal bands.

selection. The user-interface action of identifying an object or a portion of text for later operations.

serif. A small stroke at the end of the main strokes of letterforms. Typefaces with serifs are called serif typefaces and those without, sans serif typefaces.

set. The horizontal extent of a given letter. Also, the average width of the letters in a font, normally gauged by the width of a lowercase alphabet.

SGML. Standard Generalized Markup Language, an ISO standard revisable document format.

shoulder. In letterpress type, the level of metal upon which the relief letter sits on a piece of type. The shoulder provides support in letterpress printing for kerns that project from adjacent pieces.

sidebearings. The spaces at the left and right of each letter in a font design that allow for the normal spacing of the letters.

signature printing. Books, magazines, pamphlets, and the like are often printed in signatures, large sheets of paper that are folded, bound, and trimmed to form the finished product. The pages must be printed out of order, half of them upside down, and on both sides, for the pages in the folded sheet to be in the right order and orientation.

simultaneous contrast. An illusion in vision in which equal light intensities appear different as a result of differing surrounding intensities.

size of type. The distance between adjacent lines of type with no extra space (leading) added between them. The type design determines how much of this overall space is actually occupied by letters when printed.

smoothing. An interpolation technique that attempts to remove jaggedness from bitmap images, which may be useful, for example, when screen bitmaps are printed at higher resolution.

sort. A piece of metal type.

space. The part of the printed page that is not occupied by print or other images. The ground or complement of the image.

sparkle. A typographic property associated with many classical, readable typefaces that is related to their typographic contrast.

spatial dithering. The method of creating halftones digitally using a bitonal output device.

spatial frequencies. The analysis of print or other images in terms of rate of variation of intensity over distance.

spelling correction. A programmed service that calls attention to words that may be misspelled and offers choices of correctly spelled words.

spline. A mathematical curve specified by a number of points and possibly tangents. Also, a drafting tool for drawing such curves.

spot size. The dimension of the region illuminated by the electron beam in a CRT. Since the spot has soft edges, the spot size is measured between the 50% luminance points.

spread. The broadening of letter features because of the spreading of ink in the printing process. For example, letters are broadened when printed through a cloth ribbon.

stem. A main (vertical) stroke in a letterform.

stroke display. An image display device that produces images by directly creating lines, arcs, and so forth, as opposed to a bitmap display. Also called a calligraphic display.

stroke font. Letterforms defined by pen (or beam) paths rather than by outline or raster.

subpixel addressing. The positioning of glyphs on a grid effectively finer than the pixel resolution of the output device, using grayscale.

subscript. Letters or symbols positioned slightly below the baseline within a line of text and generally smaller in size.

superscript. Letters or other symbols positioned slightly above the baseline within a line of text and generally smaller in size.

swash letters. Fancy alternative decorative letters, usually available only in italic capitals. For example, *ABCDEFG*

symbol. Any graphic form such as a letter, number, punctuation mark, or mathematical sign.

symmetry. The property of similarity within a letterform or between letterforms of the same design. For example, the letter 'T' in some typeface designs has right-left mirror symmetry, but does not in other faces.

tables. Rectangular arrangements of text, numbers, or other textual information. Tables generally float in documents, and may be positioned in a number of places relative to the text that refers to them.

tachistoscope. A scientific instrument used by psychologists for vision experiments to present an image or images for very short periods of time.

tangent. The direction of a curve at a specified point; also, a line through this point and oriented in this direction.

T$_E$X. A batch-formatting language developed by Donald Knuth. Notable for its careful line and page breaking, high-quality hyphenation, and capabilities for setting mathematics.

text. Any sequence of graphic symbols.

texture. (typography) The appearance of a page or block of text, perceived as a surface.

Times New Roman. A popular contemporary serifed typeface originally developed by Stanley Morison for the *London Times.* It has a relatively large x-height, and is relatively narrow (small set) for its x-height.

Tinker, Miles. Psychologist who performed legibility studies with tens of thousands of subjects under varying typographic conditions.

toner. The ink used in xerographic and other electrostatic printing processes.

troff. A batch-oriented document formatter used in the UNIX environment for phototypesetting. It is associated with nroff, another document formatter used in that environment.

Tschichold, Jan. German typographer, 1902–1974. Inventor of asymmetric typography. Standardized book designs for Penguin Books.

type. Originally metal type, now a typeface design or some typeset text.

typeface. A distinctive, visually consistent design for the symbols in an alphabet.

typesetter. A machine for setting type. Professional digital typesetters that output on photographic paper have printing resolutions between about 700 and 5000 dpi.

type size. The size of a typeface, measured from line to line, when no additional interline space is added. Digital typefaces may not have an inherent size, as did metal typefaces.

typewriter fonts. Usually monospaced typefaces, in the style of traditional typewriter typefaces, now used to indicate computer printout or a typewritten style of document.

typographer. A professional designer of type, books, magazines, and other printed matter.

typography. The art and practice of designing type, books and other printed matter according to æsthetic and scientific principles.

uppercase. A capital letter, so called because of the placement of capital letters in a printer's type case.

user interface. The component of a computer-based system that is responsible for interactions with the user of the system and that manifests all of the system's external behavior.

verso page. Left-hand page of an opening. It has an even page number.

ViewPoint. Operating system of a Xerox Corporation office workstation, with document-preparation facilities similar to the earlier Star workstation.

visibility. The degree to which letters or words can be identified and discriminated, without regard to the speed of reading.

vision. The ability of human beings (and other animals) to perceive the shape and other properties of objects around them by analyzing received light.

wavelength. The length of one cycle of a cyclic function, measured, for example, from peak to peak.

weight. Heaviness or blackness of letters. Numerically, the ratio of the widths of vertical strokes to the x-height.

widow. The last line of a paragraph that appears at the top of a page.

winding number. A method of determining whether a region is inside a curve, and thus should be inked when an outline-specified letterform is rasterized.

word processing. Preparation of text in document form. The term is now dated, suggesting text-only documents and impact printing, as opposed to typeset compound documents.

WYGINS. Acronym for What You Get Is No Surprise, a term invented by the author.

WYSIWYG. Acronym for What You See Is What You Get, used to describe interactive editing or formatting in which a facsimile of the paper output is presented on the screen; coined by Doug Engelbart.

x-height. The height of a lowercase letter 'x' in a particular font.

Xerox PARC. Xerox Palo Alto Research Center, where the Alto workstation, the Bravo editor, and other significant innovations were made.

Zapf, Hermann. German typographer who designed many contemporary typefaces, including Optima, Palatino, Melior, and Janson.

Index

Items in *italics* are also listed in the Glossary.

addressing, subpixel, 114
addressing resolution, 50
algorithmic tools for font design, 132,
    140-147
aliasing, 45, 47, 49, 52, 53
analog letterform, digitizing from, 47-
    48, 101-105
anisotropic scaling, see scaling
anisotropy, 63
anti-aliasing, see grayscale, 111-115
aperiodic dithering, 84, 85
arc-and-vector form, 125
artificial intelligence, page layout
    and, 286
ascender, 16, 99
aspect ratio, 50-51
assimilation, 24-25
asymmetry
    of beam on and off, 62-63, 65
    polarity, 64, 78-79
automatic layout, 234-279
automatic pagination, 241-244

Babbage, Charles, 49
back up, 237
bandwidth, see spatial resolution, 50,
    52-54, 56, 85
baseline, 16
Baskerville, 23, 102
Baskerville, John, 101, 103, 104
batch formatters, 224
Baudin, Fernand, 153
Bembo, 92
Bézier splines, 128
bibliographic references, 240-241

Bigelow, Charles, 25, 45, 212
bitmap font-design tools, 131, 132-
    134
bitmap fonts, 121-123
bitmap output device, 123
bitmapped display, 55
blackness, 17
blue noise, 85
Bodini, 42-43
bold (type), 17, 26, 130-131
borders, 157, 168, 207-208, 265, 267
bottom-up font design, 100, 108-109,
    197, 198
bowl, 16
Bravo, 248
breaking lines, 180-189, 203-204,
    236, 258, 260
breaking pages. *See* pagination
brightness, 69
brilliance, see typographic contrast, 93
bullet (in list), 274
Bulmer, 92

CAD. *See* computer-aided design, 146
calligraphic display, 55
cap-height, 16, 99
captions, 161
case, 20, 26
Caslon, William, 104
cathode ray tube (CRT), 56-71
    anisotropy and, 65
    chromatic aberration and, 67-68
    color, 64-71, 192
    edge detection and, 68-69
    flicker of, 58-60, 191

cathode ray tube (CRT) (*cont.*)
  image contrast and, 60-63
  interlaced scanning and, 59-60
  light emitted by, 59-63, 191
  linearity of, 58
  perceptual uniformity of color space
    and, 69
  persistence and, 58-60
  phosphor dots and, 66
  pixels and, 58, 60, 66
  polarity of, 64, 191
  random-access, 58
  raster, bit-mapped, 58
  reading from, 189-193
  refreshing of, 59-60
  resolution and, 197, 200
  shadow mask and, 66-67
  temporal resolution of, 58-59
  typography and, 192
  viewing distance and, 191-192
cell text, 13
Centaur, 92
centered (text), 165-167
CFF. *See critical-fusion frequency*,
    34
channelization, 139
Chappell, Warren, 291
character, 18, 20
character set, 15, 18
character Simulated Design (CSD),
    141
charge leaks, in laser printer, 78-79
  compensation for, 78-80
chromatic aberration, 67-68
chromaticity diagram, 69-70
CIE chromaticity diagram, 69-70
clustered dot method, 84-85
collateral font design, 100, 109-111
color, 156-157
  in fonts, 111-115
  hue, brightness, and saturation of,
    69
  of typeface, 91
color perception, deficiencies in, 71
color resolution, 56
column, in table, 261, 263-265
command style of interface, 255-256

communication
  protocols for, 288
  of typographic information, 216-219
complex writing systems, 209
compound document, 2, 153-154, 256-
    257. *See also* interchange
    formats, 224-227, *and* page-
    description languages, 227-232
comprehension, reading for, 27, 154
computed values, 271-274
computer-aided design (CAD), 146
Computer Modern, 143
conceptual model, see user interfaces,
    249-257
condensed (type), 15
cone (in retina), 28, 68
conic spline, 127
constraints, in pagination, 234-241
  in typesetting tables, 261, 263-265
continuous reading, 27
  psychology of, 285
continuous tone, 56, 82-83
continuous stroke, 136
contrast, 17
  image, 60-63
  simultaneous, 33
  typographic, 93
contrast ratio, see image contrast, 60-63
Coueignoux, Philippe, 141
counter (of a letter), 16
Courier, 214
  power spectrum of, 46
critical-fusion frequency (CFF), 34
cross-references, 240-241
CRT. *See* cathode ray tube
CSD. *See* Character Simulated
    Design, 141
cubic splines, 127
cursive (letterforms), 17-19
curves, interpolating, 127-128
  parametric, 126-127

daisy-wheel printers, 55
DDL (Document Description Lan-
    guage), 227, 229
declarative languages, 245-247
decoding (text), 20